TiVo
HACKS

Raffi Krikorian

O'REILLY®

Beijing · Cambridge · Farnham · Köln · Paris · Sebastopol · Taipei · Tokyo

TiVo Hacks
by Raffi Krikorian

Editor:	Rael Dornfest	**Production Editor:**	Sarah Sherman
Series Editor:	Rael Dornfest	**Cover Designer:**	Emma Colby
Executive Editor:	Dale Dougherty	**Interior Designer:**	David Futato

Printing History:

August 2003:	First Edition.

TiVo
HACKS

Other resources from O'Reilly

Related titles

Amazon Hacks	Mac OS X Hacks
Google Hacks	Windows XP Hacks
eBay Hacks	Linux Server Hacks
Wireless Hacks	

Hacks Series Home

hacks.oreilly.com is a community site for developers and power users of all stripes. Readers learn from each other as they share their favorite tips and tools for Mac OS X, Linux, Google, Windows XP, and more.

oreilly.com

oreilly.com is more than a complete catalog of O'Reilly books. You'll also find links to news, events, articles, weblogs, sample chapters, and code examples.

O'REILLY NETWORK

oreillynet.com is the essential portal for developers interested in open and emerging technologies, including new platforms, programming languages, and operating systems.

Conferences

O'Reilly & Associates bring diverse innovators together to nurture the ideas that spark revolutionary industries. We specialize in documenting the latest tools and systems, translating the innovator's knowledge into useful skills for those in the trenches. Visit *conferences.oreilly.com* for our upcoming events.

O'REILLY NETWORK Safari Bookshelf

Safari Bookshelf (*safari.oreilly.com*) is the premier online reference library for programmers and IT professionals. Conduct searches across more than 1,000 books. Subscribers can zero in on answers to time-critical questions in a matter of seconds. Read the books on your Bookshelf from cover to cover or simply flip to the page you need. Try it today with a free trial.

Contents

Credits

About the Author

Raffi Krikorian is an unapologetic TiVo lover and digital plumber. If you look hard enough, you can usually find him putting together a hack for some random and stray idea that sidetracked him from the last project or stray idea. He freely admits that his serious television addiction is probably getting between him and his goal of finally graduating from MIT for the second time, although he claims it's getting better. When he's not studying or watching TV, you can find him wandering around or trying something new. In whatever time is left, he tends to his wasted bits on his weblog, *http://www.bitwaste.com/wasted-bits/*.

Contributors

The following people contributed their hacks, writing, and inspiration to this book:

- Cory Doctorow (*www.craphound.com*) is coeditor of the popular weblog Boing Boing (*www.boingboing.net*) and works as a staffer for the Electronic Frontier Foundation (*www.eff.org*). He is an award-winning science fiction author, and his first novel, *Down and Out in the Magic Kingdom*, can be purchased in stores everywhere or downloaded free from *www.craphound.com/down*.

- Rael Dornfest (*http://www.raelity.org/*) assesses, experiments, programs, writes, and edits for O'Reilly & Associates, Inc. He has edited, coauthored, and contributed to various O'Reilly books. He is program chair for the O'Reilly Emerging Technology Conference. In his copious free time, Rael develops bits and bobs of freeware, including the Blosxom (*http://www.blosxom*.com) weblog application, and maintains his raelity bytes weblog.

- Josha Foust

- Greg Gardner is a software engineer who lives in San Francisco, California. He started hacking TiVos while working on a project for his company, which involved delivering digital video and photos to consumer devices. When he's not working or hacking his TiVo, Greg enjoys playing ice hockey, golfing, and traveling.

- Tobias Hoellrich, from Munich (Germany), has worked as an IT professional for the last 15 years. He spent the last 9 years at Adobe Systems in Amsterdam (The Netherlands) and San Jose (California). Since 2002, he has worked out of his home in Santa Fe (New Mexico), where he lives with his wife, Candice, and his two dogs. Aside from work, Tobias is an enthusiastic amateur photographer who has received recognition at local galleries in Santa Fe.

- Steve Jenkins (*http://www.stevejenkins.com/*) is an avid home theater junkie and TiVo hacker. He has an MBA from Brigham Young University and was the founder of two early Internet companies: WinFiles.com (formerly Windows95.com) shareware web site and VServers web hosting, both of which he sold in 1999. His most recent venture is Cheat-Codes.com, a popular online source for video game cheats, hints, and walk-throughs. When he's not wiring his hot tub so he can check the water temperature from a Web browser, Steve enjoys driving Ferraris, volunteer teaching, and, of course, tinkering with his TiVo.

- LJ lives in West Sussex, England. By day, he's an(other) IT guy. For fun, he writes TiVoWeb modules to prove both that it can be done and that his brain still works. So far, he's managed not to fry his TiVo or his brain. His latest TiVoWeb modules can be found at *www.ljay.org.uk.*

- Douglas Mayle (*http://www.mayle.org/douglas*), from Somerset, New Jersey, has worked in networking, security, and development for the last 11 years. He spent 8 years in Boston, using his experience to help start an online chocolate company, and later consulting independently. In the beginning of 2003, he moved to the south coast of France, where he now works for Metrix Systems on the internals of their systems management suite. He has spoken at Comdex and spends what little free time he has trying find new ways to use software in unexpected places.

- "Otto"

- Bill Regnery

- Glenn R. Souther (BS Computer Science, Georgia Institute of Technology; MBA Quantitative Finance, Johnson Graduate School of Management at Cornell University) is most recently employed as a Vice President in Emerging Markets Research at J.P Morgan.

- Drew Streib
- Jeff Shapiro and Michael Adberg are the guys behind WeaKnees.com (*http://www.weaknees.com*), an online resource center and Internet retailer for all things TiVo. Before dedicating themselves to helping TiVo addicts, Michael was a computer consultant and Jeff a (gasp) lawyer (although, in fairness, Jeff has a geek grounding that goes back to the AppleCat 212). Both Jeff and Michael graduated from the University of California at Berkeley, and Jeff also graduated from the University of Chicago Law School. Now, Jeff and Michael spend 95% of their time building and upgrading TiVos, and they spend the other 5% trying to convince friends and family that they have real jobs.

Acknowledgments

First and foremost, to my family, friends, and to Kelly Dobson: thank you all for believing in me and giving me the emotional support to make it through writing this book. And Kelly, thank you for being there, being my rock, and reminding me that taking a nap for a few hours is preferable to staying up all night.

TiVo, Inc., thanks for such a great box. If I didn't own one, my studies would go better, but I'm still glad I have one. I'm sure you hear this all the time, but if you ever need a spokesperson or a beta tester, I'm here.

And, speaking of beta testing, Todd Larason, thank you for beta testing this work and keeping me on the straight and narrow.

Thank you to the communities at *tivocommunity.com*, *dealdatabase.com*, and *alt.org*. It's been fun hanging out. Thanks for all the ideas, the help, and the code. Also, to my unnamed TiVo friend: thank you.

Many thanks to Tim O'Reilly and everybody at O'Reilly who even considered this a worthwhile topic to write a book on.

And lastly, more thanks than I could ever express to Rael Dornfest. Rael, you've been a great friend, a great manager, a great editor, and just an amazing person to work with. Thank you for pushing me to get this done. Thank you for all your help. Let's do it again sometime.

Preface

Forget all you think you know about watching television. Throw out the concepts of channels and lineups. VCR+ codes, your daily paper's TV listings, even the ubiquitous *TV Guide* need not apply. Primetime is a ghost of television's past.

Secede from the tyranny of the TV grid. Gone are the Sunday evenings scouring program listings, mapping out the viewing week ahead. An end to nightly feats of conflict resolution, balancing sitcoms and series against football games and specials. A mind free of cryptic codes, formerly the only way of distinguishing between new and repeat, original and syndicated. No worries about that show you forgot to record; chances are your recorder didn't. No longer do your viewing habits dictate your social life. And, best yet, never lay eyes upon a video tape again.

The TiVo is a personal video recorder (PVR), and it represents a sea change in television, far beyond the mere VCR-replacement suggested by its moniker. In addition to its recording capabilities, TiVo boasts the following abilities and features:

Control "live" TV
> PVRs are always recording whatever you happen to be watching. Rewind to catch a line missed during a particularly loud sneeze, or pause for a leisurely visit to the bathroom rather than crossing your legs and dashing during a commercial break. This is probably the most popularized, yet least interesting, feature of PVRs.

Time slipping
> Watch your favorite shows when you want to, rather than being subjected to the network executives' assigned, network-allotted time slot. Line up an evening's programming for your own personal "primetime."

The television firewall

Focus your children's television habit on interesting, educational, and age-appropriate shows, rather than whatever happens to flow past on any one particular channel. Skip those commercials or, better yet, choose programming from commercial-free channels. Lock out inappropriate channels and shows.

Season Passes

Tell TiVo to record every episode of your favorite show, no matter when or where it appears. Choose to include reruns, or ignore all but the freshest episodes.

Intelligence

VCRs are stupid creatures. Changes in programming lineup, available space, preferences for what to keep and what to ditch, and so forth go straight over their heads. The TiVo records the show, not the time slot. If your favorite show is airing at a different night this week or at a slightly different time, TiVo will catch that.

WishLists and searching

TiVo's WishList functionality allows you to find and record something even when you don't quite know what it is—actor, director, partial title—you're looking for.

Record without videotape

Reclaim drawer and closet space by ridding your household of the bushels of mislabeled, half-chewed video tapes. Plus, VCR recording quality is awful. PVRs encode digitally, offering either tunable quality or encoding at the highest quality available to them from the cable or satellite. While PVRs do indeed have a space limit, you'll seldom find yourself worrying about recording space when you go out of town for a week and don't want to miss your soaps. And, of course, that space limit isn't a hard limit, thanks to hard drive upgrades.

"It will change the way you watch TV!" is the rallying cry of the evangelical group of TiVo fanatics. You bump into these people at parties and get-togethers, trying to convince others that they have to get a TiVo, or inviting perfect strangers into their homes just to give a demonstration on how it all works.

But hacking the TiVo? Hacking a closed box that just sits under my television? Why would I ever want to do that? Or, more importantly, how do I go about doing that? That question is best answered by explaining what is under the hood.

What Is a TiVo?

You can think of the TiVo as a carefully tweaked desktop computer with a television tuner card. Instead of a Pentium or an Athlon, the original TiVo is an IBM PowerPC 403GCX–based embedded system. It uses standard IDE hard drives, with custom MPEG-2 encoding/decoding hardware, a modem, and an IR receiver. On the inside, it's running a Linux kernel. Everything the TiVo does, save the television channel tuning and the video encoding, is done in software. Everything you see on the screen, all the interactivity through the remote, and the recording scheduling is all defined in code.

But not all TiVos are the same. The original TiVo, the Series 1, is the most hackable TiVo out there; it's a box thrown together with commodity parts. The TiVo code is running on open hardware. If you feel like it, you can throw that TiVo software out the window and just home brew your own code from the bottom up. That might be a little excessive, but you get my drift.

The Series 2 TiVo, the most commonly sold TiVo today, unfortunately is not as open. To lock down the platform, TiVo, Inc. has started to add some "secrets" under the hood. While TiVo is not against people hacking their platform, they do have a media service to run, and they don't want people to freely play around with some of the stuff they intend to make money on down the road.

How to Use This Book

Hacks are generally considered quick-n-dirty, pragmatic solutions to hardware and software problems, or interesting techniques for getting a task done. TiVo, being just a shiny PC with a generalized operating system and expandable via all-but off-the-shelf parts, has proven eminently *hackable*.

Communities of TiVo hackers have sprung up on the Internet, the most well-know being the TiVo Forum (*http://www.tivocommunity.com/*). In this book, I've collected and written up some of the more useful, interesting, and cool hacks I've found. There are hardware hacks, requiring you to pop the top off your TiVo and fiddle about with the innards. There are software hacks, requiring a little less manual dexterity but no less of a sense of adventure. And, for the faint of heart, there are remote control hacks you can do from the comfort of your favorite armchair.

Don't worry, I'll guide you. Many of these hacks stand on their own, but more of them require you to do one of the other hacks first, whether it be to get you inside the box or just to enter a series of codes into a *Search by Title* field. If there's a prerequisite, there'll be a cross-reference to guide you to the appropriate hack. Feel free to flip around, following whatever interests you. I'll try to keep the map clear of obstacles.

But a couple of fair warnings before we continue. There are two types of hacks, explicitly, that you won't find in this book. The first are those that circumvent having to pay for TiVo. There are a few open source projects out there, like MythTV (*http://mythtv.sourceforge.net*), that do the same things the TiVo does, but you don't have to pay a monthly fee or a single lifetime fee to get to use it. Instead, this service queries the Internet for those valuable tidbits of information on when and what channel your television shows are on. While people have tried—and may of succeeded—to use these same techniques for the TiVo, I'm not going to talk about them. In fact, most TiVo hackers, including those that you find mentioned in this book, are not going to talk about the subject. Bypassing the TiVo, Inc. service to get television programming information into your TiVo without paying the appropriate fees is one of those shunned topics. TiVo, Inc. has built a fabulous combination of hardware, software, and service. They've embraced TiVo hacking and coexist peacefully with the hacker community. But they do need to make a living, leaving it up to every TiVo hacker to reciprocate by paying their dues and helping TiVo maintain this openness and hackability.

The second type of hacks you won't see in this book involve getting to the software insides of that new and shiny Series 2 box. Most TiVo hacking has been and continues to be done on the older and more open Series 1 boxes. There are those who've managed to gain access to the internals of the Series 2 TiVo, opening it up to many of the hacks available for the Series 1. Unfortunately, the methods to do so are beyond the scope of this book, are tricky, and are of questionable legality. Series 2 owners wishing to go beyond the remote control hacks and hard drive upgrades will most likely find newer hacks for Series 2 TiVos appearing online over time.

Caveat Hacker

You've not doubt noticed the "Do not open or you will void your warranty" sticker emblazoned across the back of your TiVo box. Well, that is true. If you open your box, you will not be able to send your TiVo into TiVo, Inc. if a problem develops.

If this is of little concern to you, you can stomach the possible consequences, or your TiVo is more than a year old and out of warranty anyway, then open her right up! There is simply no way around it for the lion's share of hacks in this book. If you're going to add a new hard drive, add networking to a Series 1 TiVo, or get a command-line prompt going, you are going to need to pull that box apart and put it back together again.

So, how hard is it really? If you are already pretty comfortable poking around inside a PC, then you should have no problem as a lot of those skills apply to what you will need to do. If not, don't worry, you're probably a quick study.

On the hardware end, about the only oddity is the need for a Torx-10 screwdriver—available at most fully stocked hardware stores—to unscrew those star-patterned screws and pop off the case. On the software end, the only price of admission is a basic working knowledge of, or willingness to learn, a little about the Unix operating system that is TiVo's brain.

All that said, let me add a few caveats before you dive in:

- TiVo sports a massive power supply that, even when unplugged, could deliver a nasty shock.

- The edges of the case are mighty sharp, so mind your head, shoulders, knees, and toes.

- Back up your TiVo before and between hacks. We put in substantial time and effort to make sure the directions we give are pretty clear, but that doesn't mean mistakes can't happen.

  Backing up is for wimps, you say? I can't emphasize enough how important it is. You do not want to end up with a $400 lemon if something goes wrong. Although you probably could find somebody out there that can give you software to restore your TiVo if something goes wrong, why should you go through all that hassle to find someone to help? Just think of backing up as an insurance policy and take the few minutes to make one of your own when we say so, and save the living on the edge for surfing or rock climbing.

- Hacks that you install may or may not be permanent. Your TiVo calls home to the TiVo service once a day and, during that time, TiVo might send an operating system update for the box that has a good chance of undoing whatever hacks you have installed. This is little more than a minor irritation, but just be warned that you might have to reinstall your hacks every once in a while. All that hard work, down the drain.

  You may think that one way of preventing this is to stop operating system updates from installing, but you might be missing some rather useful fixes, updates, and new features. When I bought my first TiVo, it did not have a Season Pass Manager until it magically showed up in one of the system updates one morning.

How This Book Is Organized

Chapter 1, *TiVo Remote Control Hacks*

> Explore what the TiVo can do even before you pop the lid. This chapter is devoted to taking a look around the TiVo and discovering what tricks you can get it to do even without rearranging the internal bits.

Chapter 2, *Adding More Hours*

> Once you become a TiVo addict (and you quickly will), you are quickly going to want more hours on your box. You are going to want to record more television shows, and sometimes save an episode or two for a long period of time. This chapter details upgrading the storage capacity of your box.

Chapter 3, *The TiVo Shell*

> While you have that lid open, why not try enabling a Bash prompt? Command-line access means your TiVo becomes that much more like any other PC in your home. The text interface and blinking cursor dramatically alters what you can twiddle and thus do with your TiVo.

Chapter 4, *Bring the Internet to TiVo*

> Your TiVo should be part of your home network. Your desktop computer should be talking to and making requests of your TiVo. Your office computer, a couple of miles down the road, should be doing the same. Bringing the Internet all the way to your TiVo is not as difficult as it sounds. This chapter will show you how and some interesting things to do once you have your TiVo online.

Chapter 5, *TiVo and the Web*

> Two solutions provide access to, and manipulation, of your TiVo over the Web: the official TiVo Home Media Option (HMO) and the open source TiVoWeb project. The former allows for remote programming and manipulation of your TiVo over the Web with all the simplicity you've come to expect from TiVo. The latter provides so much more than simple web access to your TiVo; it's a platform for Web-based TiVo-centric applications, extensible to your heart's content.

Chapter 6, *Working with Videos*

> Regular TiVo users simply record their television shows to VCR tapes when they want to save something. But by this chapter you will no longer be a regular TiVo user, so let's talk about pulling and pushing video from and to your TiVo, archiving shows in full digital splendor on your home PC or burning them to DVD.

Chapter 7, *Writing Code*

What if you want to write your own software for the TiVo? Here's a crash-course in writing programs for TiVo in Tcl and in C—and a few nifty examples along the way.

Conventions Used in This Book

The following is a list of the typographical conventions used in this book:

Italic

Used to indicate new terms, URLs, filenames, file extensions, and directories and to highlight comments in examples. For example, a path in the filesystem will appear as */Developer/Applications*.

`Constant width`

Used to show code examples, the contents of files, commands, or the output from commands.

`Constant width bold`

Used in examples and tables to show commands or other text that should be typed literally.

`Constant width italic`

Used in examples and tables to show text that should be replaced with user-supplied values.

Color

The second color is used to indicate a cross-reference within the text.

↵

A carriage return (↵) at the end of a line of code is used to denote an unnatural line break; that is, you should not enter these as two lines of code, but as one continuous line. Multiple lines are used in these cases due to page width constraints.

Menu symbols

When looking at the menus for any application, you will see some symbols associated with keyboard shortcuts for a particular command. For example, to open an old chat in iChat, you would go to the File menu and select Open... (File → Open...), or you could issue the keyboard shortcut, -O. The symbol corresponds to the key (also known as the "Command" key), located to the left and right of the spacebar on any Macintosh keyboard.

Pay special attention to notes set apart from the text with the following icons:

 This is a tip, suggestion, or general note. It contains useful supplementary information about the topic at hand.

 This is a warning or note of caution.

The thermometer icons, found next to each hack, indicate the relative complexity of the hack:

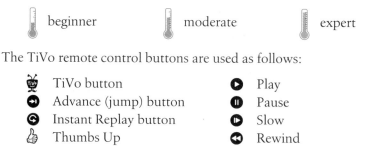

beginner   moderate   expert

The TiVo remote control buttons are used as follows:

🦃	TiVo button	●	Play
↪	Advance (jump) button	⏸	Pause
↺	Instant Replay button	▶	Slow
👍	Thumbs Up	◀	Rewind
👎	Thumbs Down	▶▶	Fast Forward
		●	Record

How to Contact Us

We have tested and verified the information in this book to the best of our ability, but you may find that features have changed (or even that we have made mistakes!). As a reader of this book, you can help us to improve future editions by sending us your feedback. Please let us know about any errors, inaccuracies, bugs, misleading or confusing statements, and typos that you find anywhere in this book.

Please also let us know what we can do to make this book more useful to you. We take your comments seriously and will try to incorporate reasonable suggestions into future editions. You can write to us at:

O'Reilly & Associates, Inc.
1005 Gravenstein Highway North
Sebastopol, CA 95472
(800) 998-9938 (in the U.S. or Canada)
(707) 829-0515 (international/local)
(707) 829-0104 (fax)

You can also send us messages electronically. To be put on the mailing list or to request a catalog, send email to:

info@oreilly.com

To ask technical questions or to comment on the book, send email to:

bookquestions@oreilly.com

The web site for *TiVo Hacks* lists examples, errata, and plans for future editions. You can find this page at:

http://www.oreilly.com/catalog/tivohks

For more information about this book and others, see the O'Reilly web site:

http://www.oreilly.com

Hack on! at:

http://hacks.oreilly.com

TiVo Remote Control Hacks

Hacks 1–19

Before we talk about popping open your box, let's focus on what we can get the TiVo software to do. Right out of the box, TiVo's software sports some hacks of its very own, which come in three flavors:

Shortcuts

TiVo has a slew of remote control shortcuts—sequences of button presses on your TiVo remote control—for navigating the TiVo menu system at high velocity.

Easter eggs

There is a cult of pride in software development, often manifested in Easter eggs—silly surprises hidden strategically for chance discovery and amusement. Think of Easter eggs as hidden treasure, buried by the programmer for other programmers, and exploring users to find and admire. Easter eggs are traditionally benign, so you should feel comfortable playing with and passing on any you might find.

Backdoor hacks

The reasons for the existence of so-called "backdoor" hacks are not fully known, but a common theory is that they are installed so that the TiVo boxes can be fully tested while at the factory. They may also provide hooks for future development. Backdoor codes can fundamentally change how TiVo behaves, and they are sometimes so powerful that they render TiVo inoperable. Be very careful when using these hacks, and be sure to back up **[Hack #24]** before giving some of the more questionable ones a whirl.

Discovering TiVo's built-in hacks was by no means easy. People like "Otto" (a well-known member of the TiVo hacking community) have repeatedly poked and prodded at their remote controls to unveil these special sequences. Once a single code is discovered, all permutations are tried to see if any variants exist, and everything is painstakingly documented at *http://*

www.dbsforums.com/cgi-bin/ultimatebb.cgi?ubb=get_topic&f=14&t=003197.
Please refer to that web page for the most up-to-date list, as Otto updates it
quite frequently.

This chapter is a compilation of the remote control sequences and backdoor
hacks discovered by the TiVo community thus far. There are a few documented key codes that we do not discuss in this chapter, just because
nobody is exactly sure what the hacks do. All we can do is encourage you to
explore—but explore carefully! Perhaps you should read about backing up
your TiVo **[Hack #24]** first.

Remote Control Hacks

The remote control hacks not only require a very specific sequence to enter
on your remote control, but the *context* (what is on your TiVo screen) when
you enter the sequence also matters a lot. For these hacks, go to any TiVo
menu screen (except Live TV or watching a recorded program), and press
the appropriate buttons in sequence on your remote control.

Note, however, that not all these hacks work on all varieties of TiVo. The
automatic TiVo OS updates add further complications; any change in the
software on the Personal Video Recorder (PVR) itself may prevent a hack
from operating. Also, there are differences in the software that runs on the
TiVo Series I, DirecTiVo Series II, etc., and these differences also prevent
certain remote control hacks from working properly. We will do our best to
note when a hack might not work on all TiVos, but keep in mind that things
may have changed since the time of this writing.

Backdoor Hacks

Backdoors are the key to accessing all the things that TiVo can do but are
not, by default, exposed through the menus or through the remote. Most of
these features were probably installed for testing and were not enabled in
the menu system, because they were deemed either not really user friendly
nor particularly useful. But who needs user friendly, anyway, when you can
hack in some more advanced functionality?

All these backdoor hacks can be entered via the remote in the same way as
all the other hacks. We do, however, need to convince TiVo to pay attention to these otherwise-disabled sequences.

All the remote control hacks in this book require you to
enable backdoor mode **[Hack #8]** enabled. In normal operation—with backdoor mode disabled—TiVo will summarily
ignore the special codes.

HACK #1   Swinging TiVo

Take a walk down memory lane with the first-time-power-up "Tarzan" video sequence.

Most likely, you still remember the first time that you powered up your TiVo. It went through some setup screens, asking you what phone numbers it should use for the daily call, whether you use cable or satellite, what channels you receive and watch, and the initial—seemingly endless—downloading of guide data. But the most memorable screen for most users was that initial video sequence featuring a Tarzan-like TiVo swinging deftly through a maze of ducts.

Want to watch it again?

On your remote control, press 🎀 → 0 (i.e., press the 🎀 button, release it, press the 0 button, and release it), and up the video comes (see Figure 1-1).

Figure 1-1. Our hero, swinging through a maze of dots

Must-Skim TV

Slide through boring baseball games, pausing only for crowd-pleasing catches and game-tying errors. Cram that unnecessarily lengthy reality show into a scant 15 minutes of onscreen viewing.

TiVo really is "TV your way." Most people assume it's just about pausing live television to visit the restroom, or watching your shows when you're good and ready to do so. But there are more tidbits to be incorporated into your television-watching modus operandi. Here are a few I find rather useful for reducing downtime in potentially engaging shows.

Sliding Straight to the Instant Replay

While the networks do a fine job of highlighting notable sports plays, it just doesn't help if you're out of the room fetching a cold one or more pretzels for your friends. If you're a sports fan and TiVo fanatic, you've no doubt discovered the ◀ button. With a flick of the thumb, you've skipped backward a few seconds to catch the splash of that San Francisco homer. Flick it again and you're back at the wind-up.

But did you know that the ◀ button, when combined with ▶, can reduce an entire game to just minutes—without missing a single crowd-pleasing catch or game-tying error? You won't even have time for that cold one! Here's what you do...

Select a game from TiVo's *Now Playing List* and start it playing. Hit the ▶ button on your TiVo remote three times to zip through the game at high speed. Now keep your eye on the network's overlaid onscreen scoreboard, while keeping your thumb hovering over the ◀ button on your remote. The second you notice a score change, click ◀ once or twice and you're right there in the action. Repeat as necessary.

Sure, it takes a trained eye, but you'll get it in no time. Forget Sports Center's take on the best plays of the day—make your own.

The 10-FF40-10 Solution

With project shows like *Trading Spaces* and *Junkyard Wars* and reality shows like *Survivor* all the rage these days, there's no end to the number of hours you can waste watching other people fixing what you should be fixing or doing what you'd never in a million years (or for a million dollars) actually do yourself.

The shows—in case you hadn't noticed—are rather formulaic:

1. Introduce the "problem."

2. Watch teams get frustrated and panic for about 30 to 40 minutes.

3. Applaud as things come together or fall apart, depending on the show.

There's a nice recipe for this kind of "Must-Skim TV":

1. Watch the first 10 minutes at normal speed, skipping commercials [Hack #4] of course.

2. Fast forward at the highest possible speed (hit three times) through the next 40 minutes, keeping one eye on the green play-bar at the bottom of the screen, the other on the action, in case there is any.

3. Watch the last 10 minutes—finished rooms, pounded bots, voting off the island, etc.—at normal speed, skipping commercials.

With minor variations on this recipe, you can compress *Antiques Roadshow* to about 15 minutes without missing any of the "action." Or, reduce *Trading Spaces* to just 30 minutes and improve its quality drastically by watching *Changing Rooms*, the original BBC version—but that's more advice than a hack. ;-)

Speed Reading

Local newscasters speak just too slowly for words? Want to skim the cream off that State of the Union Address without waiting for the morning paper to summarize it for you?

Turn on Closed Captioning [Hack #42], and hit once. You'll cruise through at twice the speed (speeding up to three s for commercials), and the Closed Captioning will keep up. Closed Captioning is perfect for skimming the news or cramming two or three of those reality shows into one hour of viewing without missing a single word. Or, if you're embarrassed, you can just claim you're working on your speed reading.

——*Rael Dornfest and Cory Doctorow*

HACK #3 Navigation Shortcuts

Remote control shortcuts mean cruising through the TiVo menu system at high velocity.

Typical TiVo menu navigation is serial, moving step-by-step from one window to another using the **Next** and **Previous** buttons. While its menu system is rather well laid out and designed for ease of use, after spending a significant amount of time with your TiVo and its remote control, the travel time and number of button presses can prove rather tedious.

Thankfully, a set of navigation shortcuts are built right in allowing you to leap between major menu items in a single bound—that is, a single button press. Table 1-1 lists known remote control shortcuts and their associated menus.

Table 1-1. TiVo remote control shortcuts

Button sequence	Menu displayed
TiVo → 1 or TiVo → TiVo	Now Playing
TiVo → 2	To Do List
TiVo → 3	WishLists
TiVo → 4	Browse By Name
TiVo → 5	Browse By Channel
TiVo → 6	Browse By Time
TiVo → 7	Record Time/Channel (manual recording)
TiVo → 8	TiVo Suggestions
TiVo → 9	Network Showcases
TiVo → ▶	Messages and Setup

The 30-Second Skip

Forget about fast forwarding through commercials; blaze through in just three to five clicks of your remote.

One of the religious differences between TiVo and ReplayTV owners is how they fast forward through commercials. While TiVo's ⏩ button will get you through those intrusive breaks soon enough, it requires some trained skill to manipulate those ⏩ and ▶ buttons while keeping a keen eye and trusting your instincts to anticipate the end of the commercials. ReplayTV, on the other hand, has a **30-second skip** button, timed specifically for skipping through commercials. Since television commercials are traditionally a multiple of 30-seconds long, ReplayTV owners just hit the **30-second skip** button three to five times to render commercials only a minor annoyance.

This feature is so effective that it has stirred up quite a bit of controversy with the networks, who are getting their hackles up, labeling commercial skipping as theft and even taking ReplayTV to court.

Don't you wish TiVo had a 30-second skip? It does, thanks to a little Easter egg magic.

The ⏭ button on the TiVo remote will bring you to the end of a program, or if you are at the end, it will bring you to the beginning. If you are fast forwarding, the ⏭ button will skip you to the next tick mark. This hack is all about repurposing that button to act as the 30-second skip.

Bring up any recorded program or Live TV. Then, enter the following sequence on your remote:

Select → ▶ → Select → 3 → 0 → Select

You'll know the combination worked when TiVo rings out three Thumbs Up sounds—that chiming "bling!" sound TiVo makes when you press the 👍 button on your remote control. Your ↦ button will now skip forward by 30 seconds.

Note that this hack is not permanent. If at any time your TiVo needs to be rebooted—after becoming unplugged or as a result of a power failure—the hack will go away and you will have to reapply it.

An Onscreen Clock
HACK #5
Turn your TiVo into a glorified and expensive clock.

Watching TV is an amazingly effective way of losing track of time. One minute it's 8 p.m. and you're watching *Friends*; the next thing you know, it's midnight and David Letterman is hurling a pencil at the camera (if you are still watching live television, that is).

Perhaps you even have a clock in the same room as your television set, but it's off in the corner and you never think to avert your gaze from the tube. This hack embeds a clock right there into your line of sight, at the bottom-right of your screen.

Enter the following sequence on your TiVo remote:

Select → ▶ → Select → 9 → Select

You will hear TiVo bling with a thumbs-up sound, and a floating white-on-black clock will appear at the bottom-right of your screen, as shown in Figure 1-2. On some versions of TiVo, you not only get the local time, but also how far you are into the show, in minutes and seconds—assuming, of course, you're watching a recorded show.

To remove the clock at any time, simply reenter the sequence and visit any TiVo menu. If you do not go to a menu, the clock will just sit there happily until you do so.

5:44:12 pm

Figure 1-2. The TiVo clock

Making the Play Bar Disappear Faster

Reduce the amount of time the play bar lingers on the screen.

So, you are a speed freak. Not only have you mastered the ⏩ button, but you also itch it to make everything faster. The one thing that particularly annoys you is that after you fast forward, then hit ▶, the play bar—that green line showing where you are in the current recording—hovers on the screen for a little longer than you really want it to.

There are two types of TiVo users: those who want as much output on the screen as possible, and the rest of us who want our screens to be as free of superfluous readout as possible. If you're in the latter category, this hack's for you.

To reduce the amount of time the play bar appears on the screen, enter the following remote control sequence:

Select → ▶ → Select → ⏸ → Select

Now give it a whirl; fast forward through a show and then push ▶. That bar should disappear right away. Undo the hack at any time by entering the sequence again.

What's Your TiVo Doing?

Out of the corner of your eye, you see TiVo's red light flicker on. Ever wonder just what your TiVo is up to?

The red light on the front of the TiVo box always raises some curiosity. "Just what is it doing? I didn't think there was anything on right now it should be recording."

The most obvious way to find out is to go to your *Now Showing* screen to check out what's being recorded, signified by the red "recording" light next to a particular show. But that means interrupting what you're currently watching. To most of us, that hardly seems like a worthwhile thing to do.

You can also peek into the mind of your TiVo. This hack overlays your currently playing show with a small information bar on the screen, which says things like Input0: InputRecording* 40 || Mode: COMPLETED (PlayRecording) when TiVo is recording—in this case, channel 40.

Select → ▶ → Select → ↩ → Select

As with the clock hack [Hack #5], reenter the button sequence, and visit any TiVo menu or live television to make it disappear again.

HACK #8 Opening the Backdoor

Open TiVo to backdoor hacks to reveal some configuration settings and features that the "untouched" TiVo does not normally allow access to.

Backdoors are the fun remote codes—the ones that require a little more knowledge to get into. You're not going to stumble upon these by accident; you have to know what you're looking for.

To use any of the backdoor remote control codes, we first have to ask TiVo to enable the as-yet-inactive backdoors code.

The one complication in enabling this mode is that it fully depends on the version of the TiVo OS your TiVo is running. To find out the version of your TiVo OS, go to the *Messages & Setup* menu and select *System Information*. You'll see a listing for "Software Version" that looks something like 3.0-01-1-010; that's what you're looking for! In this case, TiVo is running OS Version 3.0—the first two digits are the significant bits you're looking for.

Opening the Backdoor on TiVo OS 3.0 or Earlier

If your TiVo OS version is 3.0 or earlier, then armed with that version number and the listings in Table 1-2, head to the *Browse By Name* or *Search by Title* screen—the one that provides you with an alphanumeric list by which to enter letters and numbers. Using the arrows and **Select** button on your TiVo remote control, enter the appropriate backdoor code in the same way you'd usually enter the name of a show you're looking for.

> You must enter each of these backdoor codes verbatim, so pay close attention to the spaces. You can enter a space by choosing SP from the *Search by Title* or *Browse By Name* alphanumeric list.

Table 1-2. Backdoor codes for TiVos running OS 1.3 through OS 3.0

TiVo operating system version	Backdoor code
OS 1.3 in the U.S. and 1.50 or 1.51 in the U.K.	0V1T
OS 1.5.2 in the U.K.	10J0M
OS 2.0	2 0 TCD
OS 2.5 in the U.S. and 2.5.5 in the U.K.	B D 2 5
OS 2.5.2 for DirectTiVo	B M U S 1
OS 3.0	3 0 BC

Follow this by pressing the 👍 button. You will hear three thumbs-up blings, and your TiVo will briefly display Backdoors enabled!. If you check out your *System Information* screen, you'll also see a Backdoors: ENABLED! line at the top. At this point, you are in like Flynn.

The only way to disable backdoors (currently) is to reboot your TiVo.

If your TiVo is running a version of the operating system newer than 3.0, then I'm afraid you'll have to do a lot more work to open that backdoor.

Opening the Backdoor on TiVo OS 3.1 or Later

More recent versions of the TiVo operating system have started making it a little more difficult to enable backdoor mode. The previous keys were discovered by poking around TiVo's filesystem and seeking out the backdoor code itself, usually simply noted somewhere. Unfortunately, the more recent versions do not store the backdoor code "in the clear"; instead, they store a one-way, irreversible hash (read: scrambled) of the backdoor code. When you enter a potential code via *Browse By Name* or *Search by Title* as we did above, TiVo applies a special function to what you have entered and tests to see if the two hashes match up. The problem is, since the hash function is one-way, simply knowing the hash of backdoor code tells us nothing about what it is in the clear.

But it does tell us that if we know what kind of hash function the backdoor code uses (in the case of the TiVo, it uses the SHA-1 hash), then we can replace the existing hash with a new hash derived from text we do know. How about the hash of an empty string? Thankfully, Steve White has authored a utility, *backdoorpw* (*http://prdownloads.sourceforge.net/tivoutils/backdoorpw.gz?download*), that does just that.

Applying this hack is a little more complicated than the other hacks in this chapter and is going to require a few workarounds from Chapter 2. Download White's backdoor program, copy it on to a floppy disk, boot your PC using Kazymyr's bootdisk [Hack #26] with TiVo's hard drive connected [Hack #22], and then mount the floppy disk:

```
# mkdir /mnt/floppy
# mount /dev/fd0 /mnt/floppy
```

Decompress the file:

```
# cd /mnt/floppy
# gzip -d backdoor.gz
```

Then run the backdoor application on your TiVo's hard drive. Assuming that your TiVo's drive is mounted as the secondary master, use the following code:

```
# ./backdoor /dev/hdc
```

Don't worry about any damage occurring to your drive at this step. The code has a paranoia flag that, when set (which it is right now), prevents changes from being written to the drive.

Running the program should provide output very similar, but not identical, to the following:

```
Good! This is a TiVo drive
Opening MFS Application Region partition: /dev/hdc10...
searching offset 0x0fffd800
I was unable to find any occurrences of the backdoor hashes on /dev/hdc10
Opening MFS Application Region partition: /dev/hdc12...
searching offset 0x0e3fdc60
Found 96F8B204FD99534759A6C11A181EEDDFEB2DF1D4 at 0x0e41a29c
searching offset 0x0f0fda58
Found 61508C7FC1C2250E1794624D8619B9ED760FFABA at 0x0f1eb342

Found 61508C7FC1C2250E1794624D8619B9ED760FFABA at 0x0f27a2f4
searching offset 0x0fffd850
Found 3 backdoor hashes on /dev/hdc12. These will now be changed.
Patch #1 at offset 0x0e41a29c
data at 0x0e41a29c is currently '96F8B204FD99534759A6C11A181EEDDFEB2DF1D4'
data at 0x0e41a29c would be changed to
'EEA339DA0D4B6B5EEFBF5532901860950907D8AF' if we weren't paranoid
Patch #2 at offset 0x0f1eb342
data at 0x0f1eb342 is currently '61508C7FC1C2250E1794624D8619B9ED760FFABA'
data at 0x0f1eb342 would be changed to
'EEA339DA0D4B6B5EEFBF5532901860950907D8AF' if we weren't paranoid
Patch #3 at offset 0x0f27a2f4
data at 0x0f27a2f4 is currently '61508C7FC1C2250E1794624D8619B9ED760FFABA'
data at 0x0f27a2f4 would be changed to
'EEA339DA0D4B6B5EEFBF5532901860950907D8AF' if we weren't paranoid
If everything appeared okay, please rerun the program with the following
args:
./backdoor /dev/hdc y
```

The backdoor program will detect two or three hashes. In the previous output, these are the hashes:

```
data at 0x0e41a29c is currently '96F8B204FD99534759A6C11A181EEDDFEB2DF1D4'
...
data at 0x0f1eb342 is currently '61508C7FC1C2250E1794624D8619B9ED760FFABA'
...
data at 0x0f27a2f4 is currently '61508C7FC1C2250E1794624D8619B9ED760FFABA'
```

The number of hashes varies from TiVo to TiVo, but you shouldn't have more than three, unless your box has gone through a great deal of upgrades recently. It doesn't really matter, just so long as the backdoor program detects at least two hashes. Also, the offsets (e.g., 0x0e41a29c) will certainly be different, so there's no need to worry about that either.

What you should pay attention to is the format of the value inside the single quotes (e.g., 96F8B204FD99534759A6C11A181EEDDFEB2DF1D4). Make sure this value looks like the SHA hash—all uppercase, consisting of the numerals 0 through 9 and letters A through F. If the value inside the single quotes contains anything else, *do not* proceed any further, as you will most likely corrupt your TiVo's filesystem.

Provided everything looks good, rerun the program, telling it to actually write empty strings to the hash locations, like so:

```
# ./backdoor /dev/hdc y
```

The additional y flag will turn off the paranoia checks, this time writing changed hashes to the drive. Output should look something like this:

```
Good! This is a TiVo drive
Opening MFS Application Region partition: /dev/hdc10...
searching offset 0x0fffd800
I was unable to find any occurrences of the backdoor hashes on /dev/hdc10
Opening MFS Application Region partition: /dev/hdc12...
searching offset 0x0fffd878
Found 3 backdoor hashes on /dev/hdc12. These will now be changed.
Patch #1 at offset 0x0e41a29c
Patch #2 at offset 0x0f1eb342
Patch #3 at offset 0x0f27a2f4
Success! You may now put the drive back in your TiVo.
To enable backdoor mode, go into 'Search by Title' and press thumbsup.
```

The backdoor hash has been changed to an empty string. Put the drive back into your TiVo [Hack #27], revisit the *Search by Title* screen and simply press the 👍 button on your remote to open the backdoor.

Italicizing Everything
#9

If slanted type is your thing, this hack will italicize your TiVo's menus.

Maybe you are enamored with italics. Perhaps you're just in the mood for something different. Either way, after enabling backdoors [Hack #8] and entering the following sequence:

🖐 → 👍 → 🖐 → **Clear**

on a TiVo box running OS Version 3.0 or later will cause all the fonts in the menus to display in italics (see Figure 1-3).

Enter the same sequence again to change it all back.

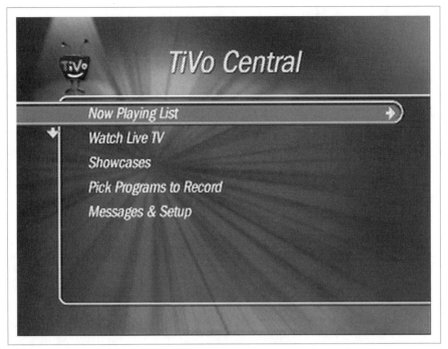

Figure 1-3. The italicized TiVo Central screen

Sorting the Now Playing List

HACK #10

If you want the sorting abilities of OS 4.0 while still using OS 3.x, then this hack is for you.

One of the major new features of TiVo OS 4.0 is the ability to sort the *Now Playing* list in more ways than just the default reverse-chronological order. OS 4.0 also allows you to sort the items in the list by expiration date or in alphabetical order.

This sorting ability is actually built into OS 3.0 too; you'll just need to enable the backdoor hack. To enable sorting, enter the following remote control sequence at the *Now Playing* screen:

▶ → 0 → ◉ → 👍

After the three thumbs-up rings, a menu bar at the bottom of the *Now Playing* list will appear, stating "Press ENTER for sort options." When you press **Enter**, your TiVo will zoom to a *Now Playing Options* screen, presenting you with the ability to sort by Newest (by record date), Expiration (by expiration date), or Alphabetical (by program name). You can also simply hit **1**, **2**, or **3** at the *Now Playing* screen as a shortcut to sort by those same options.

HACK #11 Turning Off Overshoot Protection

Turn off the overshoot protection to put fast forwarding completely under your own control.

Part of TiVo's charm is that it tries to protect you from yourself. It takes care of scheduling changes in the television shows, records new shows that you might have forgotten to request, and makes sure you don't fast forward too far when trying to get through a commercial break. But what if you want to have unmediated control over your fast forward? Well, now you can. This hack turns overshoot protection off.

The dilemma with fast forwarding is that you never know precisely where to stop. You find yourself zooming along through the commercials and watching the screen like a hawk, waiting for your program to start. Unless you're blessed with superhuman hand-eye coordination or have spent way too many hours playing twitch-reflex video games, you see your program come with the end of the commercials on the screen, inevitably overshoot by a few seconds, and therefore command your finger to hit ● a moment too late to catch the beginning of your program. Thankfully, the TiVo creators anticipated this problem and introduced *overshoot protection*; when you hit ● after fast forwarding, TiVo backs up ever so slightly, usually just enough to bring you to where you thought you should be.

But if you're a die-hard TiVo user, you might find overshoot protection akin to an automatic transmission when you'd rather prefer to drive a stick. You've probably picked up on a pattern in the way that commercials are ordered; usually right before the television show starts, the network either puts up an advertisement for itself or for one of its upcoming shows. You have the timing down to an art and just want to move overshoot protection out of the way. To do so, enable backdoors [Hack #8], then pick up your remote and enter:

Clear → Enter → Clear → 5

Reenter the sequence if you decide automatic is for you after all.

HACK #12 Controlling Overshoot Protection

Rather than turning off overshoot protection, fine-tune it to suit your fancy.

So you turn off overshoot protection [Hack #11] and find there's some value to having TiVo do some of the driving for you. You'll be happy to know there's a middle ground. Instead of turning off overshoot protection entirely, you can adjust its granularity.

Using the Node Navigator [Hack #16], carefully navigate to node number 1 and select it to access overshoot settings.

The *Set Over Shoot Value* menu, shown in Figure 1-4, shows exactly how much control your TiVo is going to give you.

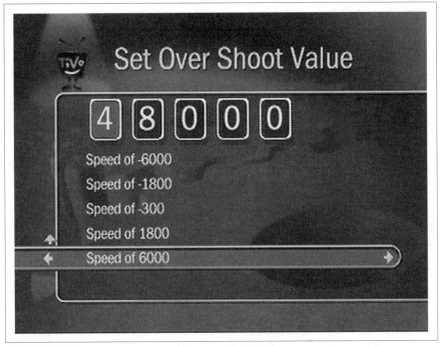

Figure 1-4. The Set Over Shoot Value menu

When you are fast forwarding or rewinding, and you hit ⊙ again, your TiVo reverses the direction for a specific number of seconds and starts playing there—that's your overshoot. The faster you are moving through the program, the larger your overshoot is set, by default.

In the *Set Over Shoot Value* menu, there are five different speeds that your TiVo has overshoot set to. If you hit ⊙ once, you zip backwards at "Speed –300". The second and third times you hit ⊙, you go back at "Speed –1800" and "Speed –6000", respectively. Likewise, if you hit ⊙ twice, you zoom ahead at "Speed 1800", and the third speed is "Speed 6000". If you play with your TiVo's remote, you'll see that there is no overshoot protection for fast forwarding just once.

To set the overshoot value for each speed, scroll down to the speed you want to change, use your remote to type in the value, and hit **Enter** to commit the value. Setting any one of these speeds to 0 will turn off overshoot protection, and every 1000 in the value set is one second of overshoot. For example, with "Speed 6000" set to 48000, if you are going through the program after hitting ● three times, hitting ● will rewind the stream 48 seconds before playing again.

If you change your values and forget the originals, don't just hope a reboot will fix it; these changes are fairly permanent. Just refer to Table 1-3 for the default values.

Table 1-3. The default values for overshoot protection in TiVo OS 3.0

Speed value	Default overshoot value
-6000	41000
-1800	14000
-300	01435
1800	15226
6000	48000

Pushing Fast Forward to Eleven

HACK #13

If TiVo's default fast forward is just not fast enough for you, this hack will satisfy your need for speed.

Now you might have made the play bar disappear quickly [Hack #6], but what if your speed desires have not yet been satisfied? Say you want to be able to blaze minutes ahead through a movie in just seconds. Or perhaps you're more the turtle and prefer to crawl forward. This backdoor hack will let you set fast forwarding to just about any speed you prefer.

After you enable backdoors [Hack #8], find yourself at the *Search by Title* screen and enter:

Enter → Enter → 1

You should see a Speed1: prompt (see Figure 1-5), and the record LED on the front of your TiVo should be lit.

Enter your preferred speed. The last two digits of the number must be 00 for an integer-multiple speed. The digits to the left of the 00 indicate how many times faster than normal playing speed the scan is running. 300 (which is 3x) is the default Speed1 scan speed; a value of 1 is super slow motion (0.01x speed).

Set the change into motion by entering:

Enter → Enter → 1

You will notice the record LED turn itself off.

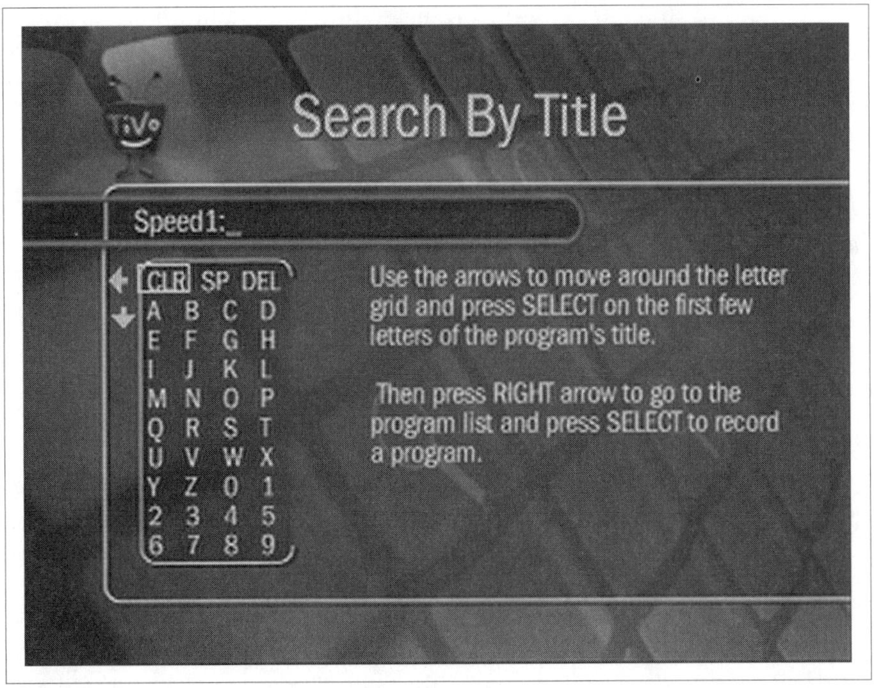

Figure 1-5. Prompting for fast-forward speed

Of course, TiVo allows you to press ⏩ up to three times, each time increasing the fast-forward speed by some factor. Set the Speed2 of the second Fast Forward press by entering:

Enter → Enter → 2

And set Speed3 for the third with:

Enter → Enter → 3

The same numerical scheme is used for all three Speed*X*: prompts. The default for the second fast forward is 2000 (or 20x), and 6000 (or 60x) is the default for the third.

TiVo will revert back to default speeds when it is rebooted.

HACK #14 Viewing Suggestions in the To Do List

TiVo has a wandering eye and is always on the lookout for what you may not have explicitly ask it to record, but which it thinks you might enjoy anyway. This hack shows you what TiVo has in mind.

Much of TiVo's magic lies in the way it watches what you watch and makes some independent decisions on other shows you might like but may not yet have noticed or thought about recording. While you might think the *To Do List* is TiVo's list of what to record, it's really TiVo's list of what you've asked it to record. This hack makes the *To Do List* reflect TiVo's list of what it intends to offer you.

To see what interests TiVo, enable backdoors [Hack #8], then enter the following backdoor hack sequence on your remote control from the *To Do List*:

> While you can remove these suggestions from the *To Do List*, this doesn't necessarily cancel the recording. The suggestion may be added back or the program may record anyway.

Reapply this hack to remove those suggestions from the list.

HACK #15   Viewing "Hidden" Recordings

Display previews, *Showcase* content, and advertising in the *Now Playing* list.

TiVo holds more than just your preferred programming; it also records content for its *Showcase* and the advertisements that periodically show up on the main *TiVo Central* screen. TiVo, Inc. contracts with some cable companies to provide this content late at night, and then instruct your TiVo to record it.

This hack lists this half hour or so of programming as "Teleworld Paid Program" in the *Now Playing* list.

> Remote control hacks are often context-sensitive. If you paid attention carefully, you'll notice that this sequence of remote button presses is the same as the sequence used to display TiVo's suggestions in the *To Do List* [Hack #14]. The sequence has an entirely different effect when applied on the *Now Playing* screen.

From the *Now Playing* screen, enter:

to see the "hidden" recordings listed in the *Now Playing* list.

Undo this hack by simply reapplying it.

You can, alternatively, see a hidden menu called *Clips on Disk* by entering:

Activating the Node Navigator

#16 Surf through all TiVo's menus—even a few you can't usually see—via this backdoor menu system.

Perhaps you want fine-grained control of overshoot protection [Hack #12]. Or maybe you want to access the advanced functionality in the WishLists [Hack #17]. To get to either of these means poking about into menus where the sun doesn't usually shine.

This is the ultimate rabbit hole through the system; this is TiVo's internal representation of where everything is. Every menu screen in the system, whether standard or otherwise hidden, is represented by a menu node. Each one of the menu nodes you see in Figure 1-6 will zip you straight to its respective menu screen on the system. What makes this particularly difficult is that the nodes are numbered, not named, which may cause you to end up in the wrong node. More than just a nuisance, this can actually make alterations to the way your TiVo software works.

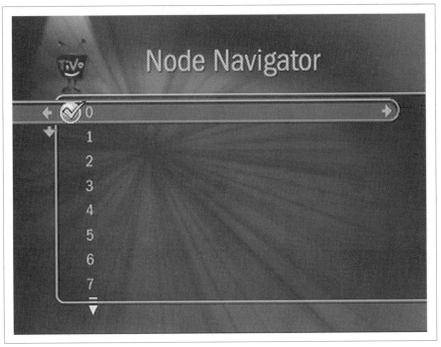

Figure 1-6. The powerful—and potentially dangerous—Node Navigator

For example, if you found the menu to set your ZIP code, but left without setting it, your programming lineup would be decimated during the next daily calling, causing your TiVo to reboot every time you tried to watch Live TV. If you do find yourself somewhere you dare not tread, hit the button to back out.

I'll say it again. The *Node Navigator* can be dangerous to play with. Simply wandering into the wrong numbered nodes on the screen could alter the TiVo software, leaving it in an unusable state and requiring a restore from backup [Hack #25].

Fine-tuning these values actually requires a little bit of bravado and some fine remote-control-handling skills, so don't slip. To bring up the *Node Navigator* menu, enable backdoors [Hack #8], then enter the following sequence on your remote control:

Clear → Enter → Clear → 6

HACK #17 Enabling Advanced WishLists

Advanced WishLists allow you to specify combinations of actors, titles, and so forth for TiVo to find and record.

TiVo's WishLists, while being pretty powerful, are limited in how granular you can get. You can ask for shows only by actor, title, director, category, or keyword—not a combination of two or more. Advanced WishLists bring the "and" to WishLists, allowing you to specify movies directed by so-and-so, starring what's-his-name.

It's not clear why TiVo exposes the Advanced WishList system—perhaps because it cannot be explained in the two to three sentences the make-it-simple philosophy the TiVo requires.

To activate the *Advanced* menu off the *Search Using WishLists* menu, start the Node Navigator [Hack #16], carefully select node 30, and select the expert interface for creating WishLists. Hit the button to jump out of the navigator.

Now, if you go to the *WishList* menu, the last item in the list should be *Advanced WishList* (you might have to scroll down past the screen). From here you can create a WishList that is any combination of actors, directors, keywords, and genres. Be as specific as you want to be. Nice, isn't it?

The Advanced WishLists hack will remain in effect after a reboot.

Turning Off the TiVo Software

#18 Turn off the software that makes your TiVo a TiVo, turning it into a $300 lemon. More precisely, you'll have a nicely packaged, almost-special-purpose Linux box.

It's not clear why you would ever want to turn off the very software that makes your TiVo a TiVo. Without the myworld program, the heart of TiVo, it's a lemon.

Either way, if you are curious, then the following simple sequence should do it:

Clear → Enter → Clear → 👎

The only way to reactivate it after turning it off is to either pull the plug on it and power it back up, or reboot it. Once you do that, your system will return to being a normal TiVo again. Or, if you have a Bash prompt on your TiVo [Hack #30], you can manually type:

```
myworld &
```

at the prompt and your television screen—and TiVo—will come back to life in a couple of seconds.

Applaud the TiVo Team

#19 Give credit where credit is due.

If you ever really wanted to know the names of all the people who gave their blood, sweat, and tears to TiVo, here is your chance meet them—virtually at least.

If you have a television with Closed Captioning (or have access to the *tivovbi* to simulate Closed Captioning [Hack #42]), turn it on and surf your way to the *Browse By Name* or *Search by Title* menu. Enter SHAGWELL as the name of the show you're looking for and press the 👍 button.

Stand up and applaud—if you're so inclined—as the names of the developers scroll by (see Figure 1-7).

This is actually a rather common so-called "Easter egg," a silly surprise hidden by a programmer or programming team for chance discovery. You'll find Easter eggs sporting the names of developers in about any computer operating system or software product—even, in the case of the original 1984 Macintosh, molded into the interior plastic shell of the computer.

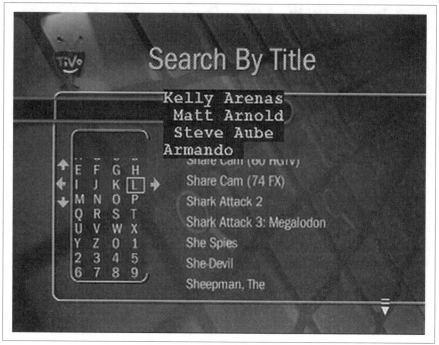

Figure 1-7. The names of TiVo developers

Adding More Hours
Hacks 20–28

Adding hours to the TiVo is no doubt one of the oldest and most obvious of all the TiVo hacks. The first TiVo to be released, the Philips HDR110 (renamed HDR112), could store a mere 14 hours of recordings at basic quality. The first technophiles to crack open their $1,000 boxes noticed right off that their units contained not only space for a second hard drive, but also a power connector and dangling ribbon connector to boot.

That was 1998. And, no, nothing much has changed since then.

No guide to adding hours would be complete without mentioning Bill "Hinsdale" Regnery, compiler and maintainer of the consummate online resource for TiVo upgraders. You can find the most up-to-date version at *http://www.newreleasesvideo.com/hinsdale-how-to*.

If this chapter seems at all daunting to you, or if you'd simply prefer someone else to take care of some or all of the nitty-gritty details for you, there are a few companies that will do just that. Ask around on *http://www. tivocommunity.com* for recommendations, or search Google for "tivo upgrade". Just be sure you pick a reputable firm; this is your beloved TiVo you're fiddling with, after all.

 This chapter was written mostly by the folks at WeaKnees (*http://www.weaknees.com*), sellers of upgrade kits and pre-upgraded TiVo units.

Basic Assumptions

Although all TiVo upgrades rely on the same tools, there is by no means one universal set of upgrade instructions. Instead, there are many variables that drive an individual upgrade. On top of these variables, there are also at least four different internal TiVo architectures: some of these PVRs come with two drives from the factory, some contain power cables and IDE ribbon connectors for a second drive, some have a bracket that can only hold a single drive, and some TiVo models may require special power management devices.

To add more to the mix, the software that powers various TiVos is not interchangeable; they may all appear to be the same, but the upgrade process varies depending on your specific model.

We're going to try to cover as many mainstream upgrades as we can, but first—because of the seemingly endless combinations—let's lay out a few specific assumptions just to reign in the scope of this chapter:

- We'll assume that you are starting with a TiVo that has never been upgraded. This way we don't have to figure out how to get around what you've already done.

- We'll also assume that your TiVo is functioning and that its drive is not corrupt. Although replacing a hard drive can solve many TiVo ailments, such as the dreaded "Sever Error has Occurred" (a.k.a. the "Green Screen of Death"), it is not possible to replace a defective drive unless you have a reliable backup of the TiVo software. And while it may be possible to search high and low to find somebody who can provide you with a backup, making one yourself is not generally possible if your original drive is not functioning. If your TiVo is misbehaving, check *http://www.weaknees.com/tivo_repair.html* and *http://www.weaknees.com/tivo_powering_up.html* for more help.

- We'll assume that you are working with and backing up a software version that is at least TiVo OS 2.5.

- Lastly, we're not going to address drive-replacement upgrades that also involve the preservation of existing recordings and settings. We hope you're not entirely wed to whatever is already recorded on your TiVo; while there is a chance that when you finish this process your recordings will still be there, there are no guarantees.

Don't worry if your upgrade-to-be veers widely from these assumptions; most assuredly, there are still options open to you. Just try out the WeaKnees interactive guide at *http://tivo.upgrade-instructions.com* for more varieties.

Gathering Some Information

Before diving right in, it's best to lay out all the options and figure out exactly what you are going to be doing. This way you are not making decisions while your TiVo is sitting open on your bench. Be a boy scout: always be prepared.

What TiVo Model Do You Have?

Most of you probably know exactly what model you have; you're probably the type that memorized everything about your TiVo while you were waiting for it to finish its setup for the first time. But if you don't know, you can find the information right on the back of your TiVo recorder itself. Plus, on some TiVos, the model is even listed at the top of the *System Information* screen. While mine doesn't list its model number in the *System Information* screen, by looking at the back I found out that my TiVo-branded 60-hour Series 2 is model TCD140060.

As of this writing, TiVo units come in four varieties of internal architecture. These four configurations determine both the parts you'll need to complete your upgrade and also the physical installation procedure. Although removing, replacing, and adding drives is roughly the same for each model within a given architecture, the software installation instructions can vary even between TiVo models with the same internal architecture. For example, even though the Hughes GXCEBOT and the TiVo TCD140060 are from the same layout family and employ similar methods to physically upgrade, when it comes to software, the instructions vary. The four internal architectures are:

Type 1: Philips HDR series and Sony SVR-2000
> These models have space for a second drive, but only the HDR312 and HD612 come equipped with a bracket for the second drive. In a pinch, you can probably get away with simply cable-tying the hard drive down, but to play it safe you'll probably want to secure it a bit more firmly. These TiVos do, however, include an IDE cable and a power cable at the ready for a second drive.

Type 2: Sony SAT T-60, Hughes GXCEBOT, Philips DSR6000, TiVo TCD140060, and AT&T TCD130040
> All these models can accommodate a second drive and may also include power and IDE cables for a second drive, depending on model and manufacture date.

Type 3: TiVo TCD240040, AT&T TCD230040, TiVo TCD240080, Hughes HDVR2, and Philips DSR7000
> Unlike the previous two TiVo families, these models require custom-designed brackets, new IDE cables, and Y-power splitters for a second drive. On top of these requirements, some Series2 standalone models (e.g., 240040, 230040, and 240080) may also require a power management solution like the PowerTrip.

Type 4: Sony SVR-3000
> The SVR-3000 already includes a bracket for a second drive and, unlike its predecessors, it does not use Torx screws. It does, however, require new IDE and power cables to support the additional drive.

How Many Hard Drives Does Your TiVo Currently Have?

Before you go out and buy a new hard drive for your TiVo, you need to know how many hard drives your TiVo already has installed. TiVos can hold up to two hard drives, so if your box already has two, your best bet is to remove both and replace them with one or two larger drives. If you only have one drive, you have the option of adding a second drive.

In all but two cases, the TiVo model number and Table 2-1 will tell you how many drives a new TiVo has inside. If you have a Philips DSR6000 or a Sony SAT T-60, the only surefire way to determine whether you have one or two drives is to open the unit and take a look.

Table 2-1. The number of drives installed in different TiVo models

TiVo model number	Number of drives
HDR312	2
HDR612	2
DSR6000	See text following this table for more details
SAT T-60	See text following this table for more details

Short of opening the DSR6000 and the T-60, here are two rules of thumb that you can use to help determine the number of drives in those models:

Serial number method

This method is not 100% accurate, but it is reasonably reliable. Locate the serial number of your DSR6000 or your SAT T-60. For the DSR6000, usually only those with serial numbers that begin with 800 ship with dual drives; all others, such as the 801 through 805 and possibly higher, come installed with only a single hard drive. Likewise, for the SAT T-60, those with serial numbers that start with 4701 through 4703 have two drives on the inside; the rest just have one. If you have a refurbished factory unit, all bets are off.

Drive screws method

In a two-drive DSR6000 and SAT T-60, each of the drives will be secured by four screws. Two of those screw holes are visible from underneath by looking through the grills on the bottom of the unit. If you look through the grills on the left side of the TiVo (left, that is, when looking at the front) and you see two empty screw holes, you have only one drive. If you see screws, again, all bets are off and you are going to have to rely on the serial number method or opening the box to figure this out. To help you out, WeaKnees has posted some illustrative pictures at *http://www.weaknees.com/directv_tivo_drives.php*.

Should You Add to or Replace Your Drives?

If your TiVo currently has two drives, then your only upgrade option is to replace both of those drives. While it is technically possible to reuse one of those factory drives, many experts strongly discourage it. In a two-drive TiVo, both drives have to be functioning for it to operate properly. If the older, factory-installed drive fails, you will have to go back into the box later to replace it. Plus, if you keep your two factory drives together on a shelf somewhere, you will be able to use them together as a backup if your upgrade drive fails.

On the other hand, if you have a one-drive TiVo, then it's up to you whether you add a second drive, replace your single drive with a newer and larger drive, or replace your single drive with two new drives. Table 2-2 should provide some guidance in making this decision; more details can be found at *http://www.weaknees.com/add_replace.php.*

Table 2-2. Adding to versus replacing your TiVo's hard drives

	Replacing the hard drive	Adding a hard drive
Programming/Settings	You will lose your programming and settings. It is possible to retain both of these, but that is beyond the scope of this chapter.	You will retain your programming and settings.
TiVo hard drive lifespan	Depending on the age of your TiVo, you may benefit by removing an older, factory hard drive and replacing it with a new one. In addition, replacing your drive or drives will enable you to retain the factory drives as a backup if, for whatever reason, you need your new drives repaired or replaced down the road.	After the upgrade, your TiVo will have two drives—one brand-new drive and one factory drive. Because your TiVo now treats those two drives as one, they cannot be separated. If one drive fails, the good drive must be reformatted and reconfigured. By continuing to use an old factory drive, you increase the chance for failure.
Performance	A new replacement drive formatted with MFS Tools 2.0 may perform better (in terms of menu speeds, etc.) than a TiVo that has been upgraded with a second drive using BlessTiVo.	Adding a second drive using BlessTiVo will result in performance degradation that may be avoided using the MFSAdd command described in this chapter, except if a new drive is added to a very old factory drive, or if a second drive is added to a large factory drive. Additionally, the TiVo may not be unable to recover on its own from the green "Severe Error" screen.

Table 2-2. Adding to versus replacing your TiVo's hard drives (continued)

	Replacing the hard drive	Adding a hard drive
Storage space	You will not utilize the space available on the factory installed drive or drives.	You will utilize the space on your factory drive, resulting in additional storage.
Ease of upgrade	Replacing your drive requires a backup of your existing drive and/or a copy of the existing drive to the new drive. This can take 20–30 minutes solely for the backup.	If you do not back up your primary drive, then preparing a second drive takes only a few minutes and is quite easy. If you do back up your drive, then adding a second drive takes no less time than replacing an existing drive. In the end, however, your programming will be preserved.

If you have a one-drive Series 1 TiVo (HDR series, SVR-2000, DSR6000, SAT T-60, or GXCEBOT), we strongly recommend that you replace your drive. Series 2 owners should review Table 2-2 and decide based on the listed factors. However, as Series 2 TiVos age, replacing older drives becomes that much more attractive.

Should You Back Up Your TiVo Before You Upgrade?

The answer is a resounding yes! We strongly recommend that you obtain a working backup of your TiVo software before upgrading your TiVo on your own. Although backing up [Hack #24] and restoring [Hack #25] will add at least an hour or two to the process, having a working backup will at least prevent you from sweating bullets. You might consider throwing caution to the wind if you are in a huge rush to upgrade and have decided to add a second drive; many experts have walked this razor's edge—installing the second drive without the backup—and have come out just fine. While we can't officially say we recommend adding a second drive without a backup, we do understand the urge to give it a skip.

Getting Everything Together

We know you're anxious to pop the top off that box, but it behooves you to take a moment to get everything you'll need together in one place so that you don't find yourself running frantically to the hardware store for a Torx screwdriver while your TiVo sits dismantled on your bench. Also, what would a hard drive upgrade be without the hard drive?

A Hard Drive

The most important, and costliest, part of a TiVo hard drive upgrade is the hard drive itself. Although most major hard drives are generally reliable, there are a number of factors—such as price, warranty, noise, and speed—that you should consider:

Finding the best price

> Price comparison sites offer a convenient way to find drive deals and we have found Price Watch (*http://www.pricewatch.com*) to be the best resource. You might also try *http://www.froogle.com*. Be careful, however; drive performance is often significantly hampered due to poor packaging from discounters. Unfortunately, many discount vendors simply mail out drives wrapped in bubble wrap and tossed into a box of peanuts or shredded paper. Drive manufacturers universally discourage this. Reputable distributors enclose their drives in plastic casing or anti-static bags, surrounded on all sides with foam cushioning. This provides the best protection for your new drive.

Finding the best warranty

> As of October 1, 2002, most major drive manufacturers—such as Maxtor, Seagate, and Western Digital—cut their warranty down from three years to one year for most basic EIDE hard drives. Some higher-end drives from these manufacturers still carry a three-year warranty. In addition, as of now, Samsung still has a full three-year warranty on its drives. Just something to keep in the back of your mind as you search for a drive.

Finding the right drive

> A basic search of most TiVo community forums will reveal a wide array of opinions regarding drives, often with very little consensus. As drive technology, models, and reliability change frequently, a quick visit to the TiVo community message boards or other hard drive review sites would probably be prudent. As of this writing, TiVos ship with 5400 RPM drives, and, although higher rotational speeds such as 7200 RPM might be tempting, they may not offer any additional benefit when installed in your TiVo. The stock TiVo kernel can only use about 170 GB per disk, so don't bother getting a disk much larger than that. Also, remember to check out how loud the drive you're looking at is; it may be a turnoff to watch a romantic movie in your living room while your TiVo is loudly clicking and whirring away.

A Spare Computer

No matter what, you're going to need an Intel-based PC that you are willing to pop open and get inside of. That PC should be equipped with a CD-ROM drive (a floppy drive will do in a pinch) and with as many free IDE slots as there are drives you plan to install. Don't forget that your CD-ROM—if you are using one—needs to remain connected during all this, so you lose an IDE slot right there.

If you intend to back up the TiVo's software, you are going to need an IDE hard drive installed in your PC (not one of the TiVo drives, or soon-to-be TiVo drives) that has a partition formatted as DOS/Windows FAT32—like that of your average Windows 95/98 install. To be safe, this partition should have at least 1.25 GB free, although backups can be done into as little as 150 MB. One final caveat: this drive has to be installed as the primary master on the PC's IDE bus.

> If finding an Intel-based PC sounds alien to you, chances are you're a Mac-lover. Unfortunately, your capabilities are severely limited. Check out *http://www.macupdate.com/info.php/id/9934*, where you can get Eric Wagner's MacTiVo Blesser. With it, you can use your Mac to bless a second drive for use in an HDR-series TiVo, SVR-2000, Philips DSR-6000, Sony SAT T-60, or Hughes GXCEBOT. Everything said later in "Adding a Second Drive the Quick-n-Dirty Way" [Hack #26] about using BlessTiVo in the Series 1 TiVos applies to the MacTiVo Blesser. You are limited, however, to only being able to *add* a new drive to your TiVo, because the software needed to *replace* one of your PVR's hard drives does not yet exist. If you just can't bear to touch a PC, check out one of the many upgrade companies that will send you an upgrade drive preformatted with the proper software.

Some Software

All the software required to upgrade your TiVo is free and publicly available for download. Grab yourself a copy of the CD-ROM (*http://hellcat.tyger.org/MFS/2.0/mfstools2noJ.iso*) or floppy version of Steven Lang's MFS Tools 2.0 (*http://www.newreleasesvideo.com/hinsdale-how-to/Mfstools2floppy.zip*). If you are adding a second drive and not planning to make a backup, then you can probably get away with grabbing BlessTiVo instead; you'll find the CD version at *http://www.9thtee.com/tbdv2_6i.iso*, and a floppy version is available at *http://www.sonnik.com/tivo/downloads/upgradeav3.2.zip*.

Download the software and burn the CDs using any basic CD-burning software package (Adaptec Easy CD Creator works well, as does Nero).

Configure the CD software to burn as an ISO image. If you have difficulties, use data mode 1, block size 2048.

If you've opted to use the floppy versions instead, unzip the downloaded file, run *MakeDisk.bat*, and put a blank 1.44 MB floppy disk in your drive. Follow the prompts to create a bootable floppy.

Other Accessories

The last of the hardware you're going to need are some screwdrivers and an assortment of cables and mounting brackets for the TiVo itself. Table 2-3 lists TiVo models and the accessories needed to complete the upgrade. Model numbers denoted with an "(A1)" refer to adding a second drive to a one-drive TiVo, "(R1)" refers to replacing the drive with a new drive, and "(R2)" refers to replacing the installed drive with two new drives.

Be sure to get everything you need before starting the upgrade.

Table 2-3. Assorted hardware—screwdrivers, cables, and mounting equipment—for each TiVo model

TiVo model	Torx T10	Torx T15	Drive screws	IDE cable	Y-power	Series 1 bracket (optional)	TwinBreeze (or equivalent)	PowerTrip (recommended)
130040(A1)	X	X	X	X	X			
130040(R1)	X	X						
130040(R2)	X	X	X	X	X			
140060(A1)	X	X	X	X	X			
140060(R1)	X	X						
140060(R2)	X	X	X	X	X			
230040(A1)	X	X		X	X		X	X
230040(R1)	X	X						
230040(R2)	X	X		X	X		X	X
240040(A1)	X	X		X	X		X	X
240040(R1)	X	X						
240040(R2)	X	X		X	X		X	X
240080(A1)	X	X		X	X		X	X
240080(R1)	X	X						
240080(R2)	X	X		X	X		X	X
DSR6000(A1)	X	X	X					
DSR6000(R1)	X	X						

Table 2-3. Assorted hardware—screwdrivers, cables, and mounting equipment—for each TiVo model (continued)

TiVo model	Torx T10	Torx T15	Drive screws	IDE cable	Y-power	Series 1 bracket (optional)	TwinBreeze (or equivalent)	PowerTrip (recommended)
DSR6000(R2)	X	X	X					
DSR7000(A1)	X	X		X	X		X	
DSR7000(R1)	X	X						
DSR7000(R2)	X	X		X	X		X	
GXCEBOT(A1)	X	X	X	X	X			
GXCEBOT(R1)	X	X						
GXCEBOT(R2)	X	X	X	X	X			
HDR112(A1)	X					X		
HDR112(R1)	X	X						
HDR112(R2)	X	X				X		
HDR212(A1)	X					X		
HDR212(R1)	X	X						
HDR212(R2)	X	X				X		
HDR312/HDR612(R1)	X	X						
HDR312/HDR612(R2)	X	X				X		
HDR3120X(A1)	X					X		
HDR3120X(R1)	X	X						
HDR3120X(R2)	X	X				X		
HDVR2(A1)	X	X		X	X		X	
HDVR2(R1)	X	X						
HDVR2(R2)	X	X		X	X		X	
SAT T-60(A1)	X	X	X	X[a]				
SAT T-60(R1)	X	X						
SAT T-60(R2)	X	X	X	X[a]				
SVR-2000(A1)	X					X		
SVR-2000(R1)	X	X						
SVR-2000(R2)	X	X				X		
SVR-3000(A1)			X	X	X			
SVR-3000(R1)								
SVR-3000(R2)			X	X	X			

[a] In some cases.

What are all those bits and bobs?

Torx screwdrivers

All upgrades (other than upgrades of the Sony SVR-3000) require at least a Torx T-10 screwdriver and, possibly, a Torx T-15 as well. Torx screwdrivers should be available at any hardware store, but if you have difficulty finding an actual screwdriver, Torx bits for cordless screwdrivers are quite common.

IDE cable

If you are considering adding a second drive to your one-drive TiVo (or replacing your drive(s) with two new drives), then you might need a new IDE cable (see Figure 2-1). If the already-installed cable has an extra connector on it, then a new cable is not needed. Where a new cable is required, a standard ATA/66 18" flat IDE cable, spaced at 0"–12"–18", should work. When purchasing an IDE cable, be sure that all of the connectors have all 40 holes open. Some connectors have only 39 open holes and one blocked hole. If you do end up with such a cable, you can often dislodge the last hole using a hot safety pin or other sharp object. Keep in mind that if you purchase a standard 18" IDE cable you will almost always have to reverse the cable to make it fit properly in your TiVo. In other words, the blue end of the connector (which is typically the motherboard connector) must be attached to the master drive for the cable to work.

Y-power cable

If you plan to house two hard drives inside your TiVo yet do not have a free power port, then you will need a power splitter (see Figure 2-1). The splitters are standard 5.25" IDE hard drive power splitters and are available at major computer stores or online. In addition, some professional upgraders sell Y-power adapters and IDE cables that are premeasured for use in TiVos.

Drive screws

Certain TiVo models require four standard #6-32 hard drive screws to mount a second drive. Other models require some other means of mounting the second drive; depending on your mounting solution, you may need different sized screws.

Mounting bracket

Certain models of TiVo do not have mounting hardware for a second hard drive. Mounting brackets for the HDR-series and the SVR-2000 are available both at *http://www.9thtee.com* and at WeaKnees, while custom-engineered brackets for models like the TiVo TCD 240040 and Hughes HDVR2 are currently available only from WeaKnees, at *http://www.weaknees.com/twinbreeze.php*.

Power management

Certain Series 2 standalone TiVo models have power supplies that have a maximum load of 38W. Hard drives take between 20W and 30W to spin up, but they then settle down to an average draw of about 5W. The 38W power supply in these particular units was not designed to handle the startup of two drives at once. To work around this power budget, WeaKnees sells the PowerTrip (at *http://www.weaknees.com/powertrip. php*, shown in Figure 2-1). The PowerTrip essentially delays the startup of the master drive for about 7–10 seconds, thereby reducing the peak total draw on the power supply.

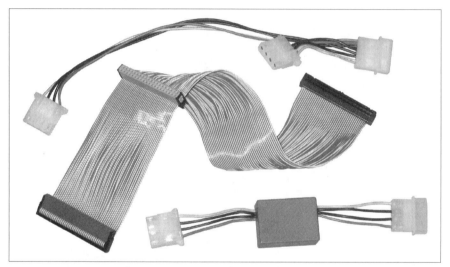

Figure 2-1. From top to bottom, a Y-power adapter, an IDE cable with two connectors, and the PowerTrip from WeaKnees.

Many online retailers do sell upgrade kits that contain tested hard drives, cables, tools, and instructions; these kits can potentially save you a lot of time and heartache. You can still have the fun of installing everything yourself, but you don't have to worry that you forgot to buy something in preparation.

However, do some research before you buy a hard drive, a mounting bracket, or any other TiVo part. Take a close look at what is being sold and make sure it won't make your TiVo look like it's being held together by duct tape or otherwise cause it to overheat. Ask around on some TiVo forums and make sure you are making an intelligent decision.

Opening the Box
#20 Pop the top off your TiVo unit.

Now it's time to get down and dirty. Let's pop that box open.

First things first: unplug the power cord from your TiVo and wait five minutes for it to discharge. Do not—I repeat, *do not*—plug the TiVo back in until you are all finished.

> The TiVo, just like any desktop computer, has a pretty large power supply mounted inside its case. No matter how long you leave the TiVo unplugged, it can still hold a sizeable charge. Be careful to avoid it as best you can, trying not to brush a stray elbow against it, lest you find out just how far you can jump.

In addition to protecting yourself from your TiVo's power supply, be very careful of static electricity, which can destroy your TiVo's internal parts. A good idea before you begin is to touch a large grounded metal surface with your hands to dissipate any electricity your body has built up. It's a very bad idea to open your TiVo up on a carpet.

Depending on your TiVo's lineage (see "What TiVo Model Do You Have?" earlier in this chapter for the four types of TiVo architectures), it'll have a different number of screws on the back to remove with your screwdriver. TiVos of type 1 have three Torx screws on the back, type 2s have four Torx screws on the back that are surrounded by the top of the TiVo's case, and Tivos based on type 3 architecture also have four Torx screws. The Sony SVR-3000 (the sole member of type 4) is a beast of a different color: it has two Philips screws on the back, surrounded by silver from the top of the case. Remove these screws and the two large-head screws on each side of the unit.

Once the screws are removed, you have to remove the lid; this sometimes doesn't actually turn out to be as easy as it sounds. The tried and true method is to place the TiVo on the floor and to kneel down with your knees at the front of the TiVo. Place your palms on the top-side edges of the TiVo, toward the middle of the TiVo's cover, and push toward the back of the TiVo. Start with a small push, but don't be surprised if you have to use the force of your entire body to jar the lid loose. If this method fails, you can try using a flathead screwdriver or similar device between the top-front of the TiVo and the lid. Eventually, you will jar the cover loose, and it will slide back and then up. Remove the cover from the TiVo.

And you're in.

Removing TiVo's Hard Drive or Drives

#21   To access the internals of your TiVo, you're going to have to pull out its hard drive.

After opening your TiVo [Hack #20], you should clearly see your TiVo's one or two hard drives (depending on your model of TiVo). The challenge now is to know how to pull them out. Each one of the TiVo architectures (see "What TiVo Model Do You Have?" at the beginning of this chapter) is subtly different, so just to be sure you're armed with enough information; we'll carefully go through how to operate on each.

> TiVo's hard drives are usually pretty close to the power supply. As you attempt to remove the drives, be sure to avoid touching the possibly charged power supply.

Removing the Hard Drive from a Type 1 TiVo

If your TiVo has only one drive inside (see Figure 2-2), you will see a gray IDE ribbon cable that runs from the green motherboard to a plastic holder on the hard drive. You're going to have to remove that ribbon cable from the hard drive on the top left. With a two-drive TiVo, you will see both hard drives and the single ribbon cable that connects each drive together and to the motherboard. Completely remove that cable from the hard drive or drives by gently pulling on it. A hard drive also has a white, inch-wide power connector attached to it. Remove that connector, too.

Now to carefully free the cables. If your TiVo had only one drive when it left the factory, the power connector for the second drive should be tied down with cable ties and may be tucked underneath the motherboard. You need to slide it out from under the motherboard and cut those ties; be very careful not to cut any of the wires. Next, if the IDE cable is clipped onto a clip next to your hard drive, you'll want to remove the cable from the clip. Don't worry about removing the clip in this case as it is secured with double-sided tape. You may also have to remove a small rubber band or another cable tie in order to free the IDE ribbon cable.

Using your Torx T10 screwdriver, carefully unscrew the two screws that secure the existing hard drive and hard drive bracket to your TiVo. These two screws are located toward the front-bottom of the TiVo, where the drive sits. If you have a two-drive TiVo, remove two screws on each of the two drive brackets. Take note of where the drive is located in your TiVo and how the bracket sits; you will be replacing it in the same place later. Now that everything is loose, remove the drive and bracket by sliding the drive and bracket toward the back of the TiVo and lifting out the bracket/drive combination.

Figure 2-2. A TiVo of architecture type 1, with only one hard drive

Finally, carefully unscrew the four Torx T15 screws located underneath the drive that secure the drive to the drive bracket. Lather, rinse, and repeat if you have two drives.

Removing the Hard Drive from a Type 2 TiVo

With the cover off, and looking underneath the front lip of the TiVo, you will be able to see one or two hard drives; an IDE ribbon cable that runs from the green motherboard to the drive(s); a red, black, and yellow power cable that runs from the power supply to the hard drive(s); and a red and blue (or red and black) fan cable that runs from the hard drive bay to the motherboard, as shown in Figure 2-3.

First, gently remove the fan cable from the motherboard by pulling straight up and out.

If you have a Sony SAT T-60, consider yourself unlucky at this point. You're going to have to locate a very pesky screw that connects the drive bay to the case. Look behind the power supply and you should see it. You're going to need a Torx L-key of size 10 or 15 to do this job—you can find one at almost any hardware store. Some TiVo hackers have reportedly used a business card to cover the power supply's capacitors while removing the screw with a screwdriver; you might want to do the same to save you from the nasty

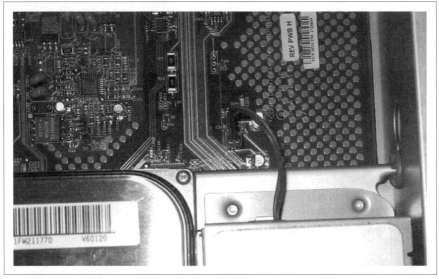

Figure 2-3. The fan cable running to the motherboard in a type 2 TiVo

shock. Be patient, and take care when removing the screw. But at the same time, rejoice, as we're not going to bother putting this screw back later on.

Orient yourself so that you are looking at the front of the TiVo. Using your Torx screwdriver, unscrew and remove the two screws on the left side of the drive bracket, as shown in Figure 2-4. Also, while you're at it, remove the gold inserts from the blue grommets and keep the screws and inserts together.

Now you should be able to lift the drive bay up from the left and slide it out of the two holes on the right side of the drive bay, as shown in Figure 2-5. As you slide it up and out, take care not to damage the drive and power cable that are still connected. You should grab the right side of the bracket with your free hand so that the drive bay doesn't slam down into the motherboard as you pull it up and out.

With everything out, remove the power connector or connectors (there should be one connected to each drive on the bay). These cables are sometimes difficult to remove. Just have patience and wiggle them back and forth, as they will eventually jiggle right out. Also, remove the gray hard drive ribbon cable from each hard drive by pulling on the hard plastic connector. Now you can remove the four screws connecting each hard drive to the drive bay and pull out the hard drives. Don't confuse these screws with the screws you removed from the back of the TiVo.

Figure 2-4. The two screws to remove when extracting the hard drive bay from a type 2 TiVo

Removing the Hard Drive from a Type 3 TiVo

Finding yourself with the cover off and looking to the front-right of your TiVo, you should be able to see one hard drive; a gray IDE ribbon cable that runs from the green motherboard to the hard drive; and a red, black, and yellow power cable that runs from the power supply to the hard drive.

Reach in, and carefully jiggle the power cable until it comes free and remove gray IDE cable from the hard drive. Please take great care not to jar or dislodge any of the other cables running around the inside of the TiVo.

Figure 2-5. Pulling the hard drive bracket up and out to the left

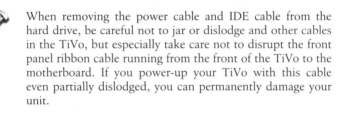

When removing the power cable and IDE cable from the hard drive, be careful not to jar or dislodge and other cables in the TiVo, but especially take care not to disrupt the front panel ribbon cable running from the front of the TiVo to the motherboard. If you power-up your TiVo with this cable even partially dislodged, you can permanently damage your unit.

Using your Torx screwdriver, unscrew and remove the two bracket screws located at the front-right of the TiVo that connect the hard drive bracket to the lower bracket. Once the screws are removed, you will be able to slide the drive and bracket toward the power supply, and then up and out of the TiVo (see Figure 2-6). Note the ribbon connector attaching the front panel to the motherboard; under no circumstances should you disturb that connector.

You can now safely remove the four screws connecting the hard drive to the hard drive bay. Take care not to confuse these screws with the four screws you removed from the TiVo's lid.

Removing the Hard Drive from a Type 4 TiVo

The SVR-3000 follows steps similar to those used with the TiVo TCD 140060 and other TiVos based on architecture type 2, with a few slight changes.

Figure 2-6. Pulling the hard drive out a type 3 TiVo

Looking underneath the front lip of the TiVo, you will be able to see the hard drive; an IDE ribbon cable that runs from the green motherboard underneath the drive to the hard drive; a red, black, and yellow power cable that runs from the power supply to the drive; and a fan cable that runs from the hard drive bay to the motherboard.

Gently remove the fan cable from the motherboard by pulling straight up and out. Next, using your index and middle fingers, reach down between the front of the hard drive and the front of the TiVo to remove the power cable from the hard drive.

Now, to free the drive bay, use a Phillips-head screwdriver to unscrew the four black drive bracket screws securing the bay to the TiVo chassis. It's best to set these black screws aside so that you don't confuse them with the other screws you have removed from your TiVo so far. You should now be able to lift the drive bay up and out. With one hand holding the bracket, use your other hand to remove the IDE cable connecting the hard drive to the TiVo.

You can now place the bay upside-down on a table. Use your Phillips-head screwdriver to remove the four very short, silver screws connecting the drive to its bay, and set them aside so that they do not get mixed up with the other screws.

Installing TiVo's Hard Drive in Your PC

With the drive out of the box, mount it in your PC, ready for booting into TiVo with keyboard and monitor attached.

At this point, you should have opened your TiVo [Hack #20] and pulled out your hard drive [Hack #21]. If you have a two-drive TiVo, you'll have both drives out of the TiVo, just itching to be backed up. Let's wire that drive into your PC.

Inspect the PC you've acquired for this task to figure out exactly where this drive transplant is going to be installed, What free slot are you going to connect this drive into? Don't forget, if you plan to back up your TiVo drive [Hack #24], then you need to have a FAT32-formatted hard drive installed. On top of that, if you have a CD-ROM drive, you must keep it connected if you intend to use a bootable CD version of the software mentioned in the "Some Software" section of "Getting Everything Together" at the beginning of this chapter .

If your TiVo has two drives, connect both to your PC.

> Do not install your TiVo's hard drive as the primary master on the IDE bus. Instead, install it in any of the other three locations. None of the software we are going to use supports having your TiVo's drive as the primary master.

You'll also need to have the right jumper settings on each TiVo hard drive before you install it into your PC. Turn your hard drive to orient its label upwards and its empty connectors facing you. From this vantage point, you will see one or more small plastic jumpers on the back. Jumper settings can be a little confusing. To make your life a little easier, there are diagrams affixed to the tops of all TiVo drives—it just might take some time to get accustomed to them. Note that Western Digital drives have different jumper settings for "single or master" and for "master with slave." Just read carefully. If you need to change the jumper positions, gently remove the jumper with the end of a paper clip or tweezers and move it to the proper position.

Throughout the remaining hacks in this chapter, we're going to use hdX or hdY to refer to the location of a drive in the PC. In both of those notations, the X and Y are variables that refer to either a, b, c, or d, depending on where the applicable drive is actually installed. You Linux-users out there should recognize the naming scheme as the way your Linux box names its IDE drives. The rest of you shouldn't be worried; just refer to Table 2-4 for guidance.

Table 2-4. The mapping between IDE position of a hard drive and naming scheme

IDE location of the drive	Hard drive name
Primary master	hda
Primary slave	hdb
Secondary master	hdc
Secondary slave	hdd

When your TiVo's drive or drives are installed in your computer, note their positions on the IDE bus and associated hard drive names.

Using MFS Tools for Backup and Restore

#23 If you need to back up or restore your TiVo software, you are going to need to use MFS Tools.

MFS Tools is the TiVo backup and restore program. You should get familiar with using it so you can use it in a pinch, but pray that you never have to use it, except the one time that you want to upgrade the hard drives in your TiVo. To begin, you'll need to get your TiVo's hard drive installed in a PC [Hack #22].

Check Your BIOS Settings

Without some modification, your PC may not boot from the CD or the boot floppy. If you are using the boot CD, you will want to set your BIOS to boot from the CD. Likewise with the floppy: make sure that the BIOS tells the computer to boot from the floppy. Most BIOS configuration menus are reached by hitting the Delete key on your keyboard just as the first signs of life flicker across your computer's screen when booting up. Consult your BIOS manual (usually in the box with a new PC or available online from the PC vendor) for instructions on setting your PC to boot from CD or floppy rather than the primary master hard drive (drive C to you Windows users).

While the version of the Linux operating system that runs from the MFS Tools CD or boot floppy will recognize the full capacity of the larger drives, some earlier versions of the BIOS will not recognize hard drives above a certain size. You may have to adjust your BIOS settings so that the drive recognition parameter for your TiVo drive or drives is set to "none" rather than "auto." Do not alter the BIOS setting for your FAT32 drive.

Boot MFS Tools 2.0 CD or Floppy

Insert the MFS Tools CD or floppy, hold your breath, and boot your computer. If you are using the CD, you will see the following output when you start:

```
default setup: Kernel with DMA enabled, but no byteswapping.
nodma same as above, but with DMA disabled.
swap DMA disabled, byte swapping enabled.
dmaswap DMA enabled, byte-swapping enabled. (Dangerous)
boot:
```

At the boot: prompt, hit the Return/Enter key on your keyboard. You'll see several pages of scrolling gobbledygook, and you should eventually see a /# prompt.

Floppy users shouldn't see the boot: prompt; after a minute or so of scrolling, you will just see the # prompt.

Verify Drive Sizes

Press Shift-PgUp repeatedly to scroll back through all that output. Among other things, you'll see whether or not the PC recognized your TiVo hard drive or drives. It is critical at this stage to verify that the full size of your TiVo drive was recognized. As you scroll up, you should see something like the following:

```
hda: WDC WD450-AA-00BAA0, ATA DISK drive
hdb: IDE/ATAPI CD-ROM 48X, ATAPI CD/DVD-ROM drive
hdc: QUANTUM FIREBALL CX13.6A, ATA DISK drive
ide0 at 0x1f0-0x1f7,0x3f6 on irq 14
hda: 87930864 sectors (45021 MB) w/2048 KiB Cache, CHS=19929/255/63,
UDMA(33)
hdb: ATAPI 17X CD-ROM drive, 128kB Cache, UDMA(33)
hdc: 26760384 sectors (13701 MB) w/418KiB Cache, CHS=1665/255/63 UDMA(33)
```

You are looking to confirm that each of your IDE drives was recognized and that the size of each drive is reported properly. For example, with a Sony SVR-3000, you will have an 80 GB drive, so it should be recognized as about 80000 MB. Above that, check to confirm that hda and hdc both look "normal" (in the text above, one is a WDC drive recognized at 45 GB, and the other is a Quantum Fireball with 14 GB of space). If one or more of your TiVo drives is being reported as an unexpectedly small number, such as 9 or 10 MB, then your drive is locked.

Unlock Your Drive

If the size of one or more of your drives is not being reported properly, then you are going to need to get your hands on a utility that will unlock them. Generally speaking, this should be a problem only if you are using the boot floppy, as the MFS Tools 2.0 CD should unlock the drive automatically. If you are facing a locked drive, first power down your PC by hitting the Control-Alt-Delete key combination. It is important to do this rather just hitting the power, because it will give your computer a chance to put the TiVo drives into a safe state. Wait until the screen displays No more processes... or until the computer begins to reboot. This lets you know that you can safely power down the PC.

Extract *DLGCHK.EXE* from *http://www.westerndigital.com/service/ftp/dlgtools/ dlgchk.zip*. Save the file to a DOS or Windows 95/98 bootable floppy disk; do not use a Windows NT/2K/XP disk. If you do not have access to a usable boot disk, then you can probably get a usable one from *http://www.bootdisk.com*.

With your TiVo drive or drives connected, boot from your newly created boot disk. At the DOS prompt, run the *DLGCHK.EXE* program and just hit Enter until you get back to a DOS prompt.

Alternatively, the program *QUNLOCK.EXE* (*http://www.9thtee.com/ qunlock.exe*) will also work. Follow the same instructions used for *DLGCHK.EXE* to get *QUNLOCK.EXE* onto a boot disk and boot from it. Once you're at the DOS prompt, type:

```
A:\ qunlock.exe 0
```

where the number is the location of the locked drive: 0 is primary master, 1 is primary slave, 2 is secondary master, and 3 is secondary slave.

When using *DLGCHK.EXE* to unlock your TiVo's drive, do *not* power down your machine before rebooting into MFS Tools. Simply use your keyboard to reset your computer, and then quickly swap your boot floppy with the MFS Tools CD or disk. Once booted, review the output again to confirm that the drive size is being reported properly.

QUNLOCK.EXE users, on the other hand, should power down the machine. When you boot it back up, have the MFS Tools CD or floppy in the drive. Check to make sure that the drive size is being detected correctly.

And now you should be sitting at the prompt ready to back up or restore your TiVo software.

HACK #24 Backing Up Your TiVo Software

Before you get too involved in hacking your TiVo, back it up!

This is probably the most important thing you can do before you delve too far into hacking your TiVo. You don't want to be scouring the Internet frantically looking for somebody to give you their backup of the TiVo software (not only hard to find, but sometimes a beast to download) or left with a lemon underneath your television.

The backup itself needs to be made only once, and it can take up to 1.5 GB of space, although fully compressed it may be as small as 150 MB. Once you have made the backup and have confirmed that it works, feel free to burn it to a CD-R or a DVD-R somewhere and just keep it locked away for that one day when you might take your hacking a bit too far.

Install the TiVo hard drive or hard drives in your PC [Hack #22], make sure that you have a drive with about 1.5 GB of space on a FAT32 partition installed as the primary master on the IDE bus, and then boot up MFS Tools [Hack #23]. At the /# or # prompt, issue the following command:

```
# mount /dev/hda1 /mnt
```

If this command is successful, you will see another /# or # prompt and you will have mounted your FAT32 drive at the /mnt directory. If, instead, you get an error message stating that you must specify the file type, try:

```
# mount -t vfat /dev/hda1 /mnt
```

This forces MFS Tools to mount the drive as a Windows partition. If that still does not work, then you probably have to try again with a smaller FAT32 drive.

Next, we are going to back up your primary TiVo hard drive to the FAT32 drive now mounted at /mnt. There is a plethora of options to *mfsbackup*, the tool that we need to use.

If you have a one-drive TiVo, try backing up with a command similar to this:

```
# mfsbackup -9so /mnt/backup.bak /dev/hdX
```

For a two-drive TiVo you can try this:

```
# mfsbackup -9so /mnt/backup.bak /dev/hdX /dev/hdY
```

As one more complication, if you are working on a TiVo based on architecture types 3 or 4 (see "What TiVo Model Do You Have?" at the beginning of this chapter), also add a -f 4200 to that command line, making it look like this:

```
# mfsbackup -f 4200 -9so /mnt/backup.back /dev/hdX
```

This will make a compressed backup of the TiVo drive at /dev/hdX (or, in the case of the two-drive TiVo, a backup of the primary drive at /dev/hdX and a backup of the secondary drive at /dev/hdY) to a file named *backup.bak* in your FAT32 drive (it will just put it into c:\backup.bak). If your TiVo drive or drives are located somewhere else, just specify the real location instead. Also, you can name your backup anything you want; just remember what you call it.

The -9 option controls how much compression to apply; the more you compress, the longer it is going to take. For the impatient, just don't bother putting a number there—it will be fine and quick, but it will produce a large file. -5 turns out to be a pretty good compromise. The -s flag also attempts to compress the data further by shrinking the volume in the backup to the smallest it can get, given the specific data that we are asking for it to back up.

And, lastly, there is no magic in the 4200 number. It modifies the default backup procedure to increase the maximum file size that MFS Tools will back up. The minimum value for this number varies among TiVo models, and this number is high enough to ensure a reliable backup in any current type 2 or type 4 units. Essentially, this number modifies the default backup procedure to increase the maximum file size that MFS Tool will back up. Without any -f switch, the backup is likely to be unreliable in type 2 and type 4 models.

While the backup is running, you should see a progress bar tick up generally for about 5 to 25 minutes. Once it is successful, press Control-Alt-Delete and wait for the No more processes... text to appear or for your computer to start rebooting itself. You can then power down to remove the TiVo drive or drives from the PC.

Feel free to do whatever you want with that backup you just made—burn a CD, leave it on your hard drive, whatever—just keep it accessible. The one item not really covered in this hack is testing your backup to make sure it works properly. If you are replacing your factory-installed hard drive with another one, then you don't really need to test it. Simply restoring from backup [Hack #25] to the larger drives for the space increase will be that test. Inversely, if you are planning on keeping your factory drive, maybe it would be worth your time to restore your backup to another drive—temporarily installing it into your TiVo [Hack #27]—and testing the backup [Hack #28] before you go for the rest.

HACK #25 Restoring from Backup

Restore your TiVo's software from backup, whether for disaster recovery or for expanding capacity.

There are two times when restoring a backup is necessary: either you are replacing your existing drive(s) with a new hard drive (or drives), or you are repairing a corrupt TiVo hard drive.

You'll need a backup in hand, whether your own or one that you've managed to convince somebody else to give you.

Although absolutely *not* recommended, if you do get a backup from another TiVo to restore to yours, make sure that the backup comes from the same model TiVo. If you don't, disaster is sure to strike.

Restoring this backup will make the TiVo look just like it did when the backup was made; all your Season Passes and other options (*not* recorded programming, however) will be restored from deep sleep right onto your drive. If you are restoring your backup onto a drive or drives that have more space that the original drive, then you are going to use all that capacity.

You are going to need access to your backup after booting up MFS Tools [Hack #23]. It's probably best to copy the backup back onto that FAT32 drive and install that drive as the primary master in your PC.

Install the hard drives destined for the TiVo into the spare PC IDE ports [Hack #22] to get them ready to be restored, and then boot MFS Tools. At the /# or # prompt, issue the following command:

```
# mount /dev/hda1 /mnt
```

We are trying to mount the FAT32 drive in the same way as we make a backup [Hack #24]. If this command is successful, you will see another prompt. If you get an error, follow the same line of thought from that previous hack.

If you are restoring onto a single TiVo drive, start the restore process with something like this:

```
# mfsrestore -s 127 -xzpi /mnt/backup.bak /dev/hdX
```

If, on the other hand, you are restoring to two drives, run something like this:

```
# mfsrestore -s 127 -xzpi /mnt/backup.bak /dev/hdX /dev/hdY
```

If you are running with a type 3 TiVo, modify the commands to either:

```
# mfsrestore -s 127 -xzbpi /mnt/backup.bak /dev/hdX
```

or:

```
# mfsrestore -s 127 -xzbpi /mnt/backup.bak /dev/hdX /dev/hdY
```

These commands will take the backup at */mnt/backup.bak* (*c:\backup.bak* on the DOS/Windows side) and restore it to */dev/hdX* [Hack #22]. The magic is that it not only restores the backup, but also expands it. The backup made from the original TiVo is blown up to encompass the entire space of the new drive or drives. If the new drive or drives total up to more space than the original, then MFS Tools will modify the backup to take over the entire capacity. Of course, if your backup has a different name, or if the hard drive you are restoring is at a different location, then feel free to change either when typing out the commands. The -s flag actually sets up swap space on your drive. By default, only 64 MB of swap is allocated, but if you have a large amount of hard drive space, you might want a little more swap to fit it all in. Do not use more than 127 MB, and always use 127 MB if you have the space.

Both of these commands presume that the upgrade drive, *hdX* in our example, is larger than the original TiVo factory drive that the backup was made from. If that drive is the same size as the original factory drive, then you may have to remove the -s option from the command line to make sure it all fits. Don't try to make your first drive be smaller than your original drive; doing so is bound to fail.

Once the restore is complete, press Control-Alt-Delete. When your machine reboots, power down your PC and pull out the drives.

Adding a Second Drive the Quick-n-Dirty Way

HACK #26

Live on the edge and add another drive without performing a full backup of your software, or without even removing the original TiVo drive from its case.

While backing up your TiVo and restoring while expanding it onto larger space is definitely the recommended way to go about things, there are two faster options if you have a one-drive TiVo and you're willing to shave a few steps. The added benefit of this indiscretion is that you have to buy only one additional hard drive for your TiVo—instead of two—when replacing the factory drive

Using mfsadd

The one definite way to lose some steps is to cut the backup out of the picture. Pull out your TiVo's one drive [Hack #21] and install it in your PC [Hack #22] along with the new hard drive that you are going to expand your space with. Boot up MFS Tools 2.0 [Hack #23], and at the prompt type:

```
# mfsadd -x /dev/hdX /dev/hdY
```

where /dev/hdX is replaced with the IDE location of your original TiVo drive and /dev/hdY is new drive you are planning to install. This should take only a few seconds, and it will report the results and sizes of your drives. If it all looks good, then Control-Alt-Delete your system and pull the drives out. If it didn't work, then pray that you can get it working by backing up and restoring.

Using BlessTiVo

This is really flying by the seat of your pants. If you opt for this, then you don't even need to remove your TiVo's drive. Instead, you're just going to set up the new drive and then screw it right in.

You are going want to open up your TiVo [Hack #20] so you can install your new drive. Now install only your new drive in your PC [Hack #22].

Before booting your PC, make sure your BIOS is set up to boot from either the BlessTiVo CD or a floppy (see how the BIOS is set up for booting up MFS Tools [Hack #23], and mimic that). If you have it all set up, then boot away.

For those of you booting off a CD, press Enter at the boot: prompt to bring up a /# prompt. If you are booting off a floppy, you are going to see a program called *TiVoMAD*, asking you to Please enter hdb, hdc, or hdd. Just Control-C to abort that program and press Enter until you see the # prompt. Verify the sizes of your drives and unlock as necessary a la the instructions for booting up MFS Tools. If everything has gone well, enter the following at the prompt:

```
# BlessTiVo /dev/hdX
```

About 1 second will go by, and your computer will print out a message telling you, hopefully, that the drive was blessed. Mazel Tov! It will also tell you the size that your drive has been blessed to. The size of this partition should be within approximately 5–10 GB of the actual drive size, depending on the drive. Do not install your drive into your TiVo if the number reported is far too small. If this does not work for you, then pull your TiVo's hard drive [Hack #21], install it into your PC [Hack #22], and then back her right up [Hack #24] and restore it onto your new dual drives [Hack #25], because there are no short cuts for you this time around.

If BlessTiVo does not report the correct blessed size of your new drive, do *not* install it. If you do, your TiVo will not recognize the full size of the drive, and recovery will be too painstaking to be in the scope of this chapter.

If this all looks good, then Control-Alt-Delete your computer, power down, and install your new drive alongside your old drive.

Putting TiVo's Drives Back

You took those hard drives out. Now they have to go back in just right to make everything work again.

Putting your drive or drives back in, conceptually, is the reverse of pulling the drives out [Hack #21] and opening the TiVo [Hack #20] in the first place. But, as usual, there are a few subtle things to get right—we'll make sure to cover in this hack.

The first thing you should do is get your new drive or drives ready to go in. If you are placing only one drive back into your TiVo, it is generally recommended that you set its jumpers into "master." If you are installing two drives in your TiVo, one should be set as "master" and the other as "slave." Also, arrange things so the master drive can be at the end of the IDE cable and the slave drive can be installed in the middle connector.

Putting Hard Drives into Type 1 TiVos

Use the same four Torx screws to connect the new drive to the bracket that you removed from your TiVo. Take care to put it back in the same way it came out. When installed properly, you will see four bracket holes below the connectors when looking at the power and IDE cable connectors with the drive-label facing up.

If you are installing two drives, you will need that newly purchased bracket. In lieu of a bracket, cable ties will also work to secure the drive so long as you aren't planning to move your TiVo (we can promise you that if you give FedEx your precious cable-tied TiVo, your drive will be surfing all over the motherboard by the time the TiVo arrives at its final destination). If you're using a bracket, screw that bracket onto the second hard drive as you did the first one; then place it down next to the first drive.

Once you have the drive or drives installed properly, reattach the bracket by lining up the two metal prongs in the chassis with the holes in the bracket. If you have a second drive to install, place it down now before screwing either one in. Finally, secure them all in place.

Once that hardware is screwed down and mounted, connect all the power cabling. Be sure to push on the connectors with some force to be sure that they are seated properly. Next, attach the IDE cabling. As mentioned before, with two drives, put the middle connector with the slave drive and the end connector with the master. Be sure the cable is pushed in snugly, but be very careful not to bend any of the hard drive pins.

Reattach the TiVo lid, screw it shut, and wire it back up to your television.

Putting Hard Drives into Type 2 and Type 3 TiVos

If you are simply installing one drive, just reattach the hard drive to the bracket that was factory installed. If, instead, you are installing the two drives into a TiVo based on the type 2 architecture, install the second/slave drive closer to the fan. If you are installing two drives into a TiVo based on the type 3 architecture, follow the instructions that you received with the custom bracket (see "Adding to versus replacing your TiVo's hard drives," earlier in this chapter) we recommended you order. Users with type 3 TiVos should ignore the remainder of this section and instead refer to the installation instructions that came with your bracket.

The easiest way, we find, to attach a drive to the factory bracket is to turn it upside-down. Using one hand, hold the drive against the bottom of the bracket and look through the holes in the drive bay to align the screw holes. Using your hands, screw the screws into each of the four holes and use a screwdriver to tighten it all up.

If you are operating on a Sony SAT T-60, Hughes GXCEBOT, or any of the TiVos born of the type 3 architecture, and you are installing two drives, you might notice at this time that the IDE ribbon in the TiVo itself has connectors that can accommodate only one drive. It's time to take out that new IDE cable we told you to buy (see Table 2-2). Remove the existing IDE cable by pulling it up and out and insert the new cable, taking care to align the grooves in the cable with the notch in the connector.

Table 2-2 also asked you to buy a Y-power splitter if you have a Hughes GXCEBOT or any of the type 3 architecture boxes and are installing two drives, so now its time to install that also. Just connect that adapter to the end of the existing drive power cable to give you two male power connectors instead of one.

Wire up the drives with the gray hard drive cable and the power cable. Be sure to push the IDE cable snugly into each hard drive; the two-drive setup should have the master going in at the end and the slave drive in the middle. Try not to make a hard fold at any point in the cable or bend any of the hard drive cables. Next, wire the power connectors up and apply some force to make sure that a snug connection is made.

Carefully flip the drive bay over and orient yourself at the front of your TiVo. You'll need to insert the two pins on the right into the blue grommets, while at the same time watching the power connectors and the IDE ribbon cable. You will want to tuck the power cables down into the TiVo (in front of the hard drives). In the two-drive upgrade, you will also want to tuck down the portion of the hard drive ribbon cable that is between the two drives. Watch to make sure that the fan cable remains free throughout this process.

One quick word about the extra cabling in a two-drive TiVo: you'll need to play with the excess cable to be sure that it packs neatly in front of, or on top of, the drives and not below them. If you pack the cable below the drives, you might pinch it and restrict airflow to the motherboard. Ideally, you will have the excess gray cable folded on top of the drives and the power cable tucked in front of the fan housing.

Once the two pins are in the blue grommets, align the left side of the drive bay so that it is directly over the screw holes on the left side of the TiVo. Screw the two screws and the gold insert back into the holds on the left side using your Torx screwdriver.

Don't forget to reattach the fan! Insert the fan cable back into the motherboard. Reattach the lid, secure it, and start running cabling back to your TV.

Putting Hard Drives into Type 4 TiVos

If you are installing two new drives into your TiVo, the slave drive should be in the position closer to the fan and the master drive should be at the edge of the bracket. In either case, be sure to orient the drive so that the connectors are opposite the fan cable. Next, secure the whole apparatus down.

The easiest way to attach a drive to the bracket is to turn the bracket upside-down. Using one hand, hold the drive against the bottom of the bracket and look through the holes in the drive bay to align the screw holes. Using your other hand, screw the screws into each of the four holes. Use a screwdriver to tighten the screws.

If you are installing two hard drives, you are going to need to replace the IDE ribbon cable and add a Y-power adapter to your TiVo. Remove the existing IDE cable by pulling it up and out. Replace it with the new cable, taking care to align the grooves in the cable with the notch in the connector. As for the power cable, just hook up the two ends to the hard drive, but don't connect it to TiVo power yet.

Wire up the drives with the IDE cable. Remember, if you are putting in two drives, the master should be on the far end of the cable with the slave hanging off the middle.

Slide the bracket to the edge of the TiVo lid and insert the end of the IDE cable into the TiVo motherboard. Be careful to insert the cable properly. There is a groove in the blue connector that must align with the notch in the motherboard connector. Now, attach the drive power connector (the red, yellow, and black cable) from the TiVo into the power connector coming out of the drives.

Once the cables are connected, carefully flip the drive bracket over and install it into the TiVo. The drive bracket will move fairly freely inside the TiVo, and you will have to be careful to align the four holes in the TiVo with the four holes on the drive bracket. Be sure that the IDE and power cables are in front of the two drives; they should not be under the drives as you turn the bracket over.

Once the four holes are aligned and the drive bracket is installed, again make sure that the IDE and power cables are tucked under the front lip of the TiVo. It is critical that all of these cables are tucked underneath the gold and silver tabs on the lip of the TiVo, lest they get pinched. With your screwdriver, reattach the four black screws in the holes on the drive bay.

Remember to reattach the fan at this point, or your TiVo is going to get mighty hot inside.

Slide the lid on and seal her up.

HACK #28 Testing Your TiVo's New Capacity

Wondering if your new hard drives work? Let's find out.

After all that hard work and time looking at the guts of your TiVo, now it's time to find out if all that hard work paid off.

Reconnect your TiVo and plug it in. Watch it boot up. If it gets that far, then this is a really good sign! Surf your way to *TiVo Messages & Setup → System Information* and check out the line that starts with "Recording Capacity." What does it say? Mine's shown in Figure 2-7.

As a rule of thumb, your TiVo should, on average, hold about 1.2 hours per GB of hard drive storage in standalone models (without a built-in DirecTV receiver) and about 0.875 hours per GB in the DirecTV with TiVo models. If you have a total of 150 GB of storage in your standalone TiVo, you should be able to store about 180 hours of programming at basic quality. In a DirecTV with TiVo, the same 150 GB will yield up to 130 hours.

If for some reason the number is not right, go over the directions with a fine-toothed comb. But if it is right, then congrats! Time to set that Season Pass to record all the soap operas that you could ever watch.

——*Chapter by Michael Adberg and Jeff Shapiro, WeaKnees.com (© 2001-2003 Adberg Consulting LLC)*

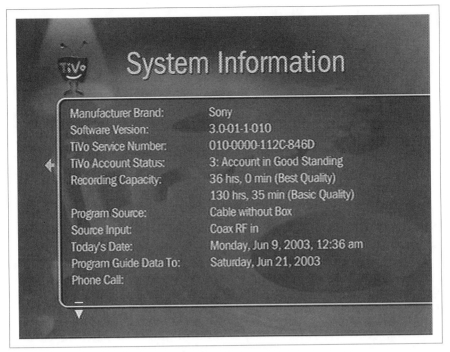

Figure 2-7. Plenty of hours of recording capacity

## CHAPTER THREE

The TiVo Shell
Hacks 29–46

We stumbled over it briefly when booting up the MFS Tools [Hack #23]. We caught a glimpse of it when we shut down TiVo's software [Hack #18]. I'm speaking about the Linux operating system humming away under the hood of your TiVo. The TiVo interface you see on your television set, TiVo's responses to your remote control, and all the gray matter that makes your TiVo a TiVo are Linux applications.

Linux, Linux, everywhere, but not a drop to drink. This chapter rectifies that by dropping you into the TiVo shell, a text-only command-line environment very much what you'd find on any Unix system (or DOS prompt, if you prefer). Here you can poke about, install software, run applications, and generally interact with TiVo from the inside out.

> TiVo's default shell is called Bash, the "Bourne-Again Shell" (*http://www.gnu.org/software/bash/bash.html*), a common variant available on just about any Unix system.

There is, however, one thing standing between you and the shell; this Linux box doesn't appear to have a keyboard. How are you to type anything on the command line without anything to type on? No worries; we'll just have to go in another way—over the serial port.

> Those of you with Series 2 machines are a little out of luck. Unlike its original Series 1 counterpart, the Series 2 has hardware encryption onboard that attempts to prevent you from running arbitrary code. The most commonly known exploit involves a hardware modification to the TiVo's motherboard, which goes well beyond the scope of this book and crosses some legality boundaries. While this chapter will focus on Series 1 software only, you're sure to see some ports to the Series 2 in the usual places online in the future.

Mounting and Working with TiVo's Drive Partitions

Before you can edit any of TiVo's configuration files, turn on the Bash shell, copy across files, and so forth, you need to understand a little about TiVo's drive partitions.

If you've performed a hard drive upgrade or simply read through Chapter 2, you probably noticed that we kept to the task at hand and never really devoted any time to what was actually on TiVo's disks. You had your hands full—literally—already, now didn't you?

In order to perform any of the feats in this chapter, you'll need at least a lay of the land when it comes to your TiVo's drives. If you're used to Unix, this will probably seem rather familiar to you; nevertheless, a quick refresher never did anyone any harm.

I'm assuming that you have gained direct access to your TiVo's drives by performing the following steps:

1. Opening your TiVo [Hack #20]
2. Removing its drive [Hack #21]
3. Mounting the drive in a spare PC [Hack #22]

If not, you'll need to do so before any of this hack is of any real use to you.

Understanding Partitions

The information on your TiVo's primary drive is stored in different sections on the disk, each called a *partition*. A standard TiVo contains 11 partitions, 3 of which (partitions 4, 7, and 9) are mountable by the Linux operating system, and are where you'll edit files and store programs for further hacking.

Before you start mounting and editing files on your TiVo's primary drive, you should understand how TiVo treats partitions 4 and 7. Both of these partitions contain copies of the *root image* of your TiVo's operating system, but only one of them—called the *active partition*—contains the *active* root image. The most current version of the TiVo OS and configuration files are stored in the active partition. The *inactive partition* contains a backup copy of the previous version of the operating system and configuration files. Depending on which partition was active when you first plugged in your TiVo, how many system software updates you've received, and the alignment of the planets, either partition 4 or partition 7 will be your currently active partition, the other being the inactive or *backup* partition. You'll figure out which is which in "Mounting Partitions" in just a moment.

When your TiVo downloads a new system software update, it writes the new, updated version to the inactive partition. When your TiVo reboots for the first time following the update, it swaps what it considers to be the active and inactive partitions (from 4 to 7, and from 7 to 4), keeping a backup of the previous version of the system software on what is now the inactive partition and running the current version on what is now the active partition.

If you've recently performed a capacity upgrade using MFS Tools [Hack #25], your TiVo will not contain a copy of the inactive partition, because it is not backed up using MFS Tools method. Don't worry! Your TiVo will automatically create an inactive partition the next time it updates its system software, and you can still use all the information in this guide without any problems.

On the other hand, if you upgraded your TiVo's recording capacity by simply adding a second drive [Hack #26] without altering your drive, you will still have both partitions on your system.

Mounting Partitions

Having booted your PC with your TiVo hard drive(s) attached, you'll need to mount the partitions before you can use them. Start by creating some new directories that will serve as mount points (think of them as parking places) for your partitions. Do so for partitions 4, 7, and 9 by typing:

```
# mkdir /mnt4
# mkdir /mnt7
# mkdir /mnt9
```

Now that you have a place to put them, mount each partition, pairing up the partition name and mount point:

```
# mount /dev/hdX4 /mnt4
# mount /dev/hdX7 /mnt7
# mount /dev/hdX9 /mnt9
```

If you've forgotten the real name of your hard drive (e.g., /dev/hdX4) refer to Table 2-4 in Chapter 2.

If all goes well, none of thee commands should produce any output. Occasionally, however, you may come across one of two error messages:

- The "checktime" error is simply Linux making note of successfully mounting an unfamiliar or unverified partition:

```
EXT2-fs Warning: checktime reached
EXT2-fs Warning: mounting unchecked file system
EXT2-fs Warning: maximal count reached
```

Every so often, Linux likes to make sure that filesystems are running well under the hood. Chances are, yours is, so pay the error no heed.

- While trying to mount partition 4 or 7, you may be warned that you're mounting a filesystem that does not exist:

```
fatfs: bogus cluster size
VFS: Can't find a valid MSDOS filesystem on dev 16:07.
fatfs: bogus cluster size
VFS: Can't find a valid MSDOS filesystem on dev 16:07.
mount: you must specify the filesystem type
```

This usually happens only if you've performed a capacity upgrade to your TiVo's drive using MFS Tools [Hack #25], which, as I've mentioned, does not back up the inactive partition.

If you receive this error while trying to mount partition 4, it means that you do not have a partition 4 and your active partition is 7. Conversely, if you receive this error while trying to mount partition 7, it means that your active partition is partition 4 and partition 7 is missing. Don't worry about the missing partition as you obviously can't mount a non-existent partition.

Poking About

While I'll give you the full tour [Hack #35] in a bit, a quick mention of what's where is probably in order:

/dev/hdX4 and /dev/hdX7
> These two directories should look pretty similar to each other, while also looking remarkably similar to the / directory on a Linux system. This should come as no surprise, since that's exactly what TiVo is! You should see familiar directories like */etc*, */dev*, and */bin*, but here they are called */mnt4/etc*, */mnt7/etc*, and so forth. That's only because we have the hard drive mounted in this odd way temporarily.

/dev/hdX9
> This is what gets mounted as the */var* directory when your TiVo is running. Files in the */var* directory constantly change when the system is running. Notice the */var/log* directory containing TiVo's log files. You'll also notice that the */tmp* directory is located here too.

Go To

If your intent was to enable the Bash shell over serial port, move on to "Enabling Bash over the Serial Port" [Hack #30].

Enabling Bash over the Serial Port

#30   The simplest way to get a prompt on your TiVo is to activate the serial port and connect your TiVo to your PC.

Since the days of yore, one of the most common and simple methods for hooking together two PCs has been to use the serial port. A garden-variety serial cable (I've collected a case of them over the years) plus a $5 null modem adapter will provide a fine, albeit slow, connection between the two machines. Fire up just about any terminal program (e.g., Windows' Hyper-Term), and you can flow text from one machine to the other.

Enabling the Bash shell so that it's available to the serial port the next time your TiVo boots requires command-line access to your TiVo drive. Yes, we know it's a catch-22—one solved by mounting the right drive partitions [Hack #29] and turning on the Bash shell. This hack assumes you've already mounted the drive partitions.

You'll be editing the *rc.sysinit* script that controls what processes and programs are started when TiVo boots up. But first, it serves you well to make backup copies of files you'll be editing, just in case something goes wrong. Type the following commands to get to and make a copy of *rc.sysinit* as *rc.sysinit.orig* (as in "original"):

```
# cd /mnt4/etc/rc.d
# cp rc.sysinit rc.sysinit.orig
```

If, in "Mounting and Working with TiVo's Drive Partitions" [Hack #29], you found that you don't have a partition 4, replace *mnt4* in the previous command with *mnt7*.

Next, we'll append (the >> bit) a command-line incantation to get the Bash shell running to the end of the *rc.sysinit* file:

```
# echo '/bin/bash --login < /dev/ttyS3 >& /dev/ttyS3 &' >> rc.sysinit
```

You're asking Bash to take its input from (< /dev/ttyS3) and send its output to (>& /dev/ttyS3) the serial port (/dev/ttyS3), instead of from the command line.

At this point, all should be set. You can delete that backup file, or not—it's up to you:

```
# rm rc.sysinit.orig
```

Most of you should have both a partition 4 and partition 7 [Hack #29]. If you do, it's a good practice to mirror a change made to the active partition on the backup partition. Perform all the previously mentioned command-line steps again, replacing *mnt4* with *mnt7*, like so:

```
# cd /mnt7/etc/rc.d
# cp rc.sysinit rc.sysinit.orig
# echo '/bin/bash --login < /dev/ttyS3 >& /dev/ttyS3 &' >> rc.sysinit
# rm rc.sysinit.orig
```

Again, removing the backup *rc.sysinit.orig* file is optional.

> Instead of the commands recommended in this hack, many guides found on the Internet recommend that you run this:
>
> ```
> echo '/bin/bash < /dev/ttyS3 >& /dev/ttyS3 &' >> rc.
> sysinit
> ```
>
> While it is completely up to you, I recommend the one with `--login` on the command line, as that will evaluate `/.profile` when the TiVo starts up.

Go To

All that remains is a little cleanup and a shut down [Hack #32]. But, before you go, it behooves you to copy over a few useful Unix utilities [Hack #31].

Copying Unix Binaries to TiVo

The shell is nothing without its utilities. What's a work environment worth if you can't do anything while you're there?

The default installation of the TiVo OS has a Bash shell and little else in the way of the utilities necessary to do anything of any use. How exciting, after all, is:

```
bash-2.02# echo *
```

Beyond the first few minutes, that is. ;-).

While you have your box open and drives mounted on your PC [Hack #29], now's a good time to bring over some of the common utilities most Unix jockeys simply assume to be there.

You are going to need a DOS- or Windows-formatted floppy disk for this one. Steve Jenkins's Newbie TiVo Hacker site offers a complete archive of useful Unix utilities for the Series 1 TiVo (*http://tivo.stevejenkins.com/downloads/tbin.tar.gz*), including *head*, *tail*, *rmdir*, *strace*, *touch*, and, most importantly, *ls*. Copy the *.tar.gz* file to the floppy. Don't run this file through any decompression programs, just copy it over as is.

Now, let's make a directory on the TiVo drive into which to put the Unix binaries. While we're at it, we'll make this the home of all our program hacks throughout the rest of this book. There are two partitions that are good candidates: */dev/hdX4* or */dev/hdX7* (these two are effectively the same, one being the backup of the other), and */dev/hdX9*.

As one of */dev/hdX4* and */dev/hdX7* is always in deep sleep while the other is running, this is probably not the best place to keep these files and your future hacks. The next time your TiVo software is upgraded, the active partition is relegated to a backup partition and will no longer be visible to your TiVo. Not to mention that the backup-partition-to-be could very well be wiped clean during a software upgrade. Poof! Any hacking you've done is history. So we'll rule out partitions 4 and 7.

Partition 9, */dev/hdX9*, on the other hand, is always visible to your TiVo and therefore appears to be a clear winner. There is, however, one caveat: if you overfill this partition, TiVo will summarily delete it and recreate it from scratch.

So, there doesn't appear to be any perfect choice. In my opinion, the lesser of two evils is to use */dev/hdX9*. Yes, we're taking the chance that we might overfill the partition and lose our work, but for the remainder of this book, this is the chance we're going to take. If, for some reason, you find that your hacks are gone, at least you'll know why.

> As it stands, there is no truly "safe" place to keep hacks on your TiVo, but Mike Baker (a.k.a. "embeem") suggests a more involved method for keeping your hacks persistent. He suggests creating *another* partition on your TiVo, convincing your TiVo to boot from that partition, and then moving on to TiVo's native partitions—all without TiVo really knowing anything about the initial bootstrap partition. Implementing these changes can be a little tricky, however. If you are interested, you'll find his post on the topic at *http://alt.org/forum/index.php?t=msg&th=17*.

Assuming you choose to use */dev/hdb9*, create a directory to house hacks, utilities, etc., like so:

```
# mkdir /mnt9/hack
```

Insert the floppy disk holding the *tivobin.tar.gz* file into your floppy drive, mount it, and copy the file over to the */mnt9/hack* directory:

```
# mkdir /floppy
# mount /dev/fd0 /floppy
# cp /floppy/tivobin.tar.gz /mnt9/hack
```

While of course you can go ahead and decompress the archive and install the Unix binaries now, let's wait to do so via the TiVo Bash shell itself **[Hack #34]**. This way, you'll be using real paths, rather than fiddling about with temporary mount points (*/mnt9* et al). There is no reason why you couldn't do that from here. However, by postponing it, you have a better shot at figuring out what is going wrong with your Bash prompt if you can't get it to show up.

Go To

You'll finish up [Hack #34] in just a moment. First, you need to clean up and shut down your PC [Hack #32], return TiVo's drives to where they belong, and get to the Bash prompt [Hack #33] over the serial line.

Clean Up and Shut Down

#32

After mounting TiVo's drives in your PC and fiddling with configuration files, you need to carefully clean up and shut down the PC to preserve your changes.

If you've made any changes to TiVo's configuration files, you must carefully unmount the TiVo partitions and shut down the PC to which your drives are connected, in order to make sure everything's saved as it should be. Do *not* just turn off your machine, or you risk leaving changes uncommitted and—worse still—leaving your TiVo partitions in an unusable state.

Unmount the partitions you mounted before, like so:

```
# cd /
# umount /mnt4 /mnt7 /mnt9
```

Of course, you should bother to unmount only the partitions you mounted in the first place; if you did not mount partition 4 at */mnt4* or partition 7 to */mnt7*, leave them out of the previous command line.

If you mounted your floppy drive to copy across the Unix utilities [Hack #31], don't forget to unmount that drive too:

```
# umount /floppy
```

> Notice that the command is umount (pronounced "yoo-mount") not unmount ("un-mount") as one might expect.

Now, you can issue an exit command to log you out of the Linux shell and return you to the Linux login prompt:

```
# exit
```

At this point, it's safe to Control-Alt-Delete your PC, watch it reboot, and, at the first sign it is returning to life (beginning to boot up again), turn it off.

Go To

Now you're ready to reinstall your TiVo's drives back into TiVo [Hack #27]. That done, if your goal has been to get the Bash shell over serial connection, carry on to connecting to your TiVo with the serial cable [Hack #33].

Connecting to TiVo Serially

#33   With your TiVo offering a Bash shell prompt over its serial port, let's tap your computer into that flow of bits.

With Bash-over-serial [Hack #30] enabled, your TiVo is spitting bits over its serial port into the ether, just waiting for someone to access its Bash prompt. Your mission, if you choose to accept it, is to get those bits to your computer. Go on, you've already done the hard bits.

On the back of your TiVo is a port labeled "serial," which is just about, but not quite, like the RS-232 serial ports on the back of a PC. The only real difference is the connector; rather than a standard serial port, TiVo's resembles a headphone jack.

> For some of you, TiVo's serial port might already be in use, to connect your TiVo unit to a cable box or satellite receiver. Unfortunately, you can't use the port simultaneously for both purposes. You can enable the prompt when you want to get access, and disable it later, but that can get to be a real hassle. There are other ways in; take a gander at "Getting Your TiVo Series 1 Online" [Hack #49].

First, let's make sure that you have the right cable to wire your TiVo to your computer. You need to get a hold of the serial control cable that shipped with your TiVo; it has a standard RS-232 serial connector on one end and what looks like a headphone plug on the other (see Figure 3-1). You're also going to need a null modem adapter (also shown in Figure 3-1), available at your local computer or electronics store. Lastly, you may also need a gender bender to get the end that attaches to your serial port to be female.

If you are contemplating connecting your TiVo to your Mac, then you will also need a serial-to-USB adapter, because your Mac does not have any serial ports. I recommend the Keyspan "High Speed" USB Adapter (*http://www.keyspan.com/products/usb/USA19W/*). Moving forward, I'll assume you are using such an adapter and have the appropriate Macintosh drivers installed.

Now that we have all the hardware we need, let's plug in and get those bits flowing. Plug the headphone-like end of the serial cable into TiVo's serial port. Connect the null modem adapter to the other end, and connect the other end of the null modem adapter to the serial port on the back of your PC. If you are connecting to a Mac, the null modem adapter plugs into your serial-to-USB adapter, which, in turn, plugs into the USB port on your Mac.

And that's it for hardware.

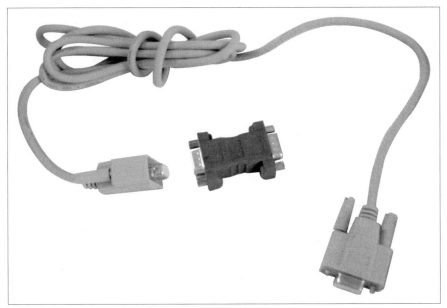

Figure 3-1. TiVo serial control cable and a null modem adapter

To talk serially to your TiVo and, thereby, the Bash shell, you are going to need the help of a simple terminal program. Use your favorite. If you don't have a favorite, there are a few popular choices: Windows has SecureCRT (*http:// www.vandyke.com*) or the inferior, but preinstalled, Hyperterminal; Macs have ZTerm (*http://homepage.mac.com/dalverson/zterm/*), which runs under both OS 9 and OS X; and Linux has Minicom (*http://packages.debian.org/stable/comm/ minicom.html*). Any one of these will do just fine.

TiVo is set up to talk at 9,600 baud and 8N1 (that's 8 data bits, 1 stop bit, and no parity bits) with no flow control. Now we'll instruct your terminal program to attach to the right port on your computer and speak the same language.

SecureCRT for Windows

Launching SecureCRT will usually present you a Connect menu; if it doesn't, select File from the Connect menu. Click the Quick Connect tool-bar button to bring up a Quick Connect dialog box. Use the same settings as those the TiVo is using (see Figure 3-2): Protocol should be serial, Port is the COM (that's communications or serial port) to which you have the serial cable connected, Baud rate is 9,600, Data bits is 8, Parity is None, and Stop bits is 1. Also, uncheck all of the Flow Control boxes.

Click the Connect button and skip to "Boot TiVo," later in this hack.

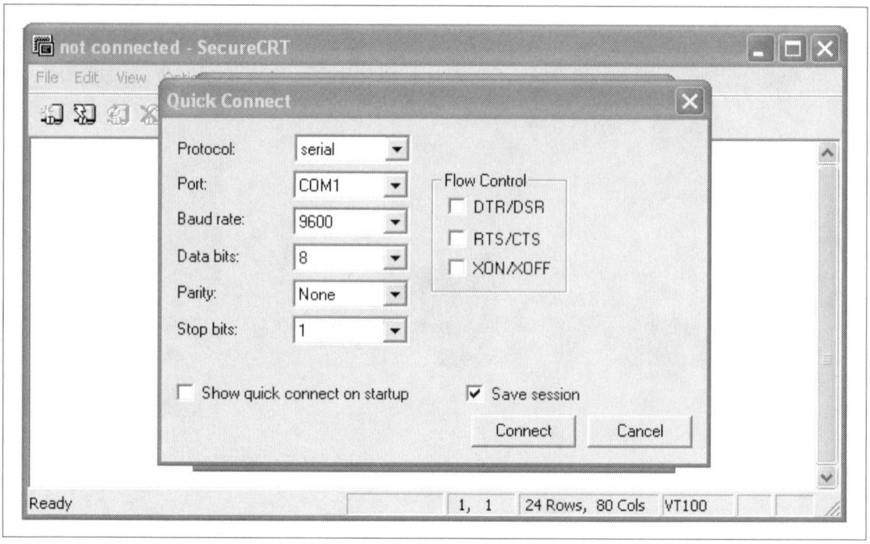

Figure 3-2. SecureCRT for Windows settings for talking to TiVo serially

ZTerm on Macintosh

Launch ZTerm on your Mac and select Settings from the Connection menu. In the resultant dialog box, shown in Figure 3-3, set things the way TiVo expects them: 9,600 Data Rate, 8 Data Bits, no Parity, and 1 Stop Bit. Uncheck both Flow Control boxes to turn off all hardware flow control.

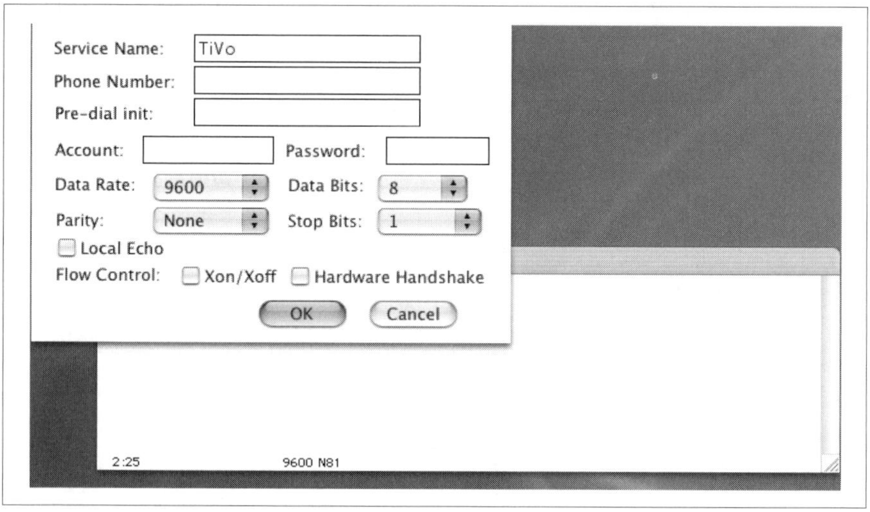

Figure 3-3. ZTerm for Macintosh settings for talking to TiVo serially

Click the OK button and skip to the "Boot TiVo" section of this hack.

Minicom for Linux

Setting up Minicom is just as simple as setting up the terminal programs for Windows and Macintosh. As root, fire up Minicom like so:

```
$ sudo minicom -s
```

You'll be prompted for your password, after which you'll be operating as root so that you'll have permission to modify and verify the serial port's settings. From the Minicom menu, select Serial Port Setup (see Figure 3-4) and configure the port to have the same options as TiVo's: set Serial Device to the */dev/tty* device into which the serial cable is plugged (in my case, */dev/ttyS1*, serial port 2), Bps/Par/Bits to 9,600 8N1, and both Hardware and Software Flow Control to No.

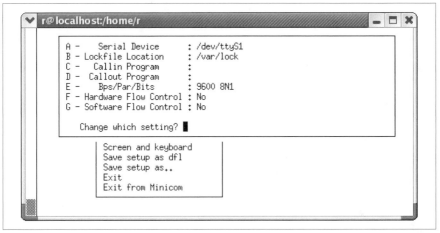

Figure 3-4. Minicom for Linux settings for talking to TiVo serially

Select Exit and save the settings. Minicom should drop you right into the terminal.

Boot TiVo

Now, turn on your TiVo (or, if it's already on, turn it off and back on) and wait through the usual "please wait a few more seconds" message appearing on your television screen. When TiVo has finished booting, you should see a shell prompt in your terminal program on your PC. If you don't, hit the Enter/Return key a few times to get TiVo's attention. If all has gone to plan, you'll see:

```
bash-2.02#
```

When you hit Enter, the cursor should move to the next line, showing another prompt, like so:

```
bash-2.02#
bash-2.02#
```

If the line wrapping appears at all jumbled—the next prompt is preceded by some amount of whitespace—clear it up by instructing Bash to try a different newline strategy:

```
bash-2.02# stty echo
```

Troubleshooting

If things don't go well and you don't see a prompt at all, start backtracking:

1. Are you sure your terminal settings are correct?
2. Are your cables in snugly on both ends? Did you include all the bits and bobs—the null modem adapter, serial-to-USB adapter (if on a Mac), etc.?
3. Did you remember to enable the Bash shell over the serial port [Hack #30]?
4. Did you add the Bash line (/bin/bash --login < /dev/ttyS3 >& /dev/ttyS3 &) to both *rc.sysinit* files if you have both a partition 4 and partition 7?

HACK #34   Installing Unix Binaries on TiVo

Continuing where we left off a little earlier [Hack #31], let's install those useful Unix utilities we copied over to TiVo's hard drive.

So you have a prompt [Hack #33], now what? By default, you don't even have the ability to do an ls (list the files in a directory). How lame is that? Not at all, really, when you consider that, from TiVo's point of view, all those human-usable utilities are superfluous for its purposes—to record television shows and play them back to you on demand. But, from a human's perspective, it's pretty lame indeed.

Let's check in on those Unix utilities you copied to your TiVo [Hack #31] and get them installed.

With your TiVo up and running, the */dev/hdX9* partition should be mounted as the */var* directory. This is easily verified, like so:

```
bash-2.02# mount
/dev/hda4 on / type ext2 (ro)
/dev/hda9 on /var type ext2 (rw)
/proc on /proc type proc (rw)
```

And there it is. Partition 9 (/dev/hda9) is mounted read-write (rw) as the */var* directory. Partition 4 (/dev/hda4) is mounted read-only (ro) as /. You'll remember it was known as */dev/hdX4* when mounted in our PC, but to TiVo it is mounted as the active primary master partition, as expected.

Now all we need to do is make our way back to the *hack* directory created earlier and unarchive that *tar* file, right? Well, yes; the only problem is that we don't yet have the tar command installed. We do, however, have cpio (read "copy input/output") with which we can manipulate the file just fine.

Expand the contents of the archive and rename the resultant directory (*tivo-bin*) to *bin* (short for "binary"):

```
bash-2.02# cd /var/hack
bash-2.02# gzip -d tivobin.tar.gz
bash-2.02# cpio -idu -h tar < tivobin.tar
bash-2.02# mv tivo-bin bin
```

As a last step, let's make sure that all the utilities are executable:

```
bash-2.02# chmod 755 bin/*
```

Now, let's give one of the utilities a whirl, shall we?

```
bash-2.02# cd bin
bash-2.02# ./ls
```

As expected, you should see a list of all the files in the *bin* directory.

The last step is to put these binaries into your path by setting the PATH variable so that your command-line shell knows where to find them. Otherwise, you'll have to specify the path to ls and its kin each time you use one of the utilities. Trust me, typing /var/hack/bin/ls each time will get really old really fast. And simply typing ls won't get you very far:

```
bash-2.02# ls
bash: ls: command not found
```

The PATH environment variable specifies which directories the Bash shell should look in when you ask it to run a command. Bash just goes down that list one directory at a time looking for the command you asked for; when it finds it, it runs it for you. Let's take a quick look at that PATH variable as it is natively:

```
bash-2.02# echo $PATH
/bin:/sbin:/tvbin:/devbin
```

Those colon-separated words are the names of the directories it'll be looking in. Notice it is not looking anywhere near your new */var/hack/bin* directory. Adding it is a piece of cake. Simply tell Bash to reexport the PATH variable, tacking on the location of your *bin* directory:

```
bash-2.02# export PATH=$PATH:/var/hack/bin
```

Taking another peek at the modified PATH, you'll see the new directories listed:

```
bash-2.02# echo $PATH
/bin:/sbin:/tvbin:/devbin:/var/hack:/var/hack/bin
```

Try that ls command again; it should work like a charm no matter where you are on the drive.

Unfortunately this change to your path is not permanent. The next time your TiVo reboots, PATH will revert to its default. What you need to do is change your path's default, accomplished by altering your profile via the aptly named *.profile* file. The *.profile* file is read whenever the Bash shell starts up, so it's a perfect place to set some preferences right off the bat for your shell session. TiVo's home directory is the / directory, so the *.profile* file should live there. Let's go ahead and create it.

Now, if you've been reading carefully, you'll remember that the partition mounted at / is still read-only. If we attempt to change anything at that mount point, TiVo will complain that we are attempting to write to a read-only location and stop us in our tracks. So, let's remount that directory as read-write:

```
bash-2.02# cd /
bash-2.02# mount -o remount,rw /
```

Now we can create that *.profile* file without any problem. Don't forget to remount the / directory as read-only again. Otherwise, you'll only confuse TiVo at some point:

```
bash-2.02# echo "export PATH=\$PATH:/var/hack/bin" >> /.profile
bash-2.02# mount -o remount,ro /
```

Note that extra backslash before the $ in $PATH. If you don't have that there, Bash will expand the value of PATH before it gets written to the file.

Whew! That was slightly painful, but worth it! You now have a rudimentary, but usable, Unix account on your TiVo. Just in case you haven't really meandered around a Unix shell before, Table 3-1 provides a quick summary of a few of the more common useful commands. For a comprehensive guide to the bash shell, check out O'Reilly's *Learning the bash Shell* (*http://www.oreilly.com/catalog/bash2/*).

Table 3-1. Unix commands to use when poking around TiVo's filesystem

Bash shell command	Purpose
ls [dir]	List files either in the current directory or a specified directory.
pwd	Print the current working directory (i.e., tell me where I am).
cd [dir]	Change directories, either to your home directory (/ in TiVo's case) or the specified directory.
cat [filename]	Print the contents of the specified filename to the terminal. Output can be redirected to another file (e.g., cat file1 > file2), concatenating (thus the name) the contents of the first onto the second.

Table 3-1. Unix commands to use when poking around TiVo's filesystem (continued)

Bash shell command	Purpose
touch [filename]	Set the modification date of a specified file to the current time. Touching a nonexistent file creates a blank or zero-length file.
mv <original> <renamed>	Rename or move a file or directory from original to renamed.
rm <filename>	Remove the specified file.
mkdir <directory>	Create a new specified directory.
rmdir <directory>	Remove a directory. This works only if the directory is empty, all its contents having already been removed using rm.

See Also

- *Learning the bash Shell (http://www.oreilly.com/catalog/bash2/)*

 ## Poking Around

#35 With a Bash prompt and some basic Unix utilities, let's get a lay of the land.

Before we really start mucking around, it's best to bring out that inner Boy Scout and whip out a map. Let's get a quick tour of the filesystem.

 No matter how hard you look around, you're not going to bump into your recorded television programs as they are not stored in this Unix-able partition. Check out Chapter 6 to figure out how to get to them.

If you go to the top-level directory on the TiVo and list all the directories, you will find a superset of those listed here. The directories and their contents may vary from TiVo model to TiVo model, but these are almost certainly going to be there:

bin

Contains most commonly used Unix programs and commands: bash, cat, cp, cpio, du, grep, gzip, ln, mkdir, mount, mv, rm, rz, sz, umount, uname, etc. This can be supplemented by bringing additional Unix binaries onboard **[Hack #31]**, **[Hack #34]**.

dev

Contains special device interfaces for the hard disks and serial ports.

etc

Contains configuration files for the Linux side of TiVo. Files in this directory specify everything from which programs should be launched on power-up to the specifics of how the system logger should run.

lib

> Holds the two libraries that all the compiled executable programs running on the TiVo are linked against, along with the kernel modules to be loaded as needed.

sbin

> Contains programs needed by the Linux operating system, including pppd, restart, route, and rsh.

tmp

> Contains temporary files.

tvbin

> Home of the programs constituting the brains of TiVo—things like myworld, the actual *TiVo* program, and *tivosh*, a TiVo-specific shell under which the various maintenance scripts slave away in the background.

tvlib

> Contains all the interesting data files used by the programs in *tvbin*. In *tvlib*, you'll find subdirectories like *font*—which contains true type fonts for everything on the screen—and *data*—which has a listing of all the actors and directors the TiVo puts up on the screen in its *famousActors* and *famousDirectors* files.

HACK #36 Moving Stuff to and from Your TiVo

Now that you have a prompt, how do you get more programs onto the TiVo for you to use?

The programs that are preinstalled on the TiVo are quite limited. There just aren't that many interesting things you can do with what you already have onboard, as there is no text editor, no compiler, or anything else of note. What we need is the ability to move things on and off the box. Enter rz/sz.

Let's rewind ourselves to the days of modems and bulletin board systems. Before the Internet became all the rave, ZMODEM, the language of rz/sz, was the way to move the files back and forth between computers. ZMODEM provides the protection of an envelope to the data in the noisy world of serial communications. Luckily, the good people at TiVo have already put rz and sz on the TiVo for us.

For the following examples, let's work with getting a copy of less [Hack #37] onto your TiVo, as you will probably want it there anyway. Grab *less-378-s1.tar.gz* (*http://prdownloads.sourceforge.net/tivoutils/less-378-s1.tar.gz?download*) and put the file onto the PC that is connected to your TiVo [Hack #33].

SecureCRT for Windows

SecureCRT seems to be made for rz and sz. Everything is automatic and simple. Any time you want to ship a file up, just type rz:

```
bash-2.02# rz
```

SecureCRT will take care of everything for you. It will present a dialog box (see Figure 3-5) from which to select the files that you want to upload. Once you have selected the files, hit the Add button, then OK to send them on their merry way. You have about 40 seconds to select all the files and ship them.

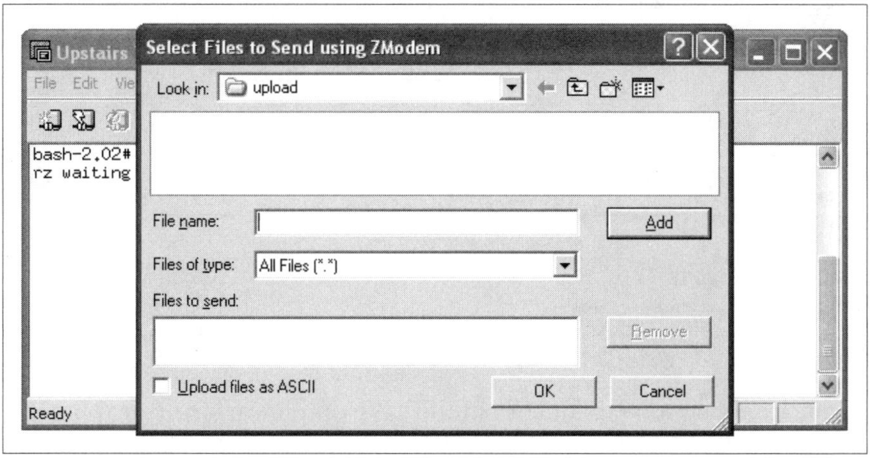

Figure 3-5. The automatic dialog box for rz in SecureCRT

Shipping files back to your PC from the TiVo is also easy with SecureCRT. Say you want to download */etc/rc.d/rc.sysinit* to tinker with offline. Just type:

```
bash-2.02# sz /etc/rc.d/rc.sysinit
```

It'll show up in the *download* subdirectory under the *SecureCRT* directory. In my case, that's *c:\Program Files\SecureCRT\download*.

ZTerm on Macintosh

With ZTerm running, any time you type rz, your TiVo will begin waiting for data to come down the line:

```
bash-2.02# rz
rz waiting to receive.*
```

When it's ready, simply press ⌘, or go to *File → Send Zmodem…*, and a dialog will pop up, allowing you to select the file that you want to move up (see Figure 3-6). Be warned, however: you only have about 30 to 40 seconds to select that file. Find the tarball containing *less*, and upload it.

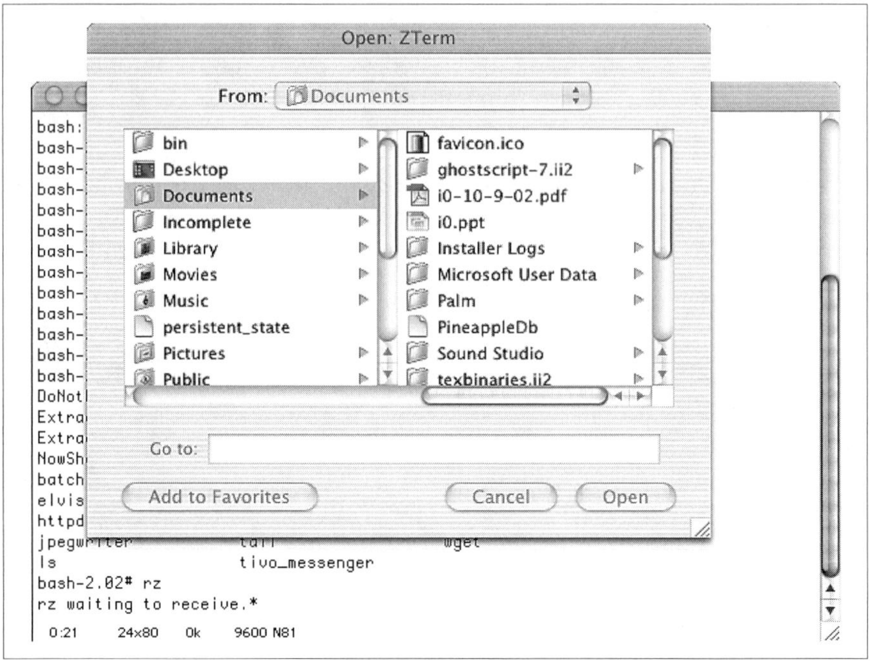

Figure 3-6. Choosing the file to send to the TiVo under ZTerm

If you are trying to grab a file from the TiVo and move it to your Mac (the reverse direction of what we did previously), just use the sz command:

```
bash-2.02# sz /etc/rc.d/rc.sysinit
```

This command will ship the */etc/rc.d/rc.sysinit* file to your PC. ZTerm will automatically receive the file and put it whatever location *Settings → Receive Folder...* is set to.

Installing the less Pager on Your TiVo
#37
Do more with less, the best way to page through and find things within a text file.

There's an old Unix saying: "less is more." It refers to two *paging* programs or commands, more and less, used to scroll through a text file a line or page at a time. While more is usually more than enough, less does all that more can and more—most notably, the ability to move and search not just forward, but also backward through a file. Indeed, less is more than more (Unix geeks just love this stuff!).

The Unix utilities package [Hack #34] doesn't have any prepackaged pagers, so I recommend you install less. Grab yourself a copy of the precompiled version for TiVo from *http://prdownloads.sourceforge.net/tivoutils/less-378-s1.tar.gz?download*. Don't expand the archive; just transfer it [Hack #36] as is to the */var/hack* directory on your TiVo and run the following commands to expand the archive, put less into place, and remove the unneeded archive:

```
bash-2.02# cd /var/hack
bash-2.02# gzip -d less-378-s1.tar.gz
bash-2.02# cd /
bash-2.02# cpio -I -H tar --make-directories < /var/hack/less-378-s1.tar
bash-2.02# rm /var/hack/less-378-s1.tar
```

This will expand less into */var/hack/bin*, where we have been putting the rest of the hacks, commands, and applications. At the same time, it is going to place a few needed libraries into */var/hack/lib*. We need to tell TiVo where to find these library files by altering the LD_LIBRARY_PATH environment variable; this is done in much the same way we edited the PATH, by modifying TiVo's *.profile* file:

```
bash-2.02# remount -o remount,rw /
bash-2.02# echo "export LD_LIBRARY_PATH=\$LD_LIBRARY_PATH:/var/hack/lib" >>
/.profile
bash-2.02# remount -o remount,ro /
```

This will help you out the next time you reboot your TiVo, but if you want it to take effect now, simply reexport LD_LIBRARY_PATH on the command line, like so:

```
bash-2.02# export LD_LIBRARY_PATH=$LD_LIBRARY_PATH:/var/hack/bin
```

Give it a whirl by taking a peek at the *rc.sysinit* file:

```
bash-2.02# less /etc/rc.d/rc.sysinit
```

To scroll forward a page at a time, hit the spacebar; hit the B key to scroll backward. You can also go forward and backward a line at a time using the down and up arrows, respectively.

Text Editing with vi on Your TiVo
#38 Nothing says text editing like vi, the default Unix editor.

When you think of text editing, you probably think Microsoft Word, Word Perfect, AppleWorks, BBEdit, Notepad, or the like. I'm afraid you won't find any of these on your TiVo. In fact, about all you have at your disposal is the echo command we used to tack commands onto the end of TiVo's *rc.sysinit*. While you can use echo to add new lines to the beginning or the end of a file, this command gets frustrating quickly when you want to add lines in the middle of a file, and it becomes nearly impossible if you want to alter a particular line.

For Unix geeks, nothing says text editing like vi or Emacs [Hack #39], but we'll get that running in just a moment. A mainstay of just about any Unix system, the vi editor is small, lightweight, and packed with geek-worthy power and functionality.

Installing elvis

Drew Streib has ported a version of elvis, a simple vi clone, to the Series 1 TiVo architecture. Grab a copy at *ftp://ftp.alt.org/pub/tivo/dtype/elvis-1.4_Tivo-1.tar.gz* and expand it on your PC. In the archive you'll find an elvis binary file. Copy the elvis binary over to your TiVo [Hack #36] and drop it into the */var/hack/bin* directory.

Make the program executable using the chmod command, like so:

```
bash-2.02# chmod 755 /var/hack/bin/elvis
```

Running elvis

On a TiVo, chances are that elvis won't "just work" at this point, but give it a shot:

```
bash-2.02# elvis
Unrecognized TERM type
```

If you get an "Unrecognized TERM type" error, your TiVo is not yet set up to properly interact with your terminal program beyond basic input/output. This is usually the case and can be fixed pretty easily. Inside the *elvis-1.4_Tivo-1.tar.gz* archive, there is a *terminfo.tar* file. Move the *terminfo.tar* file from the archive you downloaded over to your TiVo and plop it in */var/hack*. Next, make a *terminfo* directory and use cpio to unpack it and put it into place:

```
bash-2.02# mkdir /var/hack/terminfo
bash-2.02# cd /var/hack
bash-2.02# cpio -i -H tar --make-directories < terminfo.tar
```

This will supply TiVo with all the information necessary for it to display full-screen terminal programs. We just need to tell TiVo where to find the terminal information files. The easy way is to just set the TERMINFO environment variable to the */var/hack/terminfo* directory:

```
bash-2.02# export TERMINFO=/var/hack/terminfo
```

With the TERMINFO set, we should be able to use elvis by invoking it on the command line. In fact, you can give it a whirl by editing your */.profile* file to include the TERMINFO information:

```
bash-2.02# mount -o remount,rw /
bash-2.02# elvis /.profile
bash-2.02# mount -o remount,ro /
```

See Also

- *Learning the vi Editor* (*http://www.oreilly.com/catalog/vi6/*)

Text Editing with Emacs on Your TiVo

#39

Nothing says text editing like Emacs, the other default Unix editor.

Ask anybody in any Linux forum which editor is better, vi or Emacs, and you're bound to start a brawl. People love vi due to its simplicity, while Emacs people complain that using vi is too limiting. vi people complain that Emacs is bloated; Emacs people complain that vi is nonintuitive.

Let's fan the flames of this particularly geeky religious war by bringing TiVo users into the debate, shall we?

The version of Emacs for TiVo is actually called JASSPA's MicroEmacs, freely downloadable from *http://www.jasspa.com/down0212.html*. The full version of Emacs with all its ELisp files is going to be a little too much for your TiVo. Think of MicroEmacs as a version of Emacs that is packaged to be small enough to fit on one floppy.

For the TiVo, Greg Sadaway compiled nanoemacs, the smallest MicroEmacs you can get for the TiVo, and made it available at *http://alt.org/forum/index. php?t=getfile&id=44*. Grab yourself a copy, move it over to your TiVo [Hack #36], and drop it into the */var/hack/bin* directory.

I usually find it helpful to rename the program from `nec-static` to `nec` or just plain `emacs`:

```
bash-2.02# mv /var/hack/bin/nec-static /var/hack/bin/emacs
```

Also, don't forget to make the program executable, like so:

```
bash-2.02# chmod 755 /var/hack/bin/nec
```

Chances are that emacs, just like elvis, won't "just work" at this point (unless you have `elvis` [Hack #38] installed), but give it a shot:

```
bash-2.02# emacs
Unrecognized TERM type
```

If you see this error message, you will have to snag yourself a copy of `elvis` [Hack #38], pull out the *terminfo.tar* from the Series 1's archive, and install it into */var/hack/terminfo*:

```
bash-2.02# mkdir /var/hack/terminfo
bash-2.02# cd /var/hack
bash-2.02# cpio -I -H tar --make-directories < terminfo.tar
```

Don't forget to also set the TERMINFO environment variable. Why not also make the change permanent by adding it to your /.profile file?

```
bash-2.02# export TERMINFO=/var/hack/terminfo
bash-2.02# mount -o remount,rw /
bash-2.02# emacs /.profile
bash-2.02# mount -o remount,ro /
```

Displaying Images on Your TV
Hijack your television screen for displaying your own still images.

Ever considered using your TiVo to display some of your own images? Maybe you can coerce it to become your own personal slideshow viewer as you feed it JPEGs of your last family vacation? Thanks to some clever hackers, you can.

> Of course TiVo Series 2 users have a much easier time of it thanks to the Home Media Option [Hack #63] which allows you to share on your personal computer with TiVo for your viewing pleasure.

When your TiVo records a television show, it creates an MPEG file on its hard drive. MPEG is the Moving Picture Experts Group's file format for motion video; it makes use of excessive computing to squeeze every single bit of redundant data out of the video, making the smallest, yet highest quality, recording it can make. Mounted on TiVo's motherboard is an IBM MPEG CS22 Decoder. This hardware converts the MPEG-encoded video that the TiVo records to what is displayed on the TV screen.

This chip's instruction set also includes the ability to overlay the MPEG stream (read: television programming) with graphics and text. This is how the status bar is displayed on the screen during recorded video playback and when the TV guide floats over live television shows.

If you convince TiVo to send the decoder the appropriate commands, you can place whatever you wish on your television screen.

TiVo accepts only 720x480 indexed color PNG image files. Converting your images to this format requires the use of an application the likes of Photoshop (my favorite), the Gimp, or just about any other modern graphics editor.

> The Gimp (http://www.gimp.org) is a full-featured, open source, and free alternative to typically expensive graphics packages like Photoshop. While traditionally geared toward the Unix operating system, the Gimp is also available for Windows and Mac OS X.

In the graphics editor of your choice, open the image you want to put on your television screen. For this example, I'll use the cover of this book, as shown in Figure 3-7.

Figure 3-7. *The TiVo Hacks cover at the wrong resolution and sporting too many colors for TiVo's approval*

We have a few problems: the picture is 427x643 (the wrong resolution), and it's in RGB color—24-bit (or 32 if there is an alpha channel) rather than indexed color. But these problems are nothing a little image-editing magic can't fix.

First of all, shrink the image down, but keep the aspect ratio fixed so it doesn't become distorted. If your image is taller than it is wide, set the height to something like 400; if it is wider than it is tall, set its width to 640. I'm not setting it to the maximum allowed size, to give it a nice matted border. Also, some televisions hide a few pixels on the edges, and I don't want anything chopped off my cover.

I know what you're thinking: our image is now smaller than 720x480; that can't be right. True, true. Let's expand the canvas to be the right size. This will make our graphic be 720x480 pixels, but it will leave our carefully sized and colored image whatever size we decided upon, nicely centered. So, resize the canvas, add a white background, and we have our cover as shown in Figure 3-8, ready for primetime.

Figure 3-8. The TiVo Hacks cover, scaled down and placed in an image with the right dimensions

Now, change the image type from RGB to indexed and save it as a PNG file. Move that file over to your TiVo **[Hack #36]** and put it somewhere appropriate. I keep my pictures in a */var/hack/pictures* directory.

Take care not to cram your /var partition too full with lots of images, or you just may trigger TiVo's instinct to clear out this directory entirely.

The software for displaying your new image is already on the TiVo, so just type (replacing *tivo_hacks.png* with the name of the picture you wish to display):

```
bash-2.02# osdwriter /var/hack/pictures/tivo_hacks.png
```

The image should come right up on your television screen. To clear it away, just press any button on your TiVo remote control.

You have another option to get images up on the screen. Use the JPEG-writer (*http://www.allaboutjake.com/tivo/jpegwriter.html*) by Jake Bordens. Usage might be a little simpler, albeit a little less stable. Just download the archive and stick the jpegwriter in */var/hack/bin*. On the command line, pass it a JPEG, like so:

```
bash-2.02# jpegwriter /var/hack/pictures/tivo_hacks.jpg
```

The JPEG should come right up on your television screen.

Pre–TiVo OS 3.0 Series 1 users, on the other hand, have a little bit of a harder time. You all (hopefully, there are very few of you) will need Mike Hill's osdmngr, found at *http://tivo.samba.org/download/belboz/osdmngr-1.7. tar.gz*. Hill's program expects images in the TARGA (TGA) file format and will convert and output images that are in the file format your antiquated osdwriter expects. The osdwriter in Pre–OS 3.0 machines will present this file directly to the CS22 Decoder chip without ever processing it, so the osdmngr does all the processing for it.

HACK #41 Putting Text on the Screen

Ever wanted to add your own Closed Captioning to a television show? Here is your chance.

Have you ever wanted to mute your television show and put words in the mouth of the actor or actress? Maybe you just want to translate the dialog into another language. Or, more maliciously, have you ever wanted to insert your own subliminal messages into a television show? If so, then I have a utility for you.

One possible way to do this is to create an image and use osdwriter [Hack #41], but what a pain that would be. Imagine creating an image in Photoshop, copying it over to TiVo [Hack #36], and then invoking osdwriter every single time you want to put a new line of text on the screen. Ouch!

Enter Christopher Wingert's *newtext2osd* (*http://www.geocities.com/ wyngnut2k/newtext2osd-1.4.tar.gz*). This is a simple command-line program that takes any arbitrary text as an argument and plops it right on your TV screen.

Download the *newtext2osd* archive, unzip it, and you should find a single binary called *newtext2osd*. Transfer it **[Hack #36]** to your TiVo's */var/hack/bin* directory, and make it executable using the chmod command:

```
bash-2.02# chmod 755 /var/hack/bin/newtext2osd
```

Using *newtext2osd* is really easy. To display a "hello, TiVo hacker" at position (10, 10) on the screen for 10 seconds, you'd type:

```
bash-2.02# newtext2osd -s 10 -x 10 -y 10 -t "hello, TiVo hacker"
```

Figure 3-9 shows the result.

Figure 3-9. Text sent to the television screen using newtext2osd

The screen, in *newtext2osd* dimensions, is about 40x25. If your text simply won't fit, *newtext2osd* will simply complain. You can even specify the text color and background color using the –f and –b arguments, respectively. The color range is from 0–255, and you can check out the best colors in Table 3-2. This program also understands particular words as colors when passed using the --fg (foreground color) and --bg (background color) arguments. The following are recognized color names: transparent1, transparent2, transparent3, grey, white1, white2, white3, red1, green, red2, orange, turquoise, red3, yellow, black1, and black2. Play around and find a combination you like.

Table 3-2. Some of the best color values that you can pass to newtext2osd

Color value	Color
0	Clear
1	Light grey

Table 3-2. *Some of the best color values that you can pass to newtext2osd (continued)*

Color value	Color
4	White
5	Black
6	Blue
7	Green
9	Yellow
11	Red
29	Orange
34	Pink

Of course, text can overlay live television or recorded programming. And that's just the tip of the iceberg. You can also have the program watch a file or wait until the program is killed before it wipes away the text.

HACK #42 Capturing Closed Captioning

TiVo has access to Closed Captioning for the programs it records. Pipe Closed Captioning to your screen even if your TV doesn't have CC support, or capture a transcript of the show you're watching for your reference.

Television comes over the air or through the cable at 30 frames a second. The time between frames is called the Vertical Blanking Interval and is often stuffed by broadcasters with a whole mess of data. That's how that nifty VCR of yours can set its clock without your ever having to fiddle with the confusing interface for doing so manually. It's how the TiVomatic works—you know, the ability to record a television show from its commercial by pressing the 👍 button on your TiVo remote control? (Well, if you watch the commercials, that is.) Closed Captioning data—a fairly decent transcript of all that's said in the show—also comes to your television set via the Vertical Blanking Interval.

TiVo does receive, record, and sometimes process that extra information, so you can too. You'll need Mike Baker's *tivovbi* (*http://tivo.samba.org/download/mbm/tivovbi-1.03.zip*), an application for decoding, capturing, and displaying Closed Captioning received by a TiVo unit.

Download the *tivovbi-1.03.zip* file, unzip it on your PC, transfer [Hack #36] it to your TiVo's */var/hack/bin* directory, and make it executable using the chmod command:

```
bash-2.02# chmod 755 /var/hack/bin/tivovbi
```

Almost anything recorded during primetime television from a major network is bound to have Closed Captioning. Let it loose on a television show that you know has Closed Captioning by typing:

```
bash-2.02# tivovbi -xtc
```

If it all worked, you'll see something like this come flowing out onto your PC:

```
% CHANNEL CALLSIGN:
% CURRENT  RATING: TV-PG
% CHANNEL NETWORK: NBC
% CURRENT AIR DATE: 15 31 31:63:00 TAPE
```

If you don't see this output, try watching a different show to distinguish between it not working and the show just not having Closed Captioning. If indeed it isn't working, you are probably running TiVo OS 3.x or higher. Unfortunately, *tivovbi* won't work right out of the box, so we are going to have to strong-arm it.

We're going to need to load a kernel module. A kernel module is a way of extending the way an operating system works, without having to reload and reboot the entire system. The main problem here is that *tivovbi* was written for an older version of the TiVo OS. By loading this module up, it can get it to hook into the operating system again. If you are running on a standalone TiVo, grab yourself a copy of *http://tivo.samba.org/download/mbm/bin/tvbi.o*. Those of you on DirectTiVo's might want *http://tivo.samba.org/download/mbm/bin/tvbi-dtv.o*. Make yourself a new directory on your TiVo called */var/hack/modules* and stick the appropriate file in there.

Modules can be inserted into the kernel through a simple tool called insmod (or "install module"). insmod takes a kernel from the filesystem and loads it into the running kernel. Modules that are not being used can then be removed from the kernel through the *rmmod* tool, thereby also removing the functionality they bring. We're going to use insmod to load up the *tvbi.o* or *tvbi-dtv.o* modules:

```
bash-2.02# insmod -f /var/hack/modules/tvbi.o
/var/hack/modules/tvbi.o: init_module: Device or resource busy
```

Just ignore the error. You've now extended the TiVo OS to allow *tivovbi* to access the VBI information again.

Try another show with Closed Captioning and rerun *tivovbi*:

```
bash-2.02# tivovbi -xtc
```

Now you should get the output listed previously. Closed Captioning should be flowing into your terminal in time with the show dialog playing on your TV set.

Keeping a Transcript

You can actually capture the Closed Captioning and save it to a file, creating yourself a nice transcript of the show you just watched. Simply redirect the output to a file instead of to the screen. For lack of something more creative, name the file *closed-captioning.txt*, like so:

```
bash-2.02# tivovbi -xtc > closed-captioning.txt
```

When your program is done, copy the resulting *closed-captioning.txt* file over to your PC [Hack #36] and print it out for later perusal, email it to a friend, file it for later reference, and so forth. Instead of redirecting to a local file and then sending it over to your PC, you could also mount a directory on your PC [Hack #56] and start writing to files over the network.

> You can capture the Closed Captioning at higher speed by hitting the ⏩ button on your remote control. Closed Captioning will stop working if you try to go any faster than pressing the ⏩ button just once.

Showing Closed Captioning on Your Television

Even if your television set itself doesn't support Closed Captioning, you can pipe it there from TiVo using *tivovbi*:

```
bash-2.02# tivovbi -oc
```

Never miss another word of that British *East Enders* show.

 Caller ID on Your TV

HACK
#43

Only a chosen few are allowed to interrupt your favorite television show, TiVo or no. Find out who's calling without averting your eyes from the tube.

The hero and the heroine are about to kiss. The identity of the spy is mere seconds from being revealed. The fate of a major character on the show hangs in the balance. And the blasted phone rings. You could pause the program, but this is a seminal moment in television history. You could ignore the phone, but you are expecting a call about that job you were after. What to do?

If you have caller ID from your phone company and a DirecTiVo (combination DirecTV satellite and TiVo system), then you have just the combination you need to determine whether or not to reach for that phone.

> I'm afraid this hack isn't going to magically give you caller ID if you haven't requested and paid your phone company for it. We're assuming you've caller ID on the phone line into which your DirecTiVo unit is plugged.

Greg Gardner's *elseed* (*http://www.bah.org/~greg/tivo/*) displays caller ID information—recognized by your DirecTiVo through its connection to the phone line—and puts it up on your television screen for you to see. Figure 3-10 shows *elseed* in action.

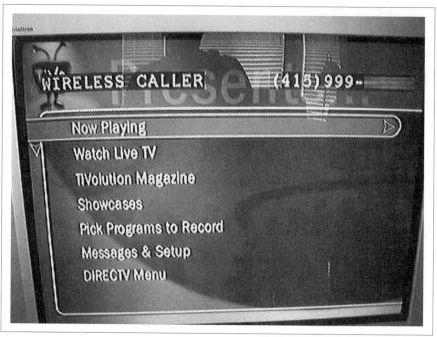

Figure 3-10. Caller ID on an incoming call, captured by elseed on TiVo and displayed on a television screen

Download the archive, extract the *elseed* binary, copy it [Hack #36] to */var/hack/bin* on your DirecTiVo, and set it as executable:

```
bash-2.02# chmod 755 /var/hack/bin/elseed
```

Give it a whirl by invoking it on the command line by hand:

```
bash-2.02# elseed -e
```

This will wait until the first phone call with caller ID comes in, pop the number up on the television, and then exit. So, pick up that cell phone, dial the line to which your DirecTiVo is hooked, and watch for your number to appear on the television screen.

Assuming that worked as expected, set up *elseed* to run automatically whenever your DirecTiVo boots. Transfer the *elseed_forever.sh* script from the *elseed* archive on your PC over to */var/hack/bin*, and use the vi [Hack #38] or Emacs editor [Hack #39] to append the following lines to your */etc/rc.d/rc.sysinit* file:

```
sleep 200
/var/hack/bin/elseed_forever.sh &
```

Or, use the echo command, like so:

```
bash-2.02# remount -o remount,rw /
bash-2.02# echo "sleep 20; /var/hack/bin/elseed_forever.sh &">> /.profile
bash-2.02# remount -o remount,ro /
```

However you choose to edit */.profile*, remount the */* partition read-write, then read-only again when you are finished, as shown in the preceding command.

Now this works just fine, displaying the telephone number and available caller information with each incoming call, but what if you want to override the information that comes from the phone company? What if, instead of her actual name, a call from your significant other could show up as "Teddy Bear" or whatever cute nickname you use? What if the phone company has nothing useful on record associated with your best friend's number?

elseed is configurable via an *elseed.conf* file. containing lines like these:

```
6175555555 A BOGUS NUMBER
5105555432 Teddy Bear
7075551234 Mom
```

Each of these lines associates a particular phone number—it *must* be a 10-digit number—with a name or bit of arbitrary text to display.

Make yourself a */var/hack/etc* directory in which to save the *elseed.conf* configuration file:

```
bash-2.02# mkdir /var/hack/etc
```

To have *elseed* pay attention to the configuration file, it has to be invoked slightly differently. Reedit your *rc.sysinit* file, changing the line:

```
/var/hack/bin/elseed_forever.sh &
```

to:

```
/var/hack/bin/elseed_forever.sh -c /var/hack/etc/elseed.conf
```

Turn your TiVo off and back on again for TiVo to launch *elseed* automatically, or start it by hand (if it's not already running) by typing the following invocation on the command line:

```
bash-2.02# elseed_forever.sh -c /var/hack/etc/elseed.conf &
```

Running the Same Thing Over and Over...

Use cron, the Unix scheduling service, to run a hack at particular times of the day, week, month, or year.

If sending TiVo email [Hack #57] isn't enough to remind you to walk your dog, or if you just want to run the same hack at regular intervals, then *cron*, the Unix scheduling service, is all you need.

Grab yourself a copy of *cron* (*ftp://ftp.dtype.org/pub/tivo/dtype/cron-3.0pl1_TiVo-2.tar.gz*), which M. Drew Streib has compiled.

Set up a directory structure to house the *cron* binary and sample *crontab* file—the actual list of scheduled events:

```
bash-2.02# mkdir /var/hack/etc
bash-2.02# mkdir /var/hack/etc/cron.d
bash-2.02# mkdir/var/hack/cron
```

Move both files over to your TiVo [Hack #36], dropping *cron* into */var/hack/bin* and *crontab* into */var/hack/etc*. Make *cron* executable:

```
bash-2.02# chmod 755 /var/hack/bin/cron
```

Now you can just start *cron* and have it run in the background:

```
bash-2.02# cron &
```

To actually schedule events, you are going to need to edit the *crontab* file directly. The syntax for this file is a little esoteric, so bear with me. Open up that file using your preferred text editor [Hacks #38, #39], and you'll see a sample line for your reference:

```
# m h dom mon dow    command
*/10 * * * *  date >> /var/hack/cron.test.out
```

The first five items on that line control the frequency of the command. These columns are the minute, the hour, the day of the month, the month, and the day of the week. You can specify each with numbers, put in a * wildcard to have the event occur at all those intervals (e.g., every minute, every hour, every day, etc.), or divide it using the / sign to have it run every nth of those intervals. Deciphering the previous line, *cron* is scheduled to run the command—in this case, output the date to a file, */var/hack/cron.test. out*—once every 10 minutes at every hour of every day of every month, regardless of the day of the week.

Back to our patient pooch. Let's say we want to send a reminder to your TV screen using *newtext2osd* [Hack #41] at 6 p.m. every weekday (just when you'd be inclined to forget and watch the evening news) and at 1 p.m. on weekend days. No problem, just add the following lines to */var/etc/crontab*:

```
0 18 * * 1-5   newtext2osd -s 10 -x 10 -y 10 -t "walk the dog"
0 13 * * 0,6   newtext2osd -s 10 -x 10 -y 10 -t "walk the dog"
```

The first line tells TiVo's *cron* to remind you at 6 p.m. (that's hour 18, military time) on weekdays (1-5, Sunday being day 0). The second line does the same for Sunday and Saturday (days 0 and 6) at 1 p.m. (hour 13).

Proof positive that Unix can indeed save the integrity of your carpets!

Hacking the Hack

Of course, you can use *cron* to schedule any of the command-line hacks in this book. Have it generate a new list of your favorite actors [Hack #91] every day to download and use on your web site. Have it clear unnecessary debug files from particular directories weekly so that your partitions [Hack #29] don't get too full. Give anything you find yourself doing on the command line on a regular basis to *cron* to handle for you; it never forgets.

Save Multiple Shows at a Time to Your VCR
#45
Dumping multiple shows in succession to your VCR is impossible with the default TiVo interface, but this is nothing a little hacking can't get around.

Ever want to save more than one television show from your TiVo to your VCR? You have to save one, wander off for the length of the show, come back, save the next…lather, rinse, repeat. All you really want to do is set your VCR to record for 8 hours—the length of a VHS tape at EP quality—tell your TiVo to play those 8 one-hour shows in succession, and leave the TiVo and VCR alone. With the default TiVo interface, you just can't do that.

But using a little hacking in the form of a batch save script, you can.

The program to make this happen has gone through many hands to reach its current state. The code was originally Mike Baker's (of TiVoVBI fame [Hack #42]), but it has since been taken over by a developer known as SuperZap. In essence, the script creates a new program that points to all the programs you want to queue up. When one program in the queue ends, it points to the next, and the next, and so on, and TiVo's never the wiser.

Grab yourself a copy of *batchsavesz1.zip* (*http://www.dealdatabase.com/forum/attachment.php?s=&postid=90390*) and unzip it on your PC. Inside, you'll find a file named *BatchSavesz1.tcl*; rename it to *batch.tcl* for short and copy it over [Hack #36] to the */var/hack/bin* directory on your TiVo. Make it executable:

```
bash-2.02# chmod 755 /var/hack/bin/batch.tcl
```

Because the authors of the script don't really have things set up on their TiVos in quite the same way as us, we'll have to make one quick change to get this hack working.

If you take a look at the *batch.tcl* file, you'll notice that in a few places it is trying to call a program called *text2osd* from the */var/hack* directory. That's an older version of *newtext2osd* we encountered while putting text on the screen **[Hack #41]** a little earlier in this chapter. To make this hack work, you have two choices: either edit the script, changing all instances of /var/hack/ text2osd to /var/hack/bin/newtext2osd, or create a symlink (symbolic link), effectively making text2osd into newtext2osd, like this:

```
bash-2.02# ln -sf /var/hack/bin/newtext2osd /var/hack/text2osd
```

Either way will work just fine.

Now for some juggling. The script needs to run from the command prompt, but it also requires you to use your remote control; so, you'll have to drive with one hand and point-and-click with the other. Navigate to the *Now Playing* menu using your TiVo remote control, and then run the script at the Bash prompt:

```
bash-2.02# batch.tcl
```

From the *Now Playing* list, select (highlight it and press the **Select** button) the program you want to save first, bringing up its description. Press the **9** button on the remote, and your command-line session should say something like this:

```
adding 1694436/-1
```

Your television screen will show something akin to Figure 3-11. The script is remembering the stream IDs for all the programs that you want to record, so it can create a metastream a little later.

Perform these same steps for all the television shows you want to queue up. Once you're done, press the **7** button on your remote. You'll see a confirmation that the various streams associated with the shows you've selected are being merged:

```
merging: 1694436/-1 1692481/-1
```

Your TV screen should now look something like Figure 3-12. Press the **1** button on the remote to leave the script.

Navigate to your *Now Playing* list again, and you'll see a new program called *multipart* (see Figure 3-13). Pop your VCR tape in, select the program and *Save to VCR*, and go have yourself a nice nap before moving on to the next chapter.

> While using the multipart feature to play multiple shows in sequence is tempting, it may not work as expected. While it may be just fine, so long as you're not touching anything, the instant you try fast forwarding or rewinding you run the risk of your TiVo rebooting itself.

Figure 3-11. The batch.tcl script, confirming a program has been added to the pending batch stream

Playing MP3s on your TiVo

#46

The Series 2 and Home Media Option allow you to play MP3s on your TiVo. Why not play them on the Series 1 as well?

Why not take advantage of that shiny box under your television to play some music when your TV-addled eyes need a rest? That's exactly what some TiVo hackers did long before the Home Media Option [Hack #63] came out for the Series 2.

> The Series 1 was not designed for playing MP3s. Its 50 MHz processor is going to be seriously strained when you execute this hack. While nothing horrible is going to happen, don't expect to get concert quality sound from your television.

Mike Baker has made a binary of *madplay* available at *http://tivo.samba.org/ download/mbm/bin/madplay*. *madplay* a small and simple Unix utility for decoding MP3s without using floating-point arithmetic, which is a good thing considering the TiVo's processor can't crunch floating-point math anyway.

Figure 3-12. The merge.tcl script, confirming that it has combined all the selected programs into one

Upload [Hack #36] the *madplay* binary to your TiVo's */var/hack/bin* directory. While you're at it, upload an MP3 file of your choosing, dropping it into */var/tmp*. Don't forget to make the program executable:

```
bash-2.02# chmod 755 /var/hack/bin/madplay
```

Try it out against that MP3 file, like so:

```
bash-2.02# madplay /var/tmp/music.mp3
```

Music to the ears! You'll probably notice the sound stuttering and the feeling that TiVo is struggling to keep up. It probably is, poor thing. I've had the best luck with MP3s that I've encoded in constant bit rate at a 32kHz sampling rate.

> Using *madplay* will leave your TiVo in a state where the menus and remote control buttons do not make any sound. Other than that, everything should work just fine. If you can't live without your sound effects, reboot your box when you're finished listening to MP3s.

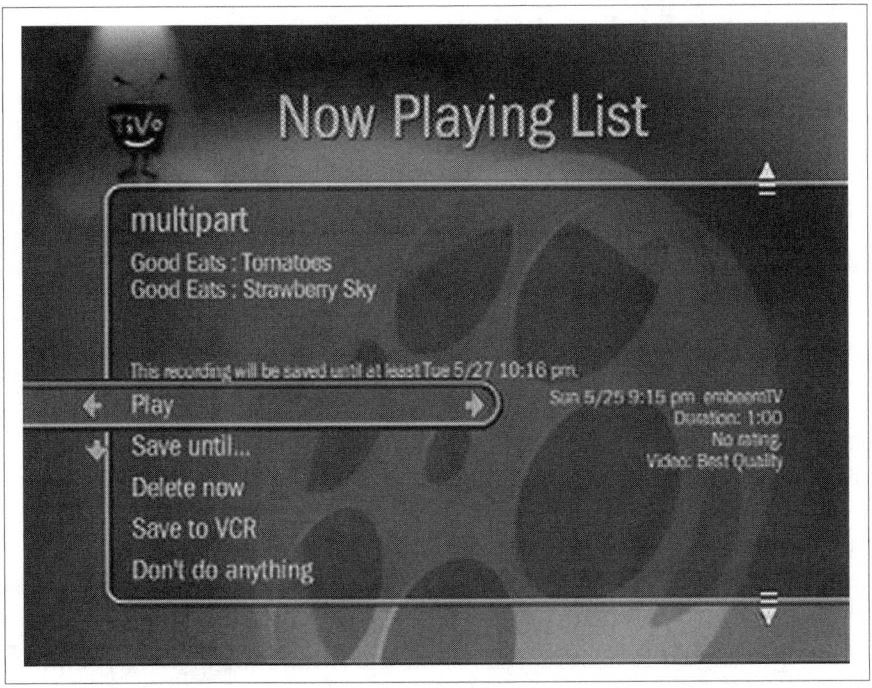

Figure 3-13. The batch.tcl-created multipart program, consisting of two shows

Don't expect to keep your entire music library on your TiVo—not even close in my case. In fact, be careful with the space in the */var* partition [Hack #29], as TiVo may suddenly decide to clean it up for you. Of course, you could always NFS mount a directory [Hack #56] and stream a MP3 to your TiVo to play.

## CHAPTER FOUR

Bring the Internet to TiVo
Hacks 47–62

While playing with the Bash prompt [Hack #30] on your TiVo is a nice adventure, it's quite limited in terms of real functionality. In the age of the networking, what we really want is all our devices linked together on the network. We want remote access, not just from a serially connected PC, but from anywhere on the Internet. We want our devices to jack into and talk to one another. And our TiVo should be no less than a first-class citizen.

Your TiVo should be part of your home network. Your desktop computer should be talking to and making requests of your TiVo. Your office computer, a couple of miles down the road, should be doing the same. Even on the go, your laptop—sitting at a WiFi access point in an airport halfway across the world—should be able to call up your TiVo.

Bringing the Internet all the way to your TiVo is not as difficult as it sounds. In fact, if you have a Series 2 Standalone TiVo, it's as simple as plugging a USB-Ethernet adapter. Things are a little more complex if you have a Series 1, but there's a gain in hackability.

Running PPP over TiVo's Serial Port

#47

Make a PPP connection over that serial cable plugged into your TiVo [Hack #33], and make your daily call over the Internet.

In this age of broadband cable and DSL connections, it may well have been a while since you heard the squawks of a modem. Cast your mind back a bit—circa 1994 through 1999 should about do it—and try recall how it all worked. Your computer was connected via serial cable to a modem, which was, in turn, connected to your phone line. To get online, your computer instructed your modem to dial your Internet Service Provider (ISP). The call was answered by a modem at the other end. After a few seconds of whistling and screaming at one-another, a connection was established between your computer and your ISP and, by association, the Internet. Primitive, but effective.

The language spoken between your computer and the ISPs was the *Point-to-Point Protocol* (PPP).

PPP is also used by your TiVo to make its daily call over its internal modem to TiVo, Inc. to download programming information, software updates, and other assorted bits. Surely your TiVo (a computer) can be coerced into making a PPP call to somewhere other than TiVo, Inc? Indeed it can—sort of. While getting TiVo's modem to make its daily call to another modem would be a neat trick, it's not particularly useful, is it? What we're actually after is using a spare PC as an intermediary for fulfilling your TiVo's needs over the Internet via your broadband connection and taking the phone call out of the equation.

Thankfully, TiVo has built-in functionality for making a serial PPP connection to another computer. Plug the TiVo serial control cable into its serial port. We'll get to the other side of the equation (your PC) **[Hack #48]** in just a moment.

Navigate TiVo's menu system to *Messages & Setup → Recorder & Phone Setup → Phone Connection → Change Dialing Options* under TiVo OS 3.x. Under OS 4.x, that's *TiVo Messages & Setup → Settings → Phone & Network Setup*. Set your Dial Prefix to ,#296 using the numeric buttons on your TiVo remote control. Use the Enter button for # ("pound" or "hash") and the ● button for , (comma).

> Your TiVo unit, version of the TiVo operating system, or remote control may use different buttons for special characters. Consult the onscreen instructions for the appropriate buttons to press.

A dial prefix of ,#296 instructs TiVo to establish a PPP connection at a speed of 9,600 baud over its serial port each time it makes its daily call. (No 9,600 baud isn't exactly speedy.) Table 4-1 provides a list of dial prefixes and their associated baud rates. It behooves you to try the slowest speed first and work your way up as you get this hack working with your PC.

Table 4-1. TiVo dialing prefixes and associated PPP connection baud rates

TiVo dialing prefix	PPP baud rate
,#296	9,600
,#238	38,400
,#257	57,600
,#211	115,200

Go To

You won't get very far without configuring your PC [Hack #48] to accept the PPP connection from your TiVo.

Accept a PPP Connection from TiVo on Your PC

Just getting the TiVo to run PPP over its serial port is not quite enough—you need your PC to accept the call and route it to the Internet.

PPP requires two computers for the communication to work, hence the Point-to-Point moniker. We've already set TiVo up [Hack #47] as the initiating end. Now we need to get the PC to answer the call, as it were, on the receiving end and route data between TiVo and the Internet.

Assuming you already have a PC with Internet access over some sort of broadband connection (cable modem, DSL, dedicated connection, etc.), and that computer has a free serial port, you're just about there. All that's left is a little configuration.

Configuring Windows

Windows XP already has all the software it needs to make this magic happen. We are, however, going to have to coerce it to interoperate properly with TiVo.

> These instructions are close, but not identical, to those necessary for Windows 2000. Reading through these Windows XP instructions should provide enough insight into how it's done to extrapolate to Windows 2000.

Just hooking the two machines—your TiVo and PC—together doesn't magically set up a PPP connection between the two. The base question is, how are these two computers going to know when to start talking to each other? Windows egotistically assumes that anybody connecting to it is going to say CLIENT over the serial line to get its attention. TiVo has no intention of doing so, instead preferring to send a ~ (tilde) to announce itself. One of the two is going to have to alter its expectations, and Windows is the pushover, so we'll make the appropriate adjustments there.

Launch Notepad, the simple Windows text editor, and open *c:\windows\inf\ mdmhayers.inf* for editing. Scroll down (quite a way) until you run into a section that looks something like this:

```
[M2700Reg] ; Null-Modem
HKR, Init, 1,, "None"
```

```
HKR, Init, 2,, "NoResponse"
HKR, Monitor, 1,, "None"
HKR, Answer, 1,, "CLIENTSERVER"
HKR, Answer, 2,, "NoResponse"
HKR, Settings, DialPrefix,, "CLIENT"
HKR,, Properties, 1, 00,00,00,00, 00,00,00,00, 00,00,00,00,
00,00,00,00,00,00,00,00, 30,00,00,00, 00,c2,01,00, 00,c2,01,00
HKR, Responses, "CLIENT",    1, 08, 00, 00, 00, 00, 00, 00,00,00,00 ; Server
side - the client is requesting a connection
HKR, Responses, "<h00>CLIENT", 1, 08, 00, 00, 00, 00, 00, 00,00,00,00 ;
Server side - the client is requesting a connection
HKR, Responses, "CLIENTSERVER", 1, 02, 00, 00, 00, 00, 00, 00,00,00,00 ;
Client side - the server has acknowledged
```

Slip the following between the last two lines in the block:

```
HKR, Responses, "~", 1, 08, 00, 00, 00, 00, 00, 00,00,00,00 ; Server side -
the client is requesting a connection
HKR, Responses, "<h00>~", 1, 08, 00, 00, 00, 00, 00, 00,00,00,00 ; Server
side - the client is requesting a connection
```

It should now look like this (inserted lines are called out in bold):

```
[M2700Reg] ; Null-Modem
HKR, Init, 1,, "None"
HKR, Init, 2,, "NoResponse"
HKR, Monitor, 1,, "None"
HKR, Answer, 1,, "CLIENTSERVER"
HKR, Answer, 2,, "NoResponse"
HKR, Settings, DialPrefix,, "CLIENT"
HKR,, Properties, 1, 00,00,00,00, 00,00,00,00, 00,00,00,00,
00,00,00,00,00,00,00,00, 30,00,00,00, 00,c2,01,00, 00,c2,01,00
HKR, Responses, "CLIENT",    1, 08, 00, 00, 00, 00, 00, 00,00,00,00 ; Server
side - the client is requesting a connection
HKR, Responses, "<h00>CLIENT", 1, 08, 00, 00, 00, 00, 00, 00,00,00,00 ;
Server side - the client is requesting a connection
HKR, Responses, "~", 1, 08, 00, 00, 00, 00, 00, 00,00,00,00 ; Server side -
the client is requesting a connection
HKR, Responses, "<h00>~", 1, 08, 00, 00, 00, 00, 00, 00,00,00,00 ; Server
side - the client is requesting a connection
HKR, Responses, "CLIENTSERVER", 1, 02, 00, 00, 00, 00, 00, 00,00,00,00 ;
Client side - the server has acknowledged
```

Save the changed file, and you have convinced your Windows machine to expect the ~ (tilde) character TiVo is planning to send.

Next, launch Windows XP's Control Panel, and from there the Phone and Modem Options. Select the Modems tab and click the Add button to launch the Add Hardware Wizard. You'll be asked whether you wish the Wizard to detect your modem, as shown in Figure 4-1.

Since we're not actually using a modem, check the "Don't detect my modem; I will select it from a list" checkbox and click the Next button to move on.

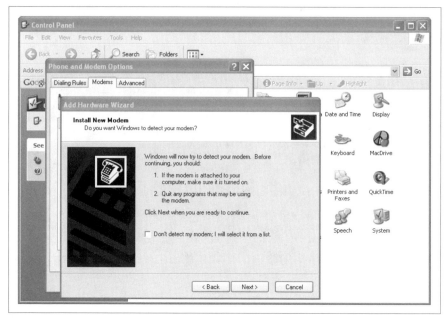

Figure 4-1. The Add Hardware Wizard asking whether or not it should detect your modem

Your computer should chug away awhile as it compiles a list of modems from which to make your selection. When it's good and ready, the wizard will show you a list of all the modems it knows (see Figure 4-2). Under Manufacturer, select "Standard Modem Types," and select "Communications cable between two computers"—that's our null modem connection—under Models. Click Next.

You'll be prompted for a COM (read: serial) port, as shown in Figure 4-3. To the question "On which ports do you want to install it?," choose "Selected ports." Then highlight the COM port to which you wired your TiVo. Click Next, and Windows will set up the connection. It should report that all went well, leaving you to click the Finish button to leave the Wizard.

The Wizard's only capable of taking care of the broad strokes; you still need to tweak and fine-tune the connection a little. Back at Phone and Modem Options, select the new "Communications cable between two computers" connection the Wizard created and click Properties to get to all its fine-tuning knobs. Select the Modem (see Figure 4-4) tab, where you'll need to make sure that the Maximum Port Speed matches the baud rate at which TiVo is set to talk **[Hack #47]**, then click OK.

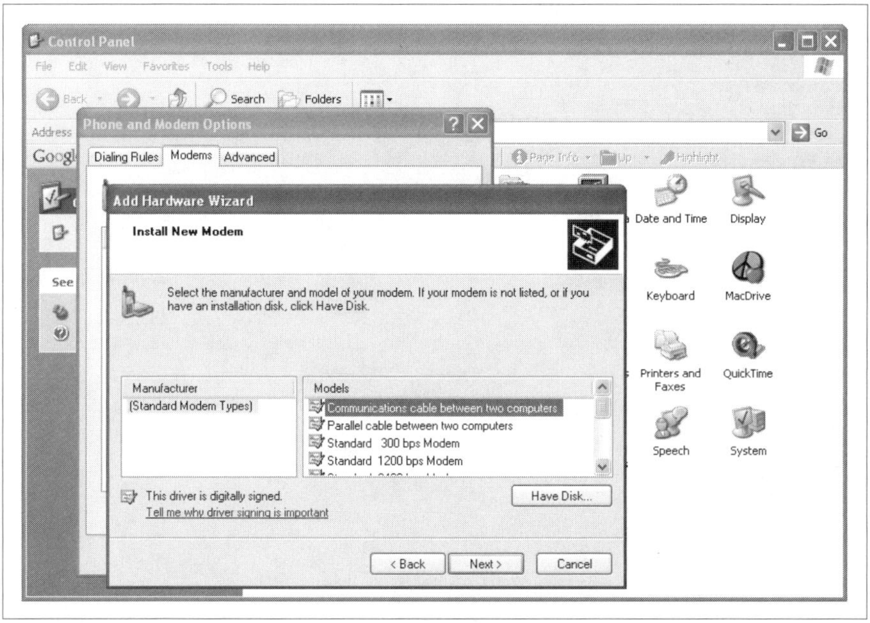

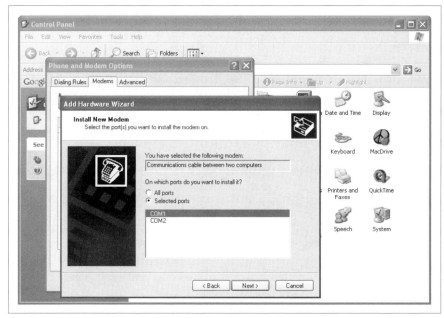

Figure 4-2. Selecting a "Communication cable between two computers"

Figure 4-3. Making sure that you have the right COM port setup

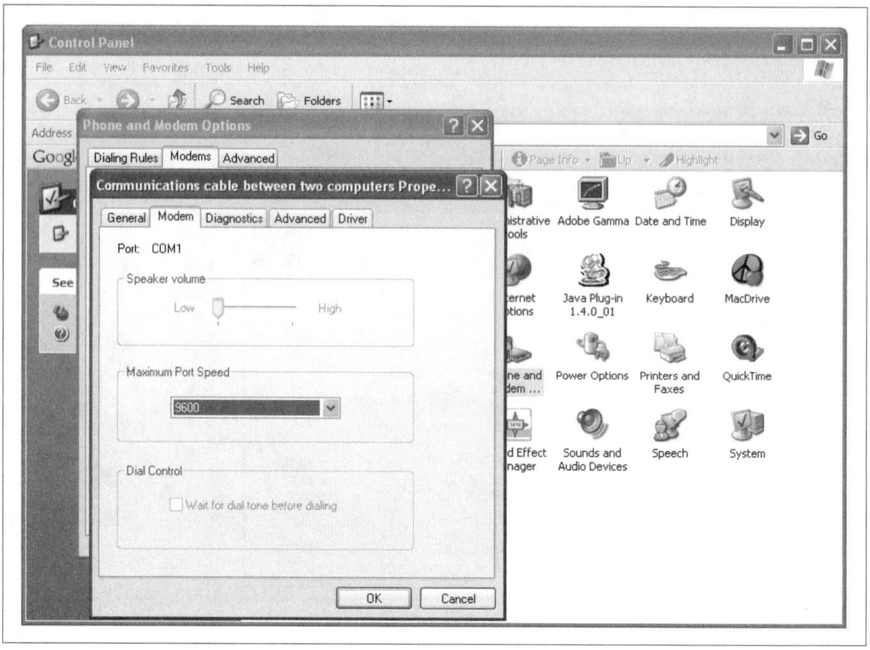

Figure 4-4. Confirming the connection's baud rate

The modem is now set up, so you can go ahead and click the OK button back at Phone and Modem Options.

With the physical connection configured, you'll now create a network connection. From the Control Panel, select Network Connections. Up comes the Network Connections window, shown in Figure 4-5. In the Network Tasks box in the left column, click "Create a new connection" to bring up the New Connection Wizard. Click Next to begin creating a new network connection.

When asked what type of network connection you want, select "Set up an advanced connection." If you read the small print, you'll see you're offered a direct connection via a serial port, which is precisely what you're trying to do. Select the option and click Next.

A dialog box asks what kind of connection you want—whether the PC is going to be receiving or sending data. Since TiVo is going to want to make an outgoing connection when it needs to make its daily call, select "Accept incoming connections" and click Next.

When asked to choose Devices for Incoming Connections (Figure 4-6), check the "Communications cable between two computers" box. That's the "modem" you just configured. Click Next again.

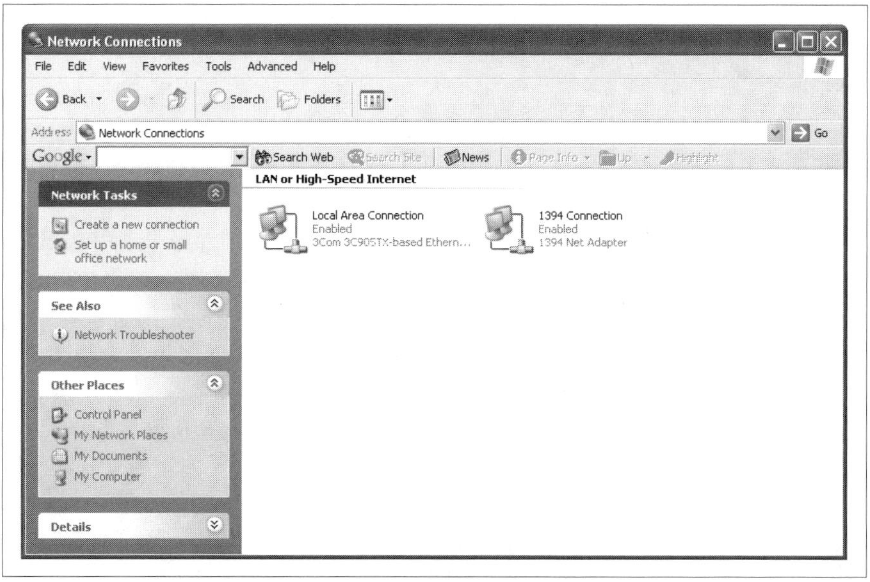

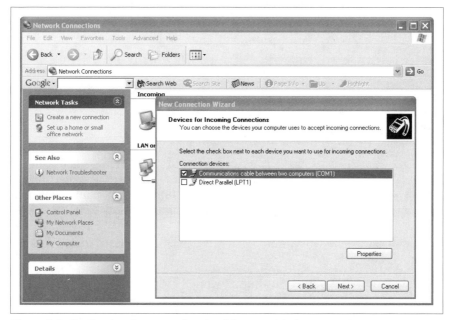

Figure 4-5. Network Connections, listing all the valid network interfaces currently configured

Figure 4-6. Configuring the proper "modem" for use with this connection

You're not going to be setting up any kind of Virtual Private Connection (VPN), so tell Windows not to allow VPNs and click—you guessed it!—Next.

The Wizard will ask you what users are allowed to connect. Since your TiVo is only using your PC as a proxy to the Net and won't be needing any kind of user privileges on the PC, just allow the Guest user. Click Next.

Now it's time to set up Networking Software and configure the PPP interface to please TiVo. Select Internet Protocol and click Properties to bring up the Incoming TCP/IP Properties dialog box shown in Figure 4-7.

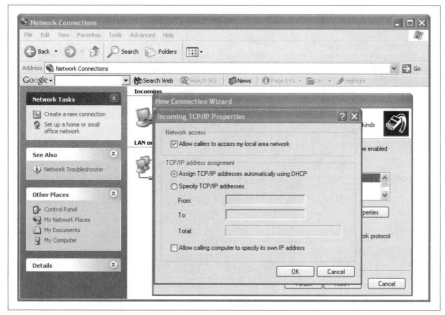

Figure 4-7. Setting up Incoming TCP/IP Properties for TiVo's direct connection

Your TiVo is expecting to use the serial connection to access your home network and the Internet. To make this possible, check "Allow callers to access my local area network." Don't worry, this isn't opening your PC to just any vagabond on the network; only the TiVo is coming in via that serial cable, nobody else.

If you have a DHCP server on your network—everybody on your home network is being assigned IP addresses by your DSL router or cable modem—then allow for TCP/IP addressing to be done automatically using DHCP by clicking the appropriate radio button. That takes the burden of configuring the TCP/IP connection off your shoulders. If you don't have a DHCP server, just select "Specify TCP/IP addresses" and put in a range of addresses that are not already being used on your network.

Chances are, if you set up your networking as shown in Figure 4-7, you'll be fine. Click OK to close the dialog box. Then click Next and Finish to dispatch the wizard, and you're almost done.

Go back to the Network Connections window, and you should now see a shiny new incoming connection. Right-click on the connection and select Properties to bring up the Incoming Connections Properties. Select the Users tab and check the "Always allow directly connected devices such as palmtop computers to connect without providing a password" checkbox, as shown in Figure 4-8. The TiVo has no notion of a password.

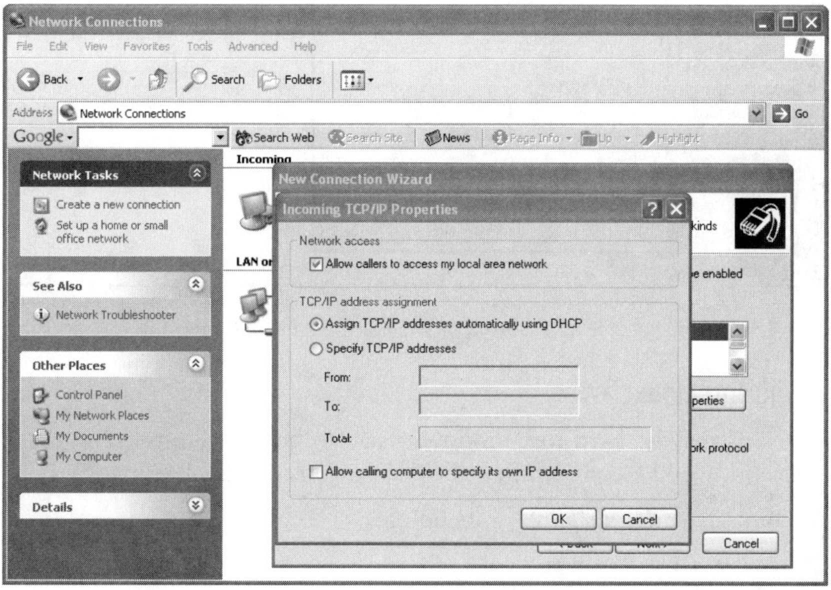

Figure 4-8. Allowing directly connected devices to connect without a password

Last step—I promise. Select the General tab in the Incoming Connections Properties dialog, select "Communications cable," and click the Properties button to bring up the dialog box shown in Figure 4-9. Turn off flow control (select "None"), as TiVo's serial port does not have the extra lines needed for any kind of hardware flow control, nor does it bother with software flow control.

Click OK and OK again, and you're done. Whew!

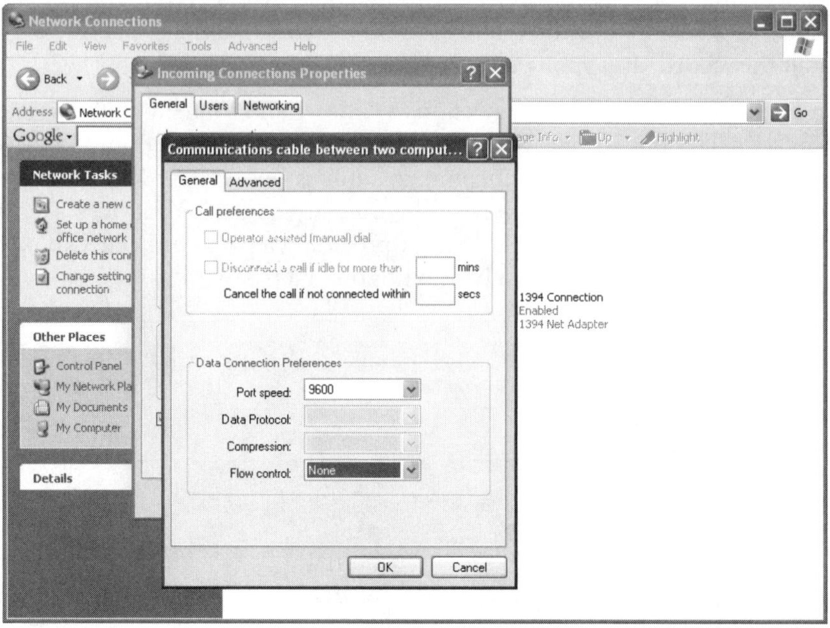

Figure 4-9. Turning off the flow control on the new direct connection

Configuring Linux

While this may be hard for Windows users to believe, Linux configuration for accepting a PPP connection from TiVo is considerably less involved.

Edit your */etc/rc.d/rc.local* file, appending:

```
echo "Enabling IP forwarding."
echo 1 > /proc/sys/net/ipv4/ip_forward

echo "Setting up TiVo connection"
/sbin/ipchains -P forward DENY
/sbin/ipchains -A forward -i eth0 192.168.1.2 -j MASQ
/usr/sbin/pppd /dev/ttyS0 9600 noauth debug proxyarp nocrtscts nobsdcomp \
nodeflate persist local lcp-max-configure 28800 192.168.1.1:192.168.1.2
```

Note that this configuration makes a couple of assumptions, both easily changeable. First, we're assuming your Internet-enabled interface is eth0 (bolded); if it's something different, change it as appropriate. Second, we're assuming 9600 baud over serial interface /dev/ttyS0; this should reflect the serial port you chose, and the baud rate should match that of the TiVo side [Hack #47]. We're assigning your Linux box a private IP address of 192.168.1.1 and your TiVo gets 192.168.1.2—at least as far as this interface is concerned.

For further guidance, consult the Home Networking mini-HOWTO (*http://
www.ibiblio.org/pub/Linux/docs/HOWTO/mini/other-formats/html_single/
Home-Network-mini-HOWTO.html*), the Linux IP Masquerade HOWTO
(*http://www.ibiblio.org/pub/Linux/docs/HOWTO/other-formats/html_single/
IP-Masquerade-HOWTO.html*), and the Linux IPCHAINS-HOWTO (*http://
www.ibiblio.org/pub/Linux/docs/HOWTO/other-formats/html_single/
IPCHAINS-HOWTO.html*).

Testing Your PPP-over-Serial Connection

Now that you've wired up your TiVo to the Internet via your PC, let's make
sure that it all works as expected.

Unplug your phone line from your TiVo; you won't be needing *that* anymore. Get TiVo to make a test call by selecting *Make Test Call* from *Messages
& Setup* → *Recorder & Phone Setup* → *Phone Connection* on OS 3.x and *TiVo
Messages & Setup* → *Settings* → *Phone & Network Setup* → *Test connection*
under OS 4.0 After a few seconds, you should see the usual messages indicat-
ing a successful connection; only this time the call's routed over the Internet. TiVo will now use this connection each time it makes its daily call.

After a successful trial at 9,600 baud, take things up a notch or two on both
the TiVo and PC ends (they must match to work) and see if you can work
your way up to downloading program data at a top speed of 115,200 baud
(see Table 4-1 for the associated TiVo dial prefixes).

——"Otto"

HACK #49 Getting Your TiVo Series 1 Online

The Series 1 TiVo was not designed with networking in mind. But being the
most hack-worthy of TiVo units means it didn't take long for some crafty
hackers to get it online.

While the Series 2 was designed from the start with networking in mind—
albeit via the USB port—the earlier Series 1 units simply were not built for a
networked world. Case closed, right? Not by a long shot! A bunch of inven-
tive Australian TiVo hackers, who simply wouldn't take "no" for an answer,
came up with a rather crafty solution: the TiVoNET.

The TiVoNET (*http://www.9thtee.com/tivonet.htm*) provides a bridge
between a PCI-shaped adapter on the Series 1's motherboard and a standard ISA slot into which you can plug in a standard Ethernet card. The
TiVoNET board has since been superceded by the TurboNET (*http://www.
9thtee.com/turbonet.htm*). Just like its predecessor, the TurboNET plugs
directly into the edge connector on a Series 1 box. Unlike the TiVoNET, the

new board does not need external power, grabbing juice right from your TiVo itself, as one would certainly hope it would. Nor do you need an additional Ethernet card to plug into it; the TurboNET board is all-in-one, plugging right into your home network via its on-board Ethernet port.

To install the TiVoNET or the TurboNET, you are going to have to mutilate your Series 1 to some degree—but only the case, mind you. As it stands, the Series 1 provides no hole through which to get an Ethernet cable out of the box. The solution: a garden-variety hack saw. I'm not kidding! Just pop the top [Hack #20], take a hack saw to the back, and open up a small port that you can sneak a cable through, as shown in Figure 4-10.

Figure 4-10. Opening up one of the mounting holes through which to snake an Ethernet cable

That done, fit your the board to the edge connector toward the front of the TiVo and push. You might need to apply a little force, as this is going to be a really tight fit. The TurboNET is a mite smaller. See Figure 4-11.

Finally, plug an Ethernet cable into your new network card, snake it out of your TiVo, and plug it into your wired home network or an Ethernet-to-WiFi bridge (the Linksys WET11 works nicely).

Some users optionally mount an Ethernet jack on the outside of their boxes (see Figure 4-12) to clean up the design of their boxes. You can grab one of these TurboNET Connect Kits from 9thtee (*http://www.9thtee.com/turbonet.htm*). Just remove the piece of double-stick tape, position the jack, press it to affix the jack to the case, and run a cable from the jack, through your hole, to the network card.

Figure 4-11. The TurboNET, fitted snugly inside the TiVo on the edge connector

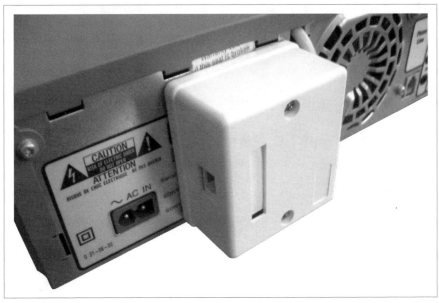

Figure 4-12. An Ethernet jack mounted on the outside of the case

If you have a Bash shell enabled on your TiVo's serial port [Hack #30], you'll do all the configuration once you shut your box; its easier that way. If you don't have Bash setup, you should do so now, as we'll walk more than halfway down that road anyway.

Don't worry if you think it's redundant to have Bash and telnet running. Think of it as a failsafe; if for any reason you can't get into your TiVo through one of those means, chances are the other one will still work.

Now that wasn't so bad, was it? Before TiVo OS Version 3.0, various configuration scripts had to be mangled and a permanent IP address had to be put into the startup scripts. All that's left nowadays is to utter a magic incantation to tell TiVo not to use its onboard modem and the phone line for its daily calls. Navigate TiVo's menu system to *Messages & Setup → Recorder & Phone Setup → Phone Connection → Change Dialing Options*, and set your Dial Prefix to `,#40` using the numeric buttons on your TiVo remote control. Use the **Enter** button for # ("pound" or "hash") and the ⏸ button for , (comma).

> Your TiVo unit, version of the TiVo operating system, or remote control may use different buttons for special characters. Consult the on-screen instructions for the appropriate buttons to press.

Somewhere on your home network you're bound to have a DHCP server handing out IP addresses to new devices coming online. Your broadband cable modem or DSL router should be providing this functionality to all the other computers in your house. It'll hand TiVo an IP address and consider it part of the family. Also, unlike running PPP [Hack #47], this connection is permanent; it's always on.

Getting Your TiVo Series 2 Online
HACK #50

The TiVo Series 2 comes with online access baked in. Plug in a USB-to-Ethernet or USB-to-WiFi adapter, and your TiVo's a first-class citizen on your home network.

While it might be useful to have your TiVo online via another computer [Hack #47], purists are sure to find it quite frustrating to see a fledgling Linux box not be able to spread its wings. Owners of the Series 2 Standalone TiVo are in luck. TiVo, Inc. has partnered with Linksys (*http://www.linksys.com/*), makers of networking and WiFi equipment for work and home, to take its users' TiVos online. TiVo recommends two adapters: the WUSB11 Version 2.6 (a WiFi 802.11b adapter from Linksys' "Instant Wireless Series") and the USB100TX USB-to-Ethernet (10/100 BaseT) adapter from their "Instant Etherfast Series."

Users have also reported success using non-TiVo USB-to-Ethernet adapters, such as these:

Linksys USB100M
Linksys USB200M
NetGear FA101
NetGear FA120
Belkin F5D5050
3Com 3C460B
Microsoft MN-110
Hawking UF200
Hawking UF100
D-Link DSB-650TX
D-Link DUB-E100
Siemens SS1001
SMC SMC2208

On the WiFi front, Table 4-2 lists non-TiVo-recommended USB-to-802.11b adapters and the TiVo service numbers with which they are most likely to work. You can find your service number with a quick trip to *TiVo Messages & Setup → System Information*. Look for it a couple of lines down from the top.

Table 4-2. Non-TiVo-recommended USB-to-802.11b adapters and associated TiVo service numbers

Initial digits of TiVo service number	Alternative USB-to-802.11b adapters
110, 130, 140	NetGear MA101 V.A, D-Link DWL-120 V.A
230, 240	D-Link DWL-120 V.D, Linksys WUSB12, Hawking WU250, Microsoft MN-510
Any	NetGear MA101 V.B, D-Link DWL-120 V.E, SMC 2662W V.2, Belkin F5D6050

That said, unless you have one of the unsupported adapters lying about your house, I'd recommend just going with one of the recommended ones.

Simply plug the adapter into the back of your Series 2 running TiVo OS 4.0 or later, and follow the onscreen directions to get it onto the network.

Figuring Out Your TiVo's IP Address

#51 Before you can even get to your now-network-enabled TiVo—let alone do anything interesting to it—you need to figure out just where it is on your home network.

All devices on the Net are ultimately accessible by IP address: a set of four numbers providing it with a unique (at least in the realm at hand) ID. Just as the postman must know the address of your house before being able to deliver your latest Amazon.com goodies, so too must you know TiVo's address on the network before you can do anything interesting with it.

Figuring out a TiVo's IP address differs by series and depends on just how you brought it online.

Series 1

As you might expect, given the hackish way in which it was made network-aware, determining the IP address on a Series 1 is a little tricky.

Nowhere in TiVo's menu system is it simply going to tell you its IP address, so let's ask nicely at the Bash prompt [Hack #30]. The ifconfig ("interface configuration") command reports on and configures a computer's network interfaces: Ethernet, WiFi, modem—anywhere the computer jacks itself into the network. In TiVo's case, usually the only interface of interest is the phone line (which we are no longer using). And now that TurboNET Ethernet card [Hack #49] we popped into place on the motherboard.

Using the ifconfig command, ask for information on eth0, the first ("zeroth" actually) Ethernet interface, like so:

```
bash-2.02# /sbin/ifconfig eth0
eth0   Link encap:Ethernet HWaddr 00:C0:F0:51:90:E9
       inet addr:192.168.0.3 Bcast:192.168.0.255 Mask:255.255.255.0
       UP BROADCAST RUNNING MULTICAST MTU:1500 Metric:1
       RX packets:6725 errors:0 dropped:0 overruns:0 frame:97
       TX packets:3953 errors:0 dropped:0 overruns:0 carrier:0 coll:0
       Interrupt:29 Base address:0x300
```

There's a lot of useful information in that output. Most importantly, TiVo does indeed recognize the TurboNET card as providing an Ethernet connection with a hardware address of 00:C0:F0:51:90:E9, as evidenced by the first line. Knowing the hardware, or MAC, address of your network card can be helpful if you're going to be bridging your TiVo onto a WiFi network that restricts access by hardware address, or if you want to configure your DHCP server to always hand the TiVo the same IP address. The second line contains the golden ticket, your TiVo's IP address: 192.168.0.3. Both the hardware and IP addresses above are for my TiVo; your numbers will obviously be different.

Series 2

Surf TiVo menus to *TiVo Messages & Setup → Settings → Phone & Network Setup* (see Figure 4-13). There, take a look at the top right and you should see some text that reads "IP address." The number after it—192.168.0.7 in my case—is your TiVo's IP address.

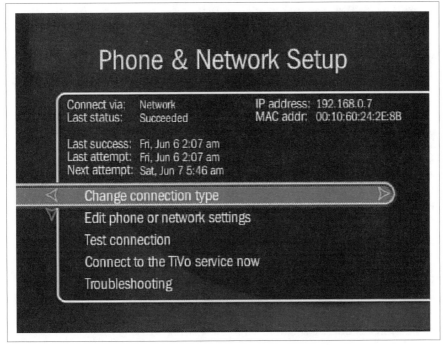

Figure 4-13. The Phone & Network Setup screen under TiVo OS 4.0, showing the IP address

Ping!

With that IP address in hand, you can give it a ping to see if your TiVo is alive—at least as far as the network's concerned. The term "pinging" borrows from the world of ships and submarines, which use sonar to locate underwater objects (usually one-another); they send out a loud "ping" sound and watch their instruments carefully, noting how the sound waves echo and bounce about and providing a virtual picture of their environment.

- Pinging your TiVo (or any other computer on the network) means sending a small chunk of data and waiting for it to echo the data back. The ping utility is available to just about any computer operating system with a network heartbeat. Get to the command line (Applications → Utilities → Terminal on Mac OS X, Start → Run... → *command* on Windows) and type (replacing *192.168.0.7* with the IP address of your TiVo):

```
$ ping 192.168.0.7
PING 192.168.0.7 (192.168.0.7): 56 data bytes
64 bytes from 192.168.0.7: icmp_seq=0 ttl=64 time=7.131 ms
64 bytes from 192.168.0.7: icmp_seq=1 ttl=64 time=3.116 ms
```

Press Control-C to stop pinging.

As long as you see echoed responses (e.g., 64 bytes from...), you can be sure your TiVo's online. If nothing comes back, your ping sitting endlessly at PING 192.168.0.7 (192.168.0.7): 56 data bytes, your TiVo's not responding and you should go back and check to make sure you're using the right IP address and took the right steps to getting your Series 1 [Hack #49] or Series 2 online [Hack #50].

Getting Telnet to Your Ethernet-Enabled TiVo

#52

Now that our Series 1 TiVo is using Ethernet [Hack #49] and is online, let's get a telnet prompt on it.

It's time to forget that primitive Bash over serial [Hack #30] connection you set up to bootstrap command-line access to your TiVo. While it will remain useful as a backup, let's face it: that connection is slow and being tied to a host PC is more hand holding than your TiVo needs. This is the age of ubiquitous networking, after all.

But before you say goodbye to that old standby, you'll use it one last time to turn on telnet, remote login capabilities from anywhere on the network. Using your serial prompt, edit [Hacks #38, #39] your *rc.sysinit* to accept telnet connections by adding the following line at the end:

```
tnlited 23 /bin/bash -login &
```

Here, I'm being a little lazy and using the echo command to append the line to *rc.sysinit* without need of a text editor:

```
bash-2.02# mount -o remount,rw /
bash-2.02# echo 'tnlited 23 /bin/bash -login &' >> /etc/rc.d/rc.sysinit
bash-2.02# mount -o remount,ro /
```

Restart your TiVo and wait for it to pass the "A few more moments please..." message on your television set. Once all appears to be up and running, use your favorite telnet application to connect to the IP address of your TiVo [Hack #51], and you're in like Flynn.

There is *absolutely no security* when telnetting to your TiVo. Not only are all your commands flowing over the network in the clear, but TiVo doesn't even ask you for a username and password.

If, for some reason, your home network isn't behind some sort of firewall, whether provided by your broadband modem or otherwise, you'll be the wiser for putting some sort of firewall in place—not just for your TiVo, but for the safety of all your computers. Until your network is reasonably protected, you won't want to open your TiVo to telnet or any other kind of network connection.

HACK #53 Fetching Files from the Web

Now that TiVo has high-speed Internet access, let's download some files from the Web.

While we now have our TiVo online [Hack #49] and can telnet to the box [Hack #52], there's still no good way to move files to and from TiVo without doing so via the serial interface using *rz/sz* [Hack #36].

> While *rz/sz* [Hack #36] will happily move files over the serial line, they don't play nicely with non-8-bit connections like the telnet interface.

Let's think about this for a bit. How does TiVo itself download stuff? Those software updates, for instance. It sets up a dialup-PPP connection to TiVo, Inc. and downloads files over HTTP. Why, then, can't we simply use the same mechanism over our higher-class permanent network connection? Well, we can.

TiVo sports a little application called *http_get*, which, as its name suggests, grabs files remotely using HTTP as its transport mechanism. One caveat is that *http_get* can't do any domain name resolution.

On top of requiring the IP address, *http_get* is actually quite finicky. Let's fiddle a bit and see what we can learn, shall we?

Let's say, for instance, you wanted to download a copy of the TiVoWeb server [Hack #65]. You'd invoke *http_get* like so:

```
bash-2.02# http_get -T 0 -C 0 -D /var/hack -U http://199.240.141.102:80/
tivoweb-tcl-1.9.4.tar.gz
```

This command asks TiVo to download the file at *http://199.240.141.102:80/ tivoweb-tcl-1.9.4.tar.gz* (-U is for URL) to the local */var/hack* [Hack #36] directory (-D is for directory). Because *http_get* was originally designed for the TiVo to use exclusively when connecting to TiVo, Inc., it also requires the –T and the –C flags, representing the serial number of the unit and the ID of the call, respectively. Simply set both to 0. Be sure to specify the URL fully. You'll get the following error if you leave off the :80 specifying the default HTTP port number:

```
connect failed, reason = Connection refused
Segmentation fault
```

You'll get the following error if you try to specify a DNS name instead of an IP address:

```
connect failed, reason = Network is unreachable
Segmentation fault
```

Not being able to specify a DNS name turns out to be more problematic than you'd think. Many web servers do something called "virtual hosting" these days. This means that many domain names actually map to the same IP address, since specifying the host name specified onboard is the only way to tell two requests for two different domains apart. Take *oreilly.com* and *oreillynet.com*, for example—for both, one of their IP addresses is 209.201.239.37. The server at that IP address knows which site you mean to visit only because your browser passes along the domain name portion of the URL as part of the HTTP request. If you don't specify a host name, the web server is either going to pick one or attempt to redirect you—the latter being something *http_get* doesn't like at all.

About the only way around this shortcoming is to download the file you're after to a machine that is accessible by IP address—one on your local network or a server out there on the Internet—and instruct TiVo to grab it from there. Of course, you can still pass files back and forth serially [Hack #36] as a last resort.

wget Things from the Web

Bring the power of GNU *wget*, the ubiquitous file fetcher, to your TiVo.

http_get [Hack #53] is quite limited in what it can do. It's biggest limitation is that it can't talk to virtual hosts. As more and more web hosting shifts away from the one web server per IP address model, this can be an impediment.

The main reason that *http_get* can't talk to virtual hosted servers is because it can't do DNS resolution, relying instead on hard-coded IP addresses in the scripts that call it. In fact, the Linux installation running on the Series 1 TiVo doesn't have support for name resolution at all.

If you desperately must have a tool that can do name resolution for the Series 1, take a look at my *wget.tcl* (*http://www.bitwaste.com/tivo/wget-tcl.tar.gz*). The archive is packaged in a similar way. Just upload it to your TiVo, put it in */var*, and extract it:

```
bash-2.02# gzip -d wget-tcl.tar.gz
bash-2.02# cd /
bash-2.02# cpio -i -H tar --make-directories < /var/wget-tcl.tar.gz
bash-2.02# chmod 755 /var/hack/bin/wget.tcl
```

This script and its supporting libraries are built upon the DNS support in the *Tcllib* (*http://tcllib.sourceforge.net*), enabling it do DNS resolution completely in Tcl. If you point the script at *hacks.oreilly.com* as in the previous command, it'll download *index.html* as before.

My *wget.tcl*, as of yet, does not handle FTP-based URLs.

Setting Up an FTP server

HACK #55

Transfer files to and from your TiVo with the ease of FTP.

FTP used to be the de facto way to move files around the Net, but HTTP is quickly catching up. However, despite the efforts of WebDAV (*http://www. webdav.org/*) and the like, an FTP server is still about the easiest way to push things to a computer. There's a plethora of client software out there for Mac, Windows, Unix, you name it. And, thanks to "sorphin," there's an FTP server for your TiVo, part of the TiVo Utilities project (*http://tivoutils. sourceforge.net/*).

Grab the FTP server for your TiVo from *http://prdownloads.sourceforge.net/ tivoutils/tivoftpd.ppc.gz?download*. With that in hand, you're faced with a classic chicken-and-egg problem: how are you to get the FTP server over to TiVo without FTP access? Hopefully you left your serial port running with Bash, because you are going to use *rz* [Hack #36].

With the downloaded file on your TiVo, unpack the daemon (read: server) and drop it into your */var/hack/bin* [Hack #36] directory as *tivoftpd*.

```
bash-2.02# gzip -d /var/hack/bin/tivoftpd.ppc.gz
bash-2.02# mv /var/hack/bin/tivoftpd.ppc.gz /var/hack/bin/tivoftpd
```

Finally, mark the program executable and start the server with:

```
bash-2.02# chmod 755 /var/hack/bin/tivoftpd
bash-2.02# /var/hack/bin/tivoftpd
```

The program will return you to your prompt immediately, with the server running quietly in the background. To test it, point your favorite FTP program at your TiVo's IP address [Hack #51].

If you are coming in from a command-line FTP program, the start of your session will look something like this:

```
Connected to tivo (192.168.0.3).
220 You are in TiVo Mode. 220 Login isn't necessary.
220 Please hit ENTER at the login/password prompts.
Name (tivo:r):
331 No Auth required for TiVo Mode.
Password:
230 Running in TiVo Mode.
Remote system type is UNIX.
ftp>
```

Like TiVo's telnet access, there is no security on the FTP daemon. Anybody can get in, upload, download, and delete files at will. Make sure that your TiVo is behind a pretty strong firewall if you plan to leave FTP running all the time.

I recommend you don't run the FTP server all the time, preferring to run it only when you need it and kill it when you're done. There is no pretty, built-in way to shut down the FTP daemon, so you'll have to do it the Unix way. Figure out the process ID of the FTP server (*tivoftpd*) and kill it:

```
bash-2.02# ps auxw | grep tivoftpd
root    1220 0.0 0.0    0    0 ?  SW  01:21   0:00 /var/hack/bin/tivoftpd
root    1233 0.0 0.0    0    0 p0 SW  01:21   0:00 grep tivoftpd
bash-2.02# kill -9 1220
```

That should take it down. If you want to check, issue the ps auxw | grep tivoftpd again, and you should no longer see any mention of the tivoftpd process.

HACK #56 Using the Same Filesystem

Rather than all this passing about of files back and forth between TiVo and your PC, mount an NFS share on your TiVo and access that networked partition as if it were local to your TiVo.

Rather than uploading MP3s [Hack #46] to your TiVo to play, or FTPing in to grab the latest version of that *Now Playing List* for incorporation into your web site [Hack #90], NFS-mount your PC's drive on your TiVo, and read and write files as if the drive were local to TiVo.

Just as we inserted a kernel module to give TiVo access to Closed Captioning [Hack #42], we can do the same to get network filesystem (NFS) support loaded into TiVo's OS. Download a copy of the kernel module (*http://themurrays.homeip.net/downloads/tivo/for_tivo/nfs-kernelmod_tivo25-1.zip*) and unzip it on your local PC. Upload the *nfs-tivo25.o* file contained therein to your TiVo and drop it into */var/hack/modules*.

> While these instructions should work about the same on Series 1 and 2 TiVos, at the time of this writing there is no NFS module for the Series 2.

To activate the kernel extension, type the following at TiVo's Bash prompt:

```
bash-2.02# /sbin/insmod -f /var/hack/modules/nfs-25.o
```

You now have the ability to mount and talk to NFS servers on your network from your TiVo. Now, let's move on to the PC side of things.

Serving NFS from Windows

There are a plethora of NFS servers out there for Windows, but one of the more popular ones is the XLink NFS Server (*http://www.xlink.com/eval.htm*). It's a breeze to setup and get working with your TiVo.

Bring up the XLink NFS Server (see Figure 4-14), and click the New button to create a new mount point. The NFS Server Export tool shown in Figure 4-15 lets you configure and set up the directory for remote mounting.

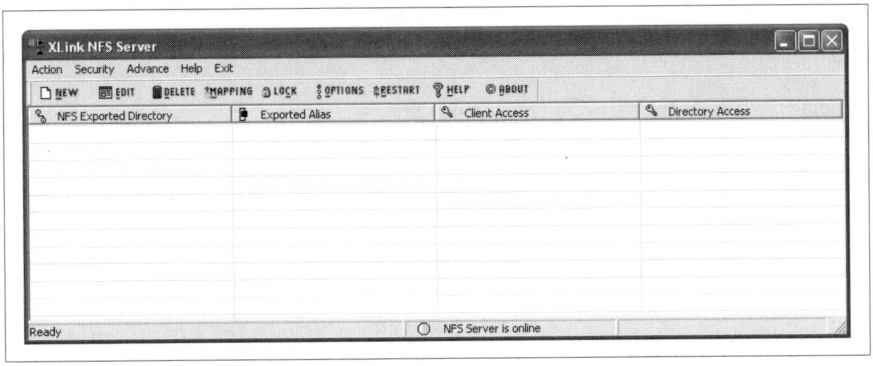

Figure 4-14. The XLink NFS Server interface

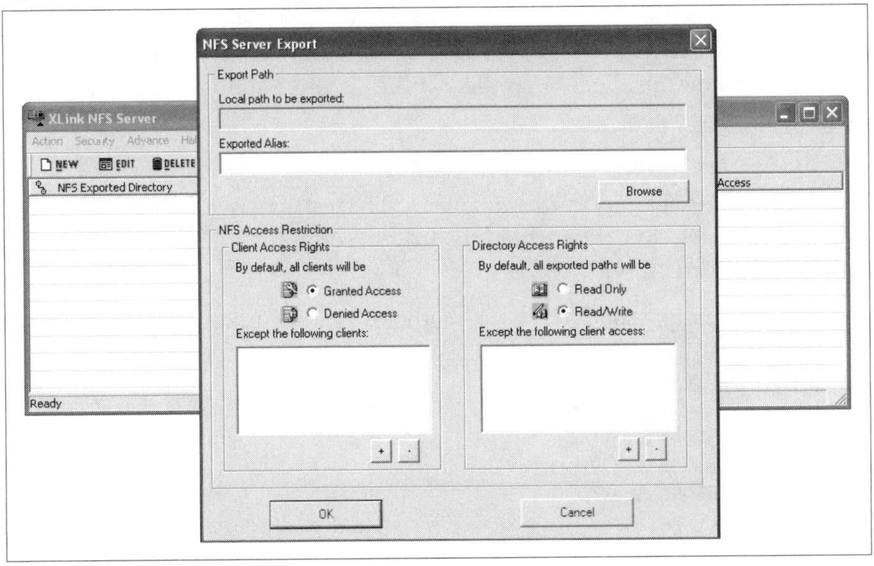

Figure 4-15. The XLink NFS Server Export tool

Setting up security on an NFS mount can be a really tricky thing. But since you are supposed to be working behind your home network's firewall, we can just ignore all that. Give all clients read/write access to the directory. This will let the TiVo mount the directory, get files, and put files over the network.

Click OK. The new mount should show up in the main XLink NFS Server window (see Figure 4-16).

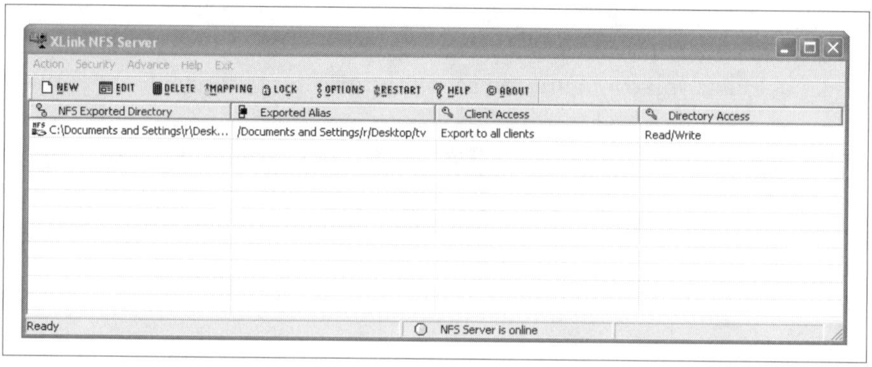

Figure 4-16. The XLink server exporting the "C:\Documents and Settings\r\Desktop\tv" directory

Serving NFS from Linux

There is no graphical tool to set up NFS mounts on Linux. On a Red Hat box, make sure that you have the *nfs-utils* RPM installed on your system; then edit your */etc/exports* file, adding the directory that you wish to allow your TiVo to mount. Such a configuration directive should look something like this:

```
/tivodir tivo.homenetwork.net(rw,no_root_squash)
```

This command will export */tivodir* over NFS, restricting access to only *tivo. homenetwork.net*. But when the TiVo does connect, it has full read/write access to that directory.

Restart *nfs* to export the NFS share, ready for remote mounting:

```
[root@localhost r]# /etc/rc.d/init.d/nfs restart
Shutting down NFS mountd:          [ OK ]
Shutting down NFS daemon:          [ OK ]
Shutting down NFS quotas:          [ OK ]
Shutting down NFS services:        [ OK ]
Starting NFS services:             [ OK ]
Starting NFS quotas:               [ OK ]
Starting NFS daemon:               [ OK ]
Starting NFS mountd:               [ OK ]
```

Mounting an NFS Share on Your TiVo

Let's assume you have an NFS server running on a PC named *nfs. homenetwork.net*, which shares a */for_tivo* directory to be mounted by your TiVo. Create a */var/mnt* directory under which to keep NFS-mounted directories. Create a subdirectory named appropriately for the machine and directory you are going to mount:

```
bash-2.02# mkdir /var/mnt
bash-2.02# mkdir /var/mnt/homenetwork
bash-2.02# mount nfs.homenetwork.net:/for_tivo /var/mnt/homenetwork
```

That's all there is to it. Now, whatever files you place into the /var/mnt/ homenetwork directory on your TiVo or the for_tivo directory on your PC will be accessible to the other.

HACK #57 Reading Email on Your TiVo

What's the point of a network connection if you can't read your email?

For many people these days, reading email is like breathing itself. The first thing they do with a network connection is grab their email. Why should your networked TiVo [Hack #49] be any different?

It shouldn't, or so answers Douglas Mayle with TPOP (http://www. networkhackers.com/tpop/), his POP3 email client for TiVo. TPOP queries a standard POP3 email server over your network connection, slurping new mail messages into TiVo's built-in message queue (Messages & Setup → Read New Messages), which is reasonably well-suited to repurposing in this way.

> As the name suggests, TPOP doesn't do IMAP. That's a pity, given that IMAP seems better suited for the task, keeping its message store on the mail server rather than locally on your TiVo.

Grab a copy of TPOP (http://www.networkhackers.com/tpop/tpop.tar.gz), transfer it to your TiVo [Hack #36], expand it, and put it into place under your / var/hack directory:

```
bash-2.02# cd /var/hack
bash-2.02# gzip -d tpop.tar.gz
bash-2.02# cpio -i -H tar < tpop.tar
bash-2.02# rm tpop.tar
bash-2.02# chmod 755 tpopd.tcl
bash-2.02# mv tpopd.tcl bin
bash-2.02# mv tpopd.conf etc
```

All that remains is to configure TPOP to know where and how to retrieve your email. Thankfully, Mayle has built all this in, allowing you to build a new configuration file from the command-line, like so:

```
bash-2.02# tpopd.tcl -c /var/hack/etc/tpopd.conf -S -s 192.168.0.1 -P 110 -u
raffi -p my_password
```

You should replace 192.168.0.1 with the IP address of your POP3 email server (sorry, TiVo doesn't do DNS resolution), 110 with the appropriate port specification (it's usually 110), and raffi and my_password with your email account's username and password. The script will overwrite the configuration file (*/var/hack/etc/tpopd.conf*) with the specified values.

Once configured, launch *TPOP*:

```
bash-2.02# tpopd.tcl -c /var/hack/etc/tpopd.conf
```

The script will start running in the background, checking your email every 10 minutes. Send yourself an email message from your usual email application, come back in a few minutes (*Messages & Setup → Read New Messages*), and read email right on your very own television screen (see Figure 4-17).

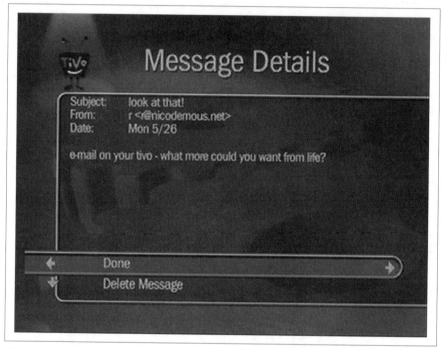

Figure 4-17. Personal email incorporated into TiVo's message queue

The TiVo interface doesn't provide any real way to respond to that email, and *TPOP* keeps itself to downloading new messages and injecting them into the queue. This means that email on the TiVo is relegated to read-only. Still, it's a rather nice trick at that!

Using the TiVo Control Station

#58 Control the various hacks you have installed on your TiVo and populate your TV screen with sports scores, weather forecasts, stock quotes, Closed Captioning, and more.

For some, TiVo—not the computer—is the central repository of all knowledge in the universe. You waste…uh, spend…many an hour seated in front of it, soaking up its bounty like a sponge. Television programming is simply not enough—you want more?

You can already browse your email [Hack #57] onscreen. If you have a Direc-Tivo, you have caller ID information [Hack #43] at your heads-up disposal. How much more do you want?

Much more.

The TiVo Control Station (TCS), available at *http://www.zirakzigil.net/tivo*, is a metahack, encompassing various other hacks applied to the Series 1 TiVo. Think of it as a backdoor hack [Hack #8], only a lot more powerful. In fact, the TCS has access to those backdoor hacks.

The TCS runs as a service on your TiVo, listening for special remote control sequences. One sequence turns on *tivovbi* [Hack #42], while others display sports scores on the screen, check the weather forecast—as if you have any intention of going outdoors any time soon ;-)—or look up stock quotes.

Setting up the TCS is a little involved, so let's go through it carefully. First, you'll need *newtext2osd* [Hack #41] and *JPEGwriter* [Hack #40] installed on your TiVo. Once you have those set up, grab a copy of the TCS at *http://www. zirakzigil.net/download/TCS_1.0.0.tar.gz*, and drop it into your */var/hack* directory [Hack #36]. Telnet in [Hack #52], and install as follows:

```
bash-2.02# gzip -d TCS_1.0.0.tar.gz
bash-2.02# cpio -i -H tar --make-directories < TCS_1.0.0.tar
bash-2.02# rm TCS_1.0.0.tar
```

This leaves you with a new */var/hack/tcs* directory, containing all the bits of the TCS you'll need. Perfect. Now, let's make sure that everything is configured properly.

Fire up your favorite text editor [Hacks #38, #39] on TiVo and edit */var/hack/tcs/config/IPAddresses*. The first three lines provide the IP addresses of three DNS name servers for the TCS to use for domain name resolution; replace the *xxx.xxx.xxx.xxx*, *yyyy.yyyy.yyyy.yyyy*, and *zzz.zzz.zzz.zzz* with the DNS server addresses used by your home network and computers. Save the modified file when you're done.

> If you're not sure where to find your local DNS servers, contact your local Internet provider and ask them for the IP addresses of their domain name servers.

Next, open the *var/hack/tcs/config/prefs* file. This is a really long file that contains every configuration option the TCS needs. Somewhere in the file you'll notice a block of lines that look something like this:

```
telnet TelnetCommand /sbin/tnlited 23 /bin/bash -login
ftp FtpCommand /tivo-bin/tivoftpd
tivoweb TivowebCommand /var/hack/tivoweb-tcl/tivoweb tcsrestart
serialbash SerialbashCommand /bin/bash </dev/ttyS3 >& /dev/ttyS3
tivovbi TivovbiCommand /var/hack/bin/tivovbi -oc
newtext2osd Newtext2osdCommand /var/hack/bin/newtext2osd
jpegwriter JpegWriterCommand /var/hack/bin/jpegwriter
text2osd Text2osdCommand /tvbin/text2osd
grep GrepCommand /bin/grep
bash BashCommand /bin/bash
ps PsCommand /var/hack/bin/ps
mkehfiles ElseedMakeFilesCommand /var/hack/tcs/bin/mkehfiles
```

These lines tell the TCS where to find all the programs it's going to control for you. All but one of these lines point to the places we've suggested you put the support programs; alter the ftp line to read:

```
ftp FtpCommand /var/hack/bin/tivoftpd
```

Hold your breath and run the TCS:

```
bash-2.02# /var/hack/tcs/startcs
```

This command should return you to the prompt immediately and—despite no confirmation at all—the TCS should be running in the background, awaiting remote control sequences.

To shut down the TCS at any time, issue the following sequence on your TiVo remote control:

9 → 9 → Clear

> Do not simply kill the TCS processes. The TiVo Control Station is built on top of *tivosh*, the underlying shell that controls most interapplication messaging in the TiVo. *tivosh* does not take well to being interrupted, so simply killing the TCS on the command line will force your TiVo to reboot itself.

So, what can the TCS do for you? The list (*http://www.zirakzigil.net/tivo/ TCSreadme.html*) is about as long as your arm—as long as mine at least. In addition to being able to stop and restart your TiVo's FTP, telnet, *tivovbi*, and *tivoweb* daemons, activate/deactivate other hacks, and sort the *Now Playing* list, you can check the weather forecast, display the latest sports scores, and look up stock quotes.

Weather Forecasts

You may recall entering your ZIP code during TiVo's initial guided setup. TiVo used that information to determine which phone numbers your TiVo should call to download programming information and software updates. The TiVo Control Station co-opts this information for determining your geographical location and finding out what the weather is like in your area.

Whilst either playing a recorded program or watching live television, point your remote control at your TiVo and hit:

8 → 2 → Clear

Don't worry that your TiVo thinks it is going to be changing channels; it will forget all about that once you hit **Clear**. While TiVo summarily ignores the seemingly useless sequence, the TCS uses your TiVo's network access to retrieve and—after a few seconds—display the current weather map, as shown in Figure 4-18.

If, instead, you issue the following remote control sequence, the TCS will retrieve and display a national weather map like the one shown in Figure 4-19:

8 → 3 → Clear

I hope you're having as nice as a day as I am.

Sports Scores

You're sitting with your significant other, watching his favorite show, and are just itching to know the final score on that Red Sox game you're missing. You could send him for a snack and flick to ESPN for a moment, but the show you're watching is live and you'd lose some of the time-slipping you've accumulated.

TiVo Control Station to the rescue! Table 4-3 lists all the sports scores the TCS can make available to you, along with their associated remote control sequences.

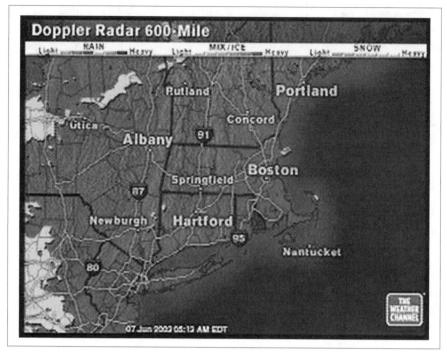

Figure 4-18. A 600-mile weather map, as displayed by the TCS

Table 4-3. TCS remote control commands for displaying sports scores

TCS remote control sequence	Sports scores displayed
6 → 0 → Clear	All the available sports scores
6 → 1 → Clear	Major League Baseball scores
6 → 2 → Clear	National Football League scores
6 → 3 → Clear	NCAA College Football scores
6 → 4 → Clear	National Hockey League scores
6 → 5 → Clear	National Basketball Association scores

For example, if you hit **6 → 4 → Clear** while watching live television or a pre-recorded program, you'll be fed all the current NHL standings, as shown in Figure 4-20.

The one caveat on all this TCS fun is that the fun is not free—at least when it comes to computing cycles, that is. All the processing devoted to keeping these modules running is being taken away from TiVo's primary job: being a personal video recorder (PVR). If you ask it to do too much, it won't be a very good PVR, because its recording and playbacks will start stuttering.

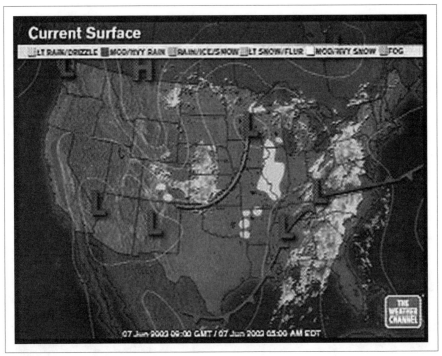

Figure 4-19. The national weather on this very rainy day in the northeast, as displayed by the TCS

Therefore, if you are an NFL nut but don't really care much for hockey, it's a good idea to disable the NFL scores module. The modules are just files located in */var/hack/tcs/modules*, so deleting what you don't want is simply a matter of deleting a file:

```
bash-2.02# rm /var/hack/tcs/modules/NHL.tcl
```

In fact, if you don't care to have any sports information available, remove all the modules:

```
bash-2.02# cd /var/hack/tcs/modules
bash-2.02# rm MLB.tcl NBA.tcl NCAAF.tcl NFL.tcl NHL.tcl SportsCommands.tcl
```

If you deleted the modules while the TCS was running, you'll have to restart the TCS before any of this will have any effect. Hit **9 → 9 → Clear** to shut down the TCS. You will have to telnet back in [Hack #33] and start the system from the command line before you can use it again.

Stock Quotes

Stocks more your game? Display the latest stock scores—quotes, that is—on your television set. Entering the remote control sequence **Clear → 7 → Clear**

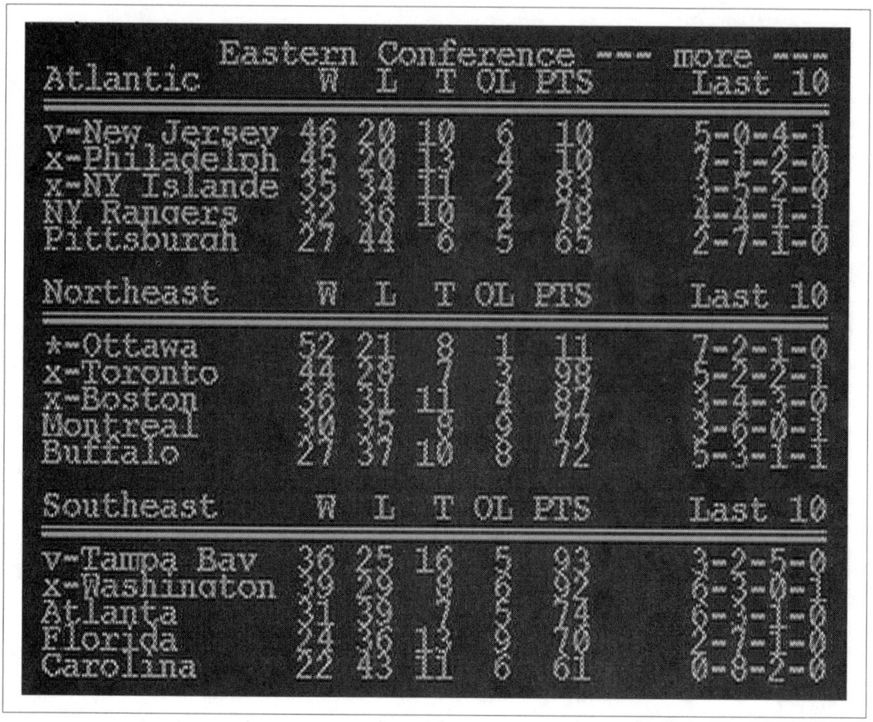

Figure 4-20. Current NHL standings, as displayed by the TCS

provides you with a screen filled with the latest stocks and indexes. Page up and down using the **Channel Up** and **Channel Down** buttons on your remote.

The indexes and stocks you see in Figure 4-21 are the default set preconfigured in the TiVo Control Station bundle.

If, instead, you have some specific ones in mind that you want to keep track of, open */var/hack/tcs/config/tickers* in your text editor:

```
^DJI Dow30
^IXIC Nasdaq
^N225 Nikkei
^FTSE FTSE
...
AGRA
AGRB
AV
AAPL Apple
CSCO Cisco
```

Feel free to alter this file as you wish, listing only the stocks you're interested in tracking. The first few lines—prepended with a ^ (caret)—are

```
        Saturday, June  7 2003  5:47am
 Index      Last     Change      High        Low

Dow30      9062.79     21.49    9215.88    9045.5
Nasdaq     1627.42    -18.59    1684.06    1625.1
Nikkei     8785.87    128.64    8814.04    8633.3
FTSE       4150.80     46.50    4178.50    4104.3
H.Kong     9694.63     55.82    9752.77    9610.8
Bovspa    13923.11    143.23   14071.32   13794.0
Bond10        3.35      0.02       3.40       3.29
Bond30        4.38     -0.01       4.44       4.36

 Stock    Last Change      High     Low    Time

AGRa       2.63    0.02    2.70    2.60   Jun 6
AGRb       2.53    0.05    2.60    2.48   Jun 6
AV         7.91    0.24    8.06    7.77   Jun 6
Apple     17.15   -0.49   18.04   17.14   Jun 6
Cisco     17.36   -0.01   18.26   17.34   Jun 6
DELL      31.35   -0.58   32.54   31.30   Jun 6
DIA       90.87    0.13   92.49   90.75   Jun 6
GE        30.30    0.53   30.52   29.86   Jun 6
HPO       22.03    0.13   22.80   21.91   Jun 6
              --- more ---
```

Figure 4-21. Stock quotes, brought to you by TCS

indexes; those without the caret character are stocks. Put the ticker symbol first on the line, followed by a human-readable version if you prefer. For example, AAPL Apple looks up the AAPL stock symbol but displays "Apple" onscreen.

> Do not list the same ticker symbol more than once in the */var/ hack/tcs/config/tickers* configuration file. If you do so, "bad things will happen," as the author puts it.

The stock quotes are probably one of the most intensive modules in the entire TCS lineup, because it grabs updates for each and every quote, every minute, Monday through Friday, 7:00 a.m. to 4:30 p.m. Ouch! If you're not planning on ever checking your stocks, disable the module by deleting the *Quotes.tcl* file:

```
bash-2.02# rm /var/hack/tcs/modules/Quotes.tcl
```

Turning Your TV into a Virtual Window

HACK
#59

It's raining in Boston, and you're stuck inside for the day. Take a virtual trip to a far-off tropical locale, without ever leaving your recliner.

It's winter time, and you're sitting at home, freezing, and wishing desperately that you could be some place warmer. While your TiVo is not going to beam you up to a tropical locale, perhaps it can provide some virtual heat.

The TiVo Home Media Option (HMO) [Hack #63] allows you to display a slideshow of your digital photos right on your television set. What about putting up live pictures from the Web, perhaps of some place you would rather be? Thanks to the dual miracles of webcams and *wget* [Hack #54], you can do just that.

Find your favorite Internet webcam—I personally like *http://www.mauimanakai.com/webcam.htm*—and figure out the URL of the image itself. You can easily do so by opening up the source of the web page on which it's displayed and doing some hunting and pecking.

Grab a copy of *wget* for your PC. Windows users will find a port at *http://space.tin.it/computer/hherold/*, while Mac OS X users will find theirs at *http://www.apple.com/downloads/macosx/unix_open_source/wget.html*. Install *wget* using the instructions provided with the application. Next, instruct it to download an image from the webcam and place it into a directory you're sharing with your TiVo through the HMO. On my Mac, I type:

```
$ wget -O /Users/r/Desktop/TiVo/webcam/image.jpg http://www.mauimanakai.com/
panasonic.jpg
```

Take a gander at the image using your TiVo's HMO *Photo* viewer. If all goes to plan, you should be transported—in mind at least—to your tropical paradise.

But a static picture won't satisfy you for long; you'll want to keep up the illusion by having a fresh version download every 5 minutes or so.

Automating Webcam Downloads with Windows

Your first instinct may be to use the *Windows Task Scheduler*. However, the smallest time interval it can work with is 1 hour. That just won't do! Thankfully, WinCron from DWG Software (*http://www.dwgsoftware.com*) is just the ticket.

Download, install, and start WinCron. If you've ever seen the command-line Unix version of *cron* [Hack #44], you'll find WinCron (shown in Figure 4-22) rather familiar, albeit slightly prettier.

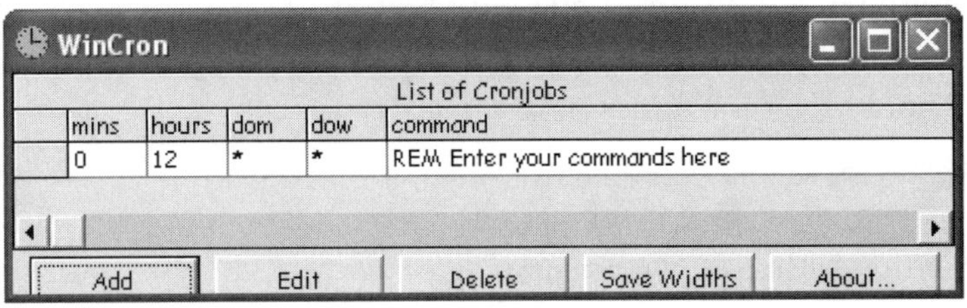

Figure 4-22. The WinCron interface

Click the Add button to bring up an interface to adding a new scheduled task (see Figure 4-23).

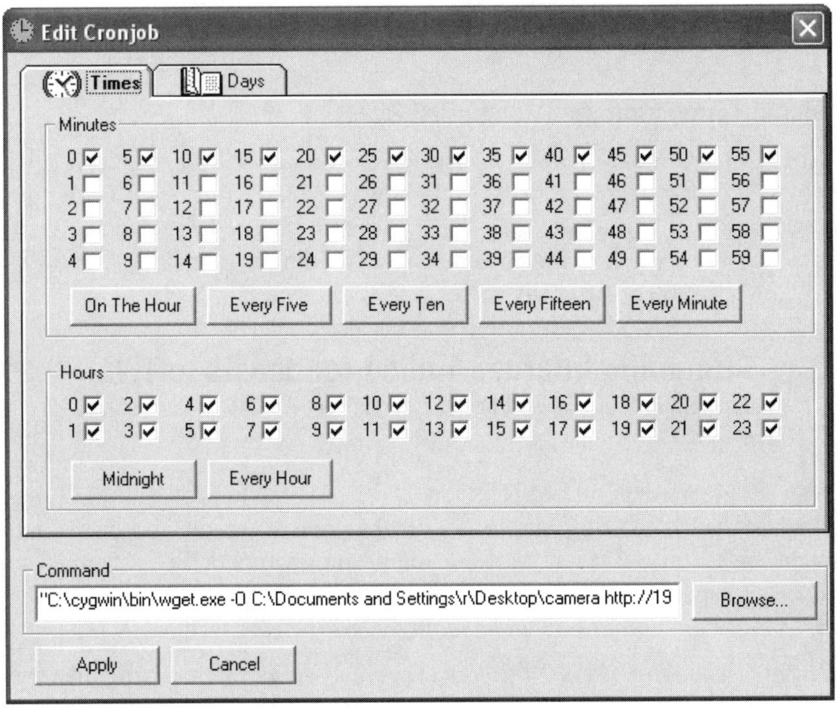

Figure 4-23. Add a new job to WinCron

Use the same *wget* command line that I used to grab the webcam image and paste it into the Command field. Make sure to specify the right path to *wget* (*wget.exe*, in this case) and pass it the right command-line arguments for output and download. Once you have all that squared away, set it up to run the command every five minutes. Click the Apply button, and that's that.

Automating Webcam Downloads with Mac OS X

Setting up this repeating task in OS X is easy using *cron* **[Hack #44]**. At the Terminal (Applications → Utilities → Terminal), type:

```
$ crontab -e
```

Up comes your existing (or a new) *crontab*—in the vi text editor, most likely. Set the last line of your *crontab* to:

```
*/5 * * * * wget -O /Users/r/Desktop/TiVo/webcam/image.jpg http://www.
mauimanaki.com/panasonic.com
```

Of course, you should replace the URL with the URL appropriate for the webcam that you are accessing, and you should also replace the download directory with the one on your Mac that the TiVo is going to be accessing. Save the updated *crontab* file and your Mac will, once every 5 minutes, download a fresh image and put it into the shared HMO directory.

Watching Time (and the Waves) Roll By

Go back to the image on your TiVo and select it as a slideshow running with repeats, as shown in Figure 4-24. This way, you'll constantly have something to look at. And just leave it. As more and more images come in, the slideshow loop will get longer and longer, making it more possible for you to dream that you are actually there.

HACK #60   Streaming Internet Audio Broadcasts to TiVo

Stream SHOUTcast Internet audio alongside your own MP3s to your HMO-enabled TiVo.

TiVo's Home Media Option (HMO) **[Hack #63]** allows you to stream MP3 music from your home PC through your TiVo to your television and home audio system speakers. But what of those online music broadcasts, streamed talk shows, and specials? The HMO can handle those too, thanks to Tobias Hoellrich's *m3ugen.pl* (*http://www.kahunaburger.com/blog/archives/000054.html*).

m3ugen.pl is a simple Perl (*http://www.perl.com*) script that generates *.m3u* files from SHOUTcast playlists. These *.m3u* files are what TiVo uses to stream music from PCs and Macs in your house to TiVo.

The Code

Save the following code to a file named *m3ugen.pl* somewhere on your PC or Mac's hard drive:

```
#!c:\perl\bin\perl.exe

use strict;
```

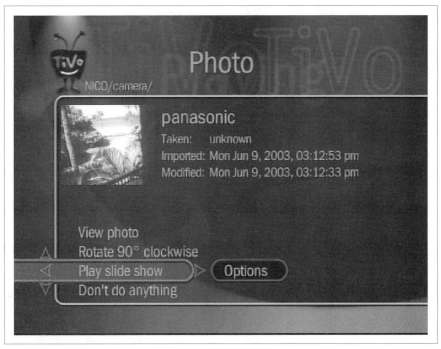

Figure 4-24. Start the slideshow of the webcam images

```perl
use HTML::LinkExtor;
use LWP::Simple;
use URI::URL;
use constant PROVIDER => qq{http://www.shoutcast.com/};
use constant DIRECTORY => PROVIDER.qq{directory/};

my $genre=$ARGV[0];
my $results=$ARGV[1];
my $outfile=$ARGV[2];
unless (defined($genre) &&
    defined($results) && $results && $results <= 25 &&
    defined($outfile)) {
  die qq{Usage:\t$0 [genre] [numresults] [outfile]\n}.
    qq{\tgenre=TopTen,House,Blues,Punk,...\n}.
    qq{\tnumresults=1..25\n}.
    qq{\toutfile=m3u output file\n};
}

my @playlists=getPlaylists(DIRECTORY.
qq{?sgenre=$genre&numresult=$results},PROVIDER);
unless (scalar(@playlists)) {
  die "No results found - unable to create playlist\n";
  exit(0);
}
@playlists=mapForTiVo(@playlists);
```

```perl
open(OUT,">".$outfile) or die "Unable to create output file - $!";
print OUT qq{#EXTM3U\n};

foreach my $entry (@playlists) {
  my($url,$title)=%$entry;
  print OUT qq{#EXTINF:,$title\n$url\n};
}
close(OUT);

sub getPlaylists {
  my($url,$base)=@_;
  my(@results);
  my $content=get($url);

  unless (defined($content) && length($content)) {
    warn qq{Unable to fetch "$url"\n};
    return @results;
  }

  my $parser=HTML::LinkExtor->new(sub {
    my($t,%a)=@_;
    return if $t ne 'a';
    push(@results,$a{href}) if($a{href}=~/filename\.pls$/i);
  });

  $parser->parse($content);
  @results = map {$_=url($_,$base)->abs;} @results;
  return @results;
}

sub mapForTiVo {
  my(@list)=@_;
  my(@results);

  foreach my $url (@list) {
    my $content=get($url);
    next unless(defined($content) && length($content));

    my($file);
    foreach my $line (split(/[\n\r]/,$content)) {
      if ($line =~ /^File\d+=(.*)$/i) {
        my $u=URI::URL->new($1);
        $u->path(""),$file=$u->abs if($u->path eq '/' || $u->path eq '');
      } elsif ($line =~ /^Title\d+\s*=(.*)$/i && defined($file)) {
        push(@results,{$file => $1});
        last;
      }
    }
  }
  return @results;
}
```

Mac OS X should alter the first line to point to the proper location of Perl:

```
#!/usr/bin/perl
```

Running the Hack

Let's say I share the path *c:\tivo\mp3* on my Windows PC with my TiVo's HMO Music option. Let's also say that I want the top 15 Punk stations from SHOUTcast (*http://www.shoutcast.com*), so I can listen to the music broadcasts of these stations through my TiVo. I'd invoke the *m3ugen.pl* at my PC's DOS prompt (Start → Run... → *command*), like so:

```
C:\> perl m3ugen.pl Punk 15 c:\tivo\mp3\Punk.m3u
```

If you don't have a copy of the Perl programming language on your system, download and install a copy of ActivePerl from ActiveState (*http://www.activestate.com/Products/ActivePerl/*).

On a Mac, sharing the path *~/tivo/mp3/Punk.m3u*, I'd run *m3ugen.pl* from the Terminal (Applications → Utilities → Terminal), as follows:

```
% perl m3ugen.pl Punk 15 ~/tivo/mp3/Punk.m3u
```

The script will visit *www.shoutcast.com*, look up the Punk category, extract the playlists of the 15 most popular Punk stations, download each individual playlist, find TiVo-compatible server entries, and generate a *Punk.m3u* file.

The HMO only likes streams with URLs of the format:

```
http://hostname:port
```

It doesn't work with more "involved " URLs like:

```
http://hostname:port/dir/dir
```

When asked to play a stream at such a URL, the HMO will simply fail to do so.

You'll then magically find a *Punk.m3u* section under *Music and Photos* → *Music* section of your HMO-enabled TiVo. Select it and listen to some of the finest punk music streamed over the Net. See Figure 4-25.

The HMO doesn't buffer streamed Internet-audio. If the stream pauses due to traffic congestion or any other problem, the HMO will just punt it and move on.

Figure 4-25. The top 15 Punk SHOUTcast stations brought to your TiVo

If Punk's not quite your cup of tea, visit *http://www.shoutcast.com* and choose a more appropriate genre from the "--Choose a genre --" pull-down list on the right side of the page. The page will refresh, and you'll end up on a page whose URL begins with *http://www.shoutcast.com/directory/?sgenre=*. The word after the = (equals sign) is what you should feed *m3ugen.pl* on the command line to find the most popular streams of that genre.

———*Tobias Hoellrich*

HACK   Watching Your Email
#61
Is a picture indeed worth a thousand words? That depends on how many words are in the picture. Render your email as PNG images, suitable for viewing via the TiVo HMO's photo sharing.

Series 2 users may not be able to check their email on their TiVo using *TPOP* [Hack #57], but this is nothing a little Perl scripting can't fix. Tobias Hoellrich comes through again with *mailrender.pl* (*http://www.kahunaburger.com/blog/archives/000052.html*). The script runs every so often, fetches any new mail from your POP3 mail server, and renders email as PNG image files for display via TiVo's Home Media Option (HMO) [Hack #63] on your TV.

In addition to Perl (*http://www.perl.com*) itself, you'll need the following Perl modules, all freely downloadable from the Comprehensive Perl Archive Network (CPAN) at *http://www.cpan.org*:

GD (*http://search.cpan.org/author/LDS/*)
An interface to the GD graphics library

Mail::Internet (*http://search.cpan.org/author/MARKOV/*)
For manipulating Internet mail messages

Mail::POP3Client (*http://search.cpan.org/author/SDOWD/*)
An interface for talking to POP3 mail servers

File::Path (*http://search.cpan.org/author/JHI/*)
For manipulating directory trees

File::Spec (*http://search.cpan.org/author/JHI/*)
For fiddling with file names

Windows users will probably find it easiest to install these modules using PPM (*http://aspn.activestate.com/ASPN/ Reference/Products/ActivePerl/faq/ActivePerl-faq2.html*), ActivePerl's package manager. Mac users, use the CPAN module (*http://search.cpan.org/author/ANDK/CPAN-1.70/ lib/CPAN.pm*).

The Code

Save the following code to a file named *mailrender.pl* somewhere on your PC or Mac's hard drive:

```
#!c:\perl\bin\perl.exe
use strict;
use File::Path;
use File::Spec;
use GD;
use Mail::POP3Client;
use Mail::Internet;

use constant DESTINATION  => q{d:\DigitalPhotos\Tivo\EMail};
use constant PREVIEW_LINES => 100;
use constant WIDTH        => 640;
use constant HEIGHT       => 480;
use constant HEADER_FONT  => gdMediumBoldFont;
use constant BODY_FONT    => gdLargeFont;

my @accounts = (
 {
 DESC    => q{thoellri@foobar.com},
 USER    => "thoellri",
 AUTH_MODE => "PASS",
```

```
  PASSWORD => "password",
  HOST    => "pop3.foobar.com"
  },
  {
  DESC    => q{tobias@somewhere.com},
  USER    => "tobias",
  AUTH_MODE => "PASS",
  PASSWORD => "password",
  HOST    => "mail.somewhere.com"
  },
);

for my $account (@accounts) {
 # erase existing messages
  rmtree([ File::Spec->catfile(DESTINATION, $account->{DESC}) ], 0, 0);
  my $pop = new Mail::POP3Client (%$account);
  unless ($pop) { warn "Couldn't connect\n"; next; }
  my $count = $pop->Count;
  if ($count <0) { warn "Authorization failed"; next; }
  next if($count == 0); # no new messages
 # create new directory for messages
  mkpath([ File::Spec->catfile(DESTINATION, $account->{DESC}) ], 0, 0711);
  for my $num (1..$count) {
    my @preview=$pop->HeadAndBody($num,100);
    my $mail=Mail::Internet->new(\@preview);
    my $header=$mail->head;
    my $image=render($mail);
    my $out=File::Spec->catfile(DESTINATION, $account->{DESC},qq{message-}.
                sprintf("%02d",$num).qq{.png});
    open(OUT, qq{>$out});
    binmode OUT;
    print OUT $image->png;
    close(OUT);
  }
  $pop->Close;
}
sub render {
  my($m)=@_;
  my $header=$m->head();
  my $im = new GD::Image(WIDTH, HEIGHT);
  # allocate some colors
  my $white = $im->colorAllocate(255,255,255);
  my $black = $im->colorAllocate(0,0,0);
  my $gray = $im->colorAllocate(20,20,20);
  my $red = $im->colorAllocate(255,0,0);
  my $blue = $im->colorAllocate(0,0,255);
  my $y=2;
  $im->string(HEADER_FONT, 5,$y, "Date:  ".$header->get('Date'),↵
  $black);$y+=10;
  $im->string(HEADER_FONT, 5,$y, "From:  ".$header->get('From'),↵
  $black);$y+=10;
  $im->string(HEADER_FONT, 5,$y, "To:    ".$header->get('To'),↵
  $black);$y+=10;
```

```
$im->string(HEADER_FONT, 5,$y, "Subject: ".$header->get('Subject'),⏎
$blue);$y+=10;
$im->string(HEADER_FONT, 5,$y, "-" x 80, $black);$y+=8;
foreach my $line (@{$m->body()}) {
  chomp($line);
  $im->string(BODY_FONT, 5, $y, $line, $gray);
  $y+=13; last if($y>=HEIGHT);
}
return $im;
}
```

Mac OS X should alter the first line to point to the proper location of Perl:

```
#!/usr/bin/perl
```

If you don't have a copy of the Perl programming language on your Windows system, download and install a copy of ActivePerl from ActiveState (*http://www.activestate.com/Products/ActivePerl/*).

You'll want to set the DESTINATION variable (highlighted in bold in the previous script) to an appropriate directory into which the script should place those generated PNG images:

```
use constant DESTINATION => q{d:\DigitalPhotos\Tivo\EMail};
```

For example, on my Mac, I might choose a space somewhere in my *Pictures* folder that I configured my HMO to read:

```
use constant DESTINATION => q{/Users/raffi/Pictures/Hacks/Tivo/Email};
```

Next, configure the script for your email particulars by changing the default settings in the @accounts array (called out in bold in the previous script). For each account, set the DESC to a reasonable description of the email account, set USER and PASSWORD to your email username and password, and set HOST to the name of my POP3 mail server.

For example, here is my setup:

```
my @accounts = (
  {
  DESC    => q{raffi@bitwaste.com},
  USER    => "raffi",
  AUTH_MODE => "PASS",
  PASSWORD => "my_password",
  HOST    => "pop.bitwaste.com"
  },
);
```

Notice that I have only one account listed. To add more, simply paste in another copy of the account settings—starting with { and ending with }— and be sure to put a , between each.

You want to set the DESC to be a description of the email account, and setting it to your email address is just fine. USER and PASSWORD are self-explanatory, and HOST is the name of your POP3 server.

Running the Hack

Run the script from the DOS prompt (Start → Run... → *command*) on your Windows PC or from the Terminal (Applications → Utilities → Terminal) under Mac OS X, like so:

```
perl mailrender.pl
```

The script will download (but not delete) your email and render a slew of PNG image files like the one shown in Figure 4-26.

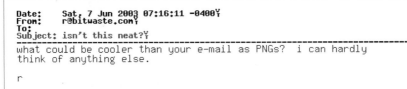

```
Date:     Sat, 7 Jun 2003 07:16:11 -0400
From:     r@bitwaste.com
To:
Subject: isn't this neat?
-------------------------------------------------------------------
what could be cooler than your e-mail as PNGs?  i can hardly
think of anything else.

r
```

Figure 4-26. An email message rendered as a PNG image by the mailrender.pl script

 You can have *mailrender.pl* regularly render your email into PNG files automatically by using Scheduled Tasks on your Windows PC (Start → Programs → Accessories → System Tools → Scheduled Tasks) or *cron* on your Mac (see O'Reilly's *Mac OS X Hacks*).

Pictures placed in your HMO-shared images directory will be snatched up by the HMO, ready to be displayed along with those family photos, as shown in Figure 4-27.

Have fun reading—or watching, to be precise—your email.

——*Tobias Hoellrich*

 ### Listen to Your Email
#62

Listen to your email as an MP3 audio stream—just because you can.

Just when you thought pictures of your email [Hack #61] was over the top, someone had to go and take it even further. Instead of rendering your email to a PNG image, let's render it to audio.

A combination of the script from "Watching Your Email" [Hack #61] and the Microsoft Speech Object Library (*http://www.microsoft.com/speech/*) reads

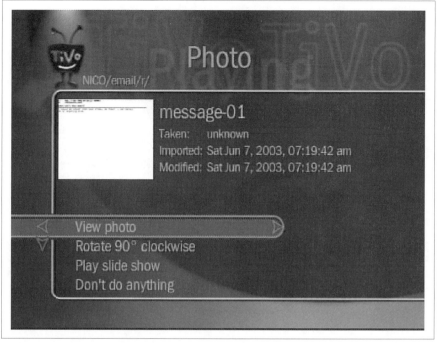

Figure 4-27. An email message in the TiVo HMO's gallery

the first few lines of each email message, rendering them as a temporary WAV audio file. That WAV file can then be converted using *bladeenc* (*http://bladeenc.mp3.no/*) or the like to an MP3 file that TiVo can understand and play. If all goes well, we can move the MP3 into an area that can be "seen" by the TiVo Media Desktop.

> Version 5 of the Microsoft Speech Object Library is installed by default under Windows XP Professional, so you won't need to install it again if you're running XP Pro.

The Code

Save the following code to a file named *mail2mp3.pl* somewhere on your PC hard drive, and follow the configuration instructions from "Watching Your Email" [Hack #61]:

```perl
#!c:\perl\bin\perl.exe

use strict;
use Cwd;
use File::Copy;
use File::Path;
```

```perl
use File::Spec;
use Mail::POP3Client;
use Mail::Internet;
use LWP::Simple;
use Win32;
use Win32::OLE;
use Win32::OLE::Const qq{Microsoft Speech Object Library};

use constant DESTINATION => q{D:\MP3\TiVo};
use constant PREVIEW_LINES => 30;

my @accounts = (
 {
 DESC    => q{thoellri@foobar.com},
 USER    => "thoellri",
 AUTH_MODE => "PASS",
 PASSWORD => "password",
 HOST    => "pop3.foobar.com"
 },
 {
 DESC    => q{tobias@somewhere.com},
 USER    => "tobias",
 AUTH_MODE => "PASS",
 PASSWORD => "password",
 HOST    => "mail.somewhere.com"
 },
);

for my $account (@accounts) {
 # erase existing messages
  rmtree([ File::Spec->catfile(DESTINATION, qq{Email}, $account->{DESC}) ],↵
    0, 0);
  my $pop = new Mail::POP3Client (%$account);
  unless ($pop) { warn "Couldn't connect\n"; next; }
  my $count = $pop->Count;
  if ($count <0) { warn "Authorization failed"; next; }
  next if($count == 0); # no new messages
 # create new directory for messages
  mkpath([ File::Spec->catfile(DESTINATION, qq{Email}, $account->{DESC}) ],↵
    0, 0711);
  for my $num (1..$count) {
    my @preview=$pop->HeadAndBody($num,100);
    my $mail=Mail::Internet->new(\@preview);
    my $mp3file=mail2mp3($mail);
    next unless defined($mp3file);
    my $out=File::Spec->catfile(DESTINATION, qq{Email}, $account->{DESC},
                   qq{message-}.sprintf("%02d",$num).qq{.mp3});
    copy($mp3file,$out);
    unlink($mp3file);
  }
  $pop->Close;
}
```

```
sub mail2mp3 {
  my($m)=@_;
  my $header=$m->head();
  my $type=Win32::OLE->new('SAPI.SpAudioFormat');
  $type->{Type}=SAFT32kHz16BitMono;
  my $stream=Win32::OLE->new('SAPI.SpFileStream');
  $stream->{Format}=$type;
  $stream->Open("output$$.wav",SSFMCreateForWrite,undef);
  my $speech=Win32::OLE->new('SAPI.SpVoice');
  $speech->{AudioOutputStream}=$stream;
  $speech->Speak(qq{From: }.$header->get('From'),SVSFDefault);
  $speech->Speak(qq{Subject: }.$header->get('Subject'),SVSFDefault);
  my($lines);
  foreach my $line (@{$m->body()}) {
    chomp($line);
    $speech->Speak($line." ",SVSFDefault);
    last if($lines++>= PREVIEW_LINES);
  }
  $speech->WaitUntilDone(-1);
  $stream->Close();
  return undef unless (-f "output$$.wav");
  # here we call out to the command line mp3 encode
  system(qq{bladeenc -quiet -nocfg -quit output$$.wav output$$.mp3});
  unlink(qq{output$$.wav});
  return undef unless (-f "output$$.mp3");
  return File::Spec->catfile(getcwd,qq{output$$.mp3});
}
```

Running the Hack

Run the script from the DOS prompt (Start → Run... → *command*) on your Windows PC or from the Terminal (Applications → Utilities → Terminal) under Mac OS X, like so:

```
perl mail2mp3.pl
```

With this magic running, your email will be downloaded but not deleted. Your computer will start silently talking to itself and recording itself (see Figure 4-28). It'll then compress all the sounds down to a basket-full-o'-MP3s that your TiVo would be content to sit and play all day and night.

See Also

- Lame, pronounced: "Lame Ain't an MP3 Encoder" (*http://lame. sourceforge.net/*)

——Tobias Hoellrich

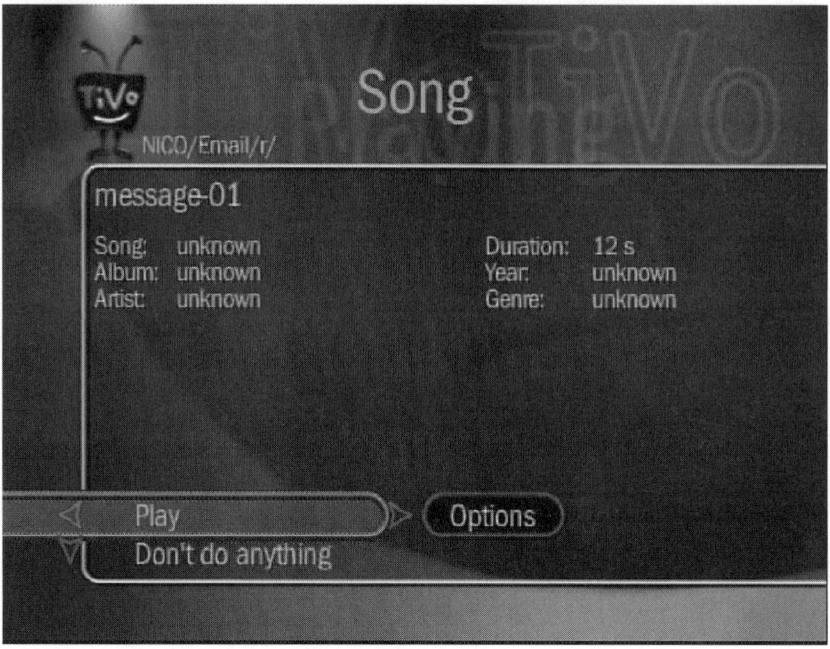

Figure 4-28. An email message as MP3 audio through the TiVo Home Media Option

TiVo and the Web
Hacks 63–80

It always happens when you're already halfway across town for that dinner date or soaring toward a week's vacation in some faraway place: you plumb forgot to set TiVo to record that awards show or season finale.

Sure, in all likelihood, TiVo knows you'd probably want to record the show in question, but it would put your mind at ease to know it's on the *To Do List*. It sure would be useful to call up your TiVo and check.

Two solutions provide access to, and manipulation, of your TiVo over the Web: the official TiVo Home Media Option (HMO) and the open source TiVoWeb project. Schedule recordings, prune your *Now Playing List*, or add season passes; about anything you can do while standing in front of your TV set can be done from any web browser anywhere in the world.

 HACK #63 ## Signing Up for the Home Media Option
Expand your Series 2's capabilities with TiVo, Inc.'s software upgrade.

The TiVo Home Media Option (HMO) is a $99 add-on (available at *http://www.tivo.com/4.9.asp*) that you can purchase for your Standalone Series 2 TiVo. The HMO brings a whole slew of features, including the ability to schedule recordings over the Web, play MP3s through your television and attached stereo system, display digital photos on your TV, and even stream television shows between Series 2 TiVos.

> Unfortunately, there is no Home Media Option support for Series 1 TiVos or DirecTiVos (TiVo/DirecTV combination) at the time of this writing.

Signing up for the Home Media Option is pretty simple.

First, get your networked Series 2 TiVo [Hack #50] onto your home broadband connection. Any high-speed connection will do just fine.

Point your browser to *http://www.tivo.com* and click the HMO link, or go directly to the HMO page: *http://www.tivo.com/4.9.asp*. You will need the email address and password you provided TiVo, Inc. when you first activated your TiVo. Don't worry if you've forgotten your password; you can either have a new password assigned and sent to your email address, or you can set everything up again by providing TiVo, Inc. with your service number. You can find that number on the *New Messages & Setup → System Information* screen.

Once you're signed up and have your TiVo connected to your home network, you will have to wait for your TiVo to connect to the service to activate itself. If you're a little impatient, you might try forcing your TiVo to connect and download the HMO option right away by having it make its Daily Call: *TiVo Messages & Setup → Settings → Phone & Network Setup → Connect to the TiVo service now*. If you notice the addition of *Photos and Music* to your *TiVo Central* menu, then the install worked.

HACK #64 Remotely Scheduling a Recording Through the HMO

With the TiVo Home Media Option, remotely scheduling a recording is as easy as going to *http://www.tivo.com* and making your selection.

Scheduling a recording via the Home Media Option (HMO) is supposed to be pretty simple, and indeed it is.

Before you can use TiVo's HMO to administer your TiVo Series 2 remotely, you'll need to log in to TiVo Central Online at *http://www.tivo.com/tco*. You'll be prompted (see Figure 5-1) for the email address and password that you used when you signed up for the HMO.

After successfully logging in, you're presented with a page for scheduling a recording (see Figure 5-2). First, choose which TiVo you want to record on; assuming you're fortunate enough to own more than one, there will be multiple choices.

In much the same manner as TiVo itself, you can *Search TV Listings* for a particular show by title, title/description, or actor/director; or, you can *Browse by Channel* for a gander at what's on TV over the next couple of days.

Advanced Search (shown in Figure 5-3) is reminiscent of the Advanced Wishlists [Hack #17]. If you choose that interface, you can set up "and" relationships in the search you want to make. Name that show *and* the actor/director *and* the category. TiVo Central Online will try to find it for you.

Figure 5-1. Logging in to TiVo Central Online

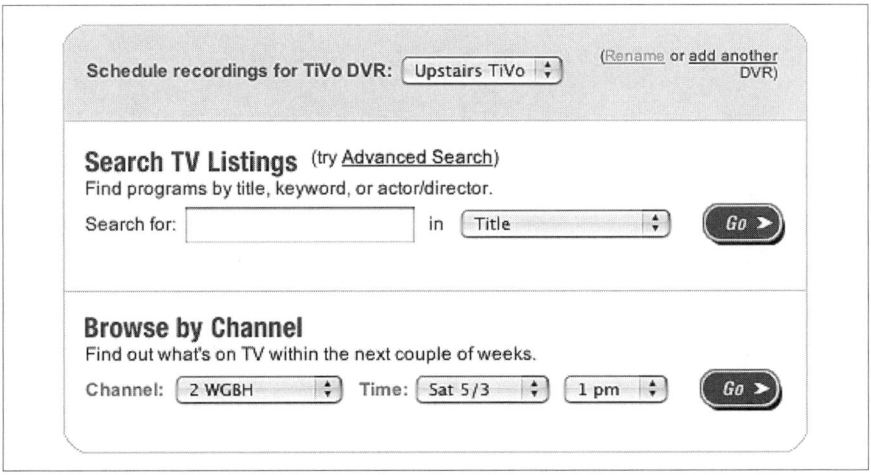

Figure 5-2. Scheduling a recording through TiVo Central Online

This site behaves just as you expect your TiVo would. Figure 5-4 shows it listing all the upcoming episodes.

Select which upcoming show you want recorded by clicking on it. You will be given the option of recording just the one episode or getting a Season Pass to it (see Figure 5-5).

The recording options (shown in Figure 5-6) are similar to the options you have when you schedule a recording on the TiVo itself: you can have the box keep the recording until space is needed, specify whether to start and

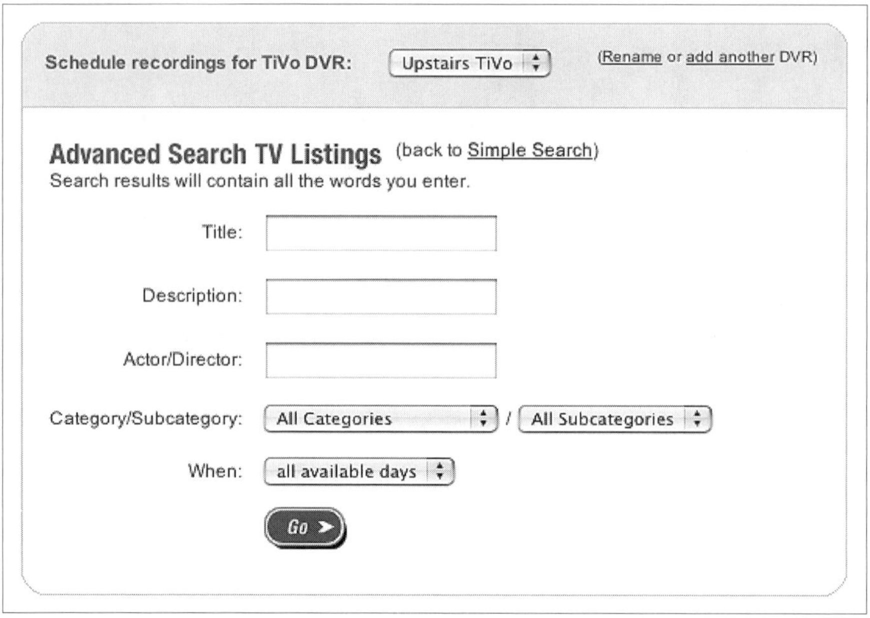

Figure 5-3. Using TiVo Central Online'sAadvanced Search interface

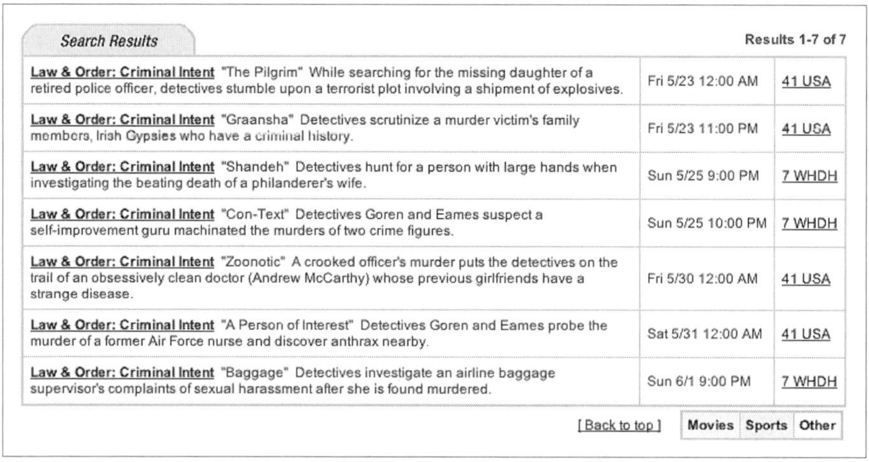
Search Results — Results 1-7 of 7

Law & Order: Criminal Intent "The Pilgrim" While searching for the missing daughter of a retired police officer, detectives stumble upon a terrorist plot involving a shipment of explosives.	Fri 5/23 12:00 AM	41 USA
Law & Order: Criminal Intent "Graansha" Detectives scrutinize a murder victim's family members, Irish Gypsies who have a criminal history.	Fri 5/23 11:00 PM	41 USA
Law & Order: Criminal Intent "Shandeh" Detectives hunt for a person with large hands when investigating the beating death of a philanderer's wife.	Sun 5/25 9:00 PM	7 WHDH
Law & Order: Criminal Intent "Con-Text" Detectives Goren and Eames suspect a self-improvement guru machinated the murders of two crime figures.	Sun 5/25 10:00 PM	7 WHDH
Law & Order: Criminal Intent "Zoonotic" A crooked officer's murder puts the detectives on the trail of an obsessively clean doctor (Andrew McCarthy) whose previous girlfriends have a strange disease.	Fri 5/30 12:00 AM	41 USA
Law & Order: Criminal Intent "A Person of Interest" Detectives Goren and Eames probe the murder of a former Air Force nurse and discover anthrax nearby.	Sat 5/31 12:00 AM	41 USA
Law & Order: Criminal Intent "Baggage" Detectives investigate an airline baggage supervisor's complaints of sexual harassment after she is found murdered.	Sun 6/1 9:00 PM	7 WHDH

[Back to top] Movies Sports Other

Figure 5-4. The results of the program listing search, showing all the shows that match the query

stop the episode on time, and pick the quality of the recording. There is one recording option that might not seem that familiar: "What priority?"

Because your TiVo is not continuously connected to TiVo, Inc.'s web site, it doesn't know exactly what shows your TiVo is already scheduled to record. Because your broadband-enabled PVR connects to TiVo, Inc. only a few times

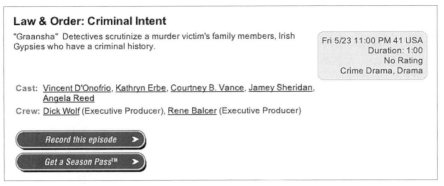

Law & Order: Criminal Intent

"Graansha" Detectives scrutinize a murder victim's family members, Irish
Gypsies who have a criminal history.

Fri 5/23 11:00 PM 41 USA
Duration: 1:00
No Rating
Crime Drama, Drama

Cast: Vincent D'Onofrio, Kathryn Erbe, Courtney B. Vance, Jamey Sheridan,
Angela Reed
Crew: Dick Wolf (Executive Producer), Rene Balcer (Executive Producer)

    Record this episode   ➤

    Get a Season Pass™   ➤

Figure 5-5. Record this episode or get a Season Pass to the show

Law & Order: Criminal Intent

"Graansha" Detectives scrutinize a murder victim's family members, Irish
Gypsies who have a criminal history.

Fri 5/23 11:00 PM 41 USA
Duration: 1:00
No Rating
Crime Drama, Drama

1. **Record this episode**

    On TiVo DVR: [Upstairs TiVo ⬍]

2. **Confirm recording options:**   Other recording options (Change)

    What priority? [Only record if nothing else conflicts ⬍]   Keep Until: Space needed
                                                                     Start: On Time
    What quality? [Use the default on the DVR ⬍]   Stop: On Time

3. **Send confirmation?**

    ☐ Yes, use this email address: [   ]   *If conflicts are
                                                                    found, e-mails
                                                                    may identify
                                                                    recordings on
                                                                    your DVR (tell
                                                                    me more).*

    Schedule It! ◯

Figure 5-6. Setting all the recording options when scheduling a show to be recorded

a day; the information the HMO has may not be as up-to-date as it would like
to be. So, if you ask the HMO to schedule a recording for you, it can't know if
there is a conflict brewing. To work around this problem, there are two
options: "Only record if nothing else conflicts" and "Cancel other programs if
necessary." These selections do exactly as they say: the first will record if there
are no other entries on the *To Do List*, and the second will trump anything
else already in the schedule.

If you ask for a Season Pass to be added to your lineup, you're presented with a similar screen, but this time you are able to modify the Season Pass options, as shown in Figure 5-7. The only thing you can't change is the ordering of your passes; to reorder your passes, you're going to have to go to your TiVo.

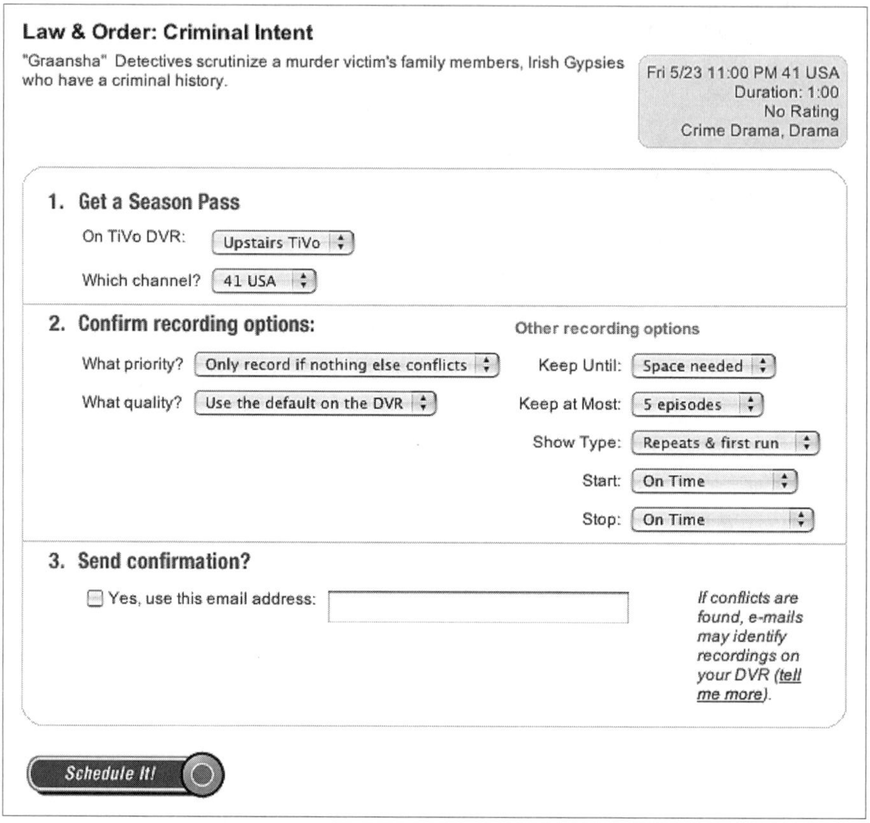

Law & Order: Criminal Intent

"Graansha" Detectives scrutinize a murder victim's family members, Irish Gypsies who have a criminal history.

Fri 5/23 11:00 PM 41 USA
Duration: 1:00
No Rating
Crime Drama, Drama

1. Get a Season Pass

On TiVo DVR: [Upstairs TiVo ⬍]

Which channel?   [41 USA ⬍]

2. Confirm recording options: Other recording options

What priority? [Only record if nothing else conflicts ⬍]   Keep Until: [Space needed ⬍]

What quality? [Use the default on the DVR ⬍]   Keep at Most: [5 episodes ⬍]

Show Type: [Repeats & first run ⬍]

Start: [On Time ⬍]

Stop: [On Time ⬍]

3. Send confirmation?

☐ Yes, use this email address: [   ]   *If conflicts are found, e-mails may identify recordings on your DVR (tell me more).*

[Schedule It! ◯]

Figure 5-7. Set the Season Pass recording options remotely through the HMO

After you have asked TiVo Central Online to schedule a show for you, TiVo, Inc. just waits for contact from your PVR. And here is the main reason that you're now using your broadband connection for your TiVo: your TiVo doesn't have to use your phone line anymore. Now, it's really simple and basically unobtrusive for your TiVo to make its Daily Call. A few times a day, sometimes as often as once an hour, your broadband-enabled TiVo will connect over the Internet and receive any of these queued-up requests from TiVo Central Online. If it receives any, it will start to incorporate them into its schedule.

If all goes as it should, the next time you turn on your TiVo you should find a message waiting for you, confirming that your request has been added to the *To Do List*. And if you check out the *To Do List*, the show will be there, as expected.

If all does not go to plan—for example, if there's a scheduling conflict—then things get a little more complicated. An hour or so after you ask the HMO to schedule a recording—probably around the time your box decides to connect to TiVo Central Online—you'll receive an email message, informing you of the conflict. A typical email of this sort looks something like this:

```
From: TiVo - Your Upstairs TiVo DVR confirmations@tivo.com
Date: Sat May 3, 2003 15:15:07 America/New_York
To:
Subject: Status of your request for "Law & Order: Criminal Intent"

Your online request for "Law & Order: Criminal Intent : Malignant" has been
received. However, this episode COULD NOT be scheduled to record because it
conflicts with a previously scheduled, higher priority recording.

Will NOT record:
 Law & Order: Criminal Intent 5/4  10:00 pm-11:00 pm    7 WHDH
 overlaps with  Alias  9:00 pm - 11:00 pm

To change which programs will and won't record, go to the
To Do List and Recording History. To get there:
-  press the TiVo button to go to TiVo Central
-  choose "Pick Programs to Record"
-  choose "To Do List"

Best regards,

TiVo
http://www.tivo.com/support
```

This is the TiVo HMO's way of performing conflict resolution. Now it's up to you to go back to TiVo Central Online and reschedule.

Because your TiVo is not constantly connected and your web browser is not talking directly to your TiVo, the remote abilities of the HMO are quite limited. There is no way for you to take a look at the *To Do List*, and there is no way for you to manage your Season Passes. In fact, you are not able to do anything except schedule a recording, and even that may not go to plan, because you have no way of knowing—until an hour has passed—whether there is a conflict. In fact, if you want to record a show that starts in 5 minutes, there is a very good chance that Remote Scheduling will not do it for you.

Those of you who want it all, take a look at TiVoWeb [Hack #65] instead.

TiVoWeb, a Web Interface to Your TiVo

#65   TiVoWeb is the TiVo interface embodied in a web browser, allowing you full
remote control of your TiVo from anywhere in the world.

Josha Foust's TiVoWeb (*http://tivo.lightn.org/*) predates TiVo's Home Media
Option (HMO) and far outstrips it in terms of features. While the HMO's
Remote Scheduling feature simply allows you to add something to your
TiVo's recording schedule over the Web, TiVoWeb is almost the full TiVo
interface embodied in a web browser. It allows direct manipulation of about
every aspect of your PVR: manipulate your Season Passes, unschedule something from the *To Do List*, undelete a program you might have accidentally
deleted, read your TiVo messages, and the list goes on and on.

A nice side effect of running TiVoWeb is the ability to manipulate your TiVo
while it's doing something else—playing back a recorded show, for instance.

Before you begin, you'll need a networked TiVo [Hack #49] with a Bash prompt
[Hack #52]. You can even use a PPP-over-serial [Hack #47] instead of the TiVo/
TurboWeb card in your Series 1.

Installing TiVoWeb

The first step is to download the TiVoWeb application code to the TiVo
itself. There are many ways to do this, probably the easiest of which is to use
the *http_get* utility [Hack #53] on the TiVo command line to grab the files from
the TiVoWeb site:

```
bash-2.02# http_get -T 0 -C 0 -D /var/hack -U http://199.240.141.102 /↵
tivoweb-tcl-1.9.4.tar.gz
```

At the time of this writing, the current version of TiVoWeb is 1.9.4; be sure to
check the TiVoWeb page for the latest, replacing tivoweb-tcl-1.9.4.tar.gz
with the appropriate filename. Notice I used an IP address (199.240.141.102) in
the download URL instead of the TiVoWeb domain name (tivo.lightn.org).
http_get does not have domain name resolution capabilities, so it won't know
where to find the TiVoWeb site.

Another option is to download the TiVoWeb application code (*tivoweb-tcl-
1.9.4.tar.gz*) to another computer, enable the FTP server [Hack #55] on the
TiVo, and upload the file.

Once the TiVoWeb application is onboard, move it into the */var/hack* directory that we have been working in all along and unpack the archive, like so:

```
bash-2.02# mv tivoweb-tcl-1.9.4.tar.gz /var/hack
bash-2.02# cd /var/hack
bash-2.02# gzip -d tivoweb-tcl-1.9.4.tar.gz
bash-2.02# cpio -H tar -i < tivoweb-tcl-1.9.4.tar
```

Unfortunately, due to updates in the TiVo operating system, the default version of TiVoWeb does not handle the newest genre information your TiVo is keeping track of. So, before going any further, we are going to have to replace the *ui.itcl* file with one that has been patched to work. Josha talks about this at *http://www.tivocommunity.com/tivo-vb/showthread. php?postid=973653#post973653* and provides code that you can paste into your *ui.itcl* file. You'll find an upgraded version at *http://tivo. kitschcamppalace.org.uk/00ui.itcl.txt*. Either download it to your PC and FTP it into your TiVo [Hack #55], or use *wget* [Hack #54] to download it directly to TiVo. Once you have it moved into */var/hack/tivoweb-tcl/modules*, install it:

```
bash-2.02# cd /var/hack/tivoweb-tcl/modules
bash-2.02# mv 00ui.itcl.txt ui.itcl
```

Starting TiVoWeb

That done, let's start the TiVoWeb server running:

```
bash-2.02# /var/hack/tivoweb-tcl/tivoweb console
```

You will see a whole slew of data scrolling by. Most of these are status and debugging messages of the TiVoWeb code, detailing its startup procedure. We'll go through these messages in a little more detail later when we want to add different extensions to the code [Hack #78]. Ignore them for now.

An "Accepting Connections" status message signals that the server has started successfully. Point your browser to the IP address of your TiVo [Hack #51], and you should see the TiVoWeb's main screen, as shown in Figure 5-8.

Poking Around TiVoWeb

The first thing you should notice is that the menu items on this front page are the same as the menu items up top. That menu bar will always be visible, giving you quick access to the entire TiVoWeb from any web page inside the site.

Your first real stop should be *User Interface*, and a page resembling Figure 5-9 will show up on your browser. This page is at the heart of controlling your TiVo; almost everything you see on your *TiVo Central* menu on your television is going to appear here. Take a poke around.

The *Info* menu shows you some random information about your TiVo, such as how much memory is being used and a calculated guess about how much space is currently allocated to television shows. If you want to guess what your TiVo is doing, take a gander at the *Logs* and from there you can see what your box is noting. *MFS* lets you browse through a representation of

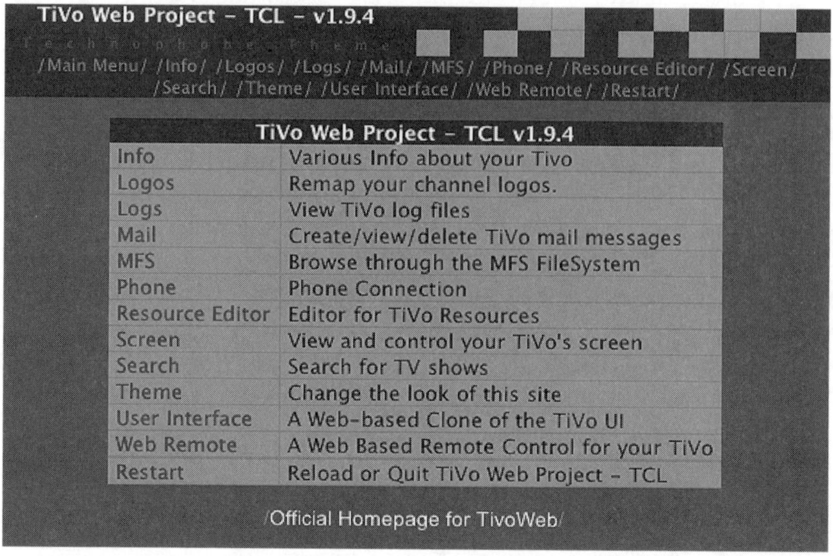

Figure 5-8. The TiVoWeb main page

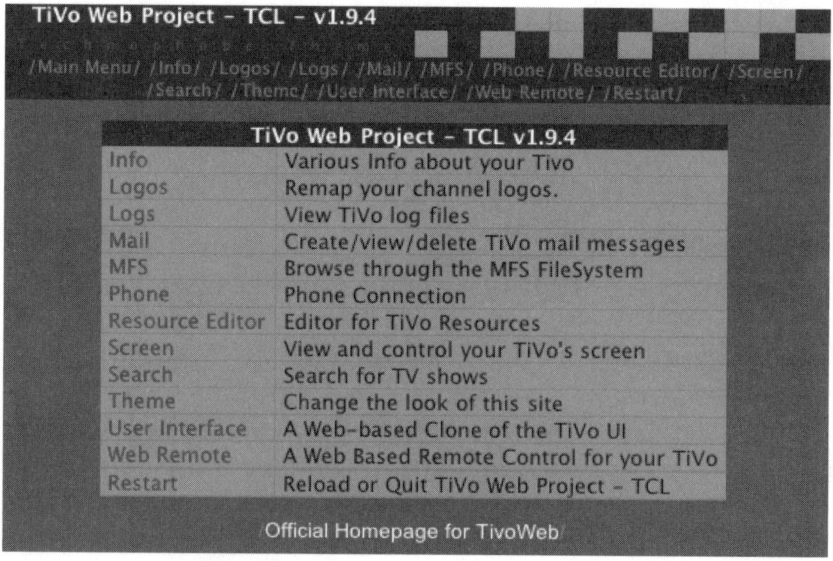

Figure 5-9. The User Interface menu

the MFS filesystem and, finally, the *Resource Editor* exposes a few of TiVo's internal variables for editing [Hack #97]. As for the rest of them, I'll get to them in a bit.

Stopping TiVoWeb

To shut down the TiVoWeb web server, visit the *Restart* menu, either from the main web page or menu bar at the top of the page, and select Quit. The server will shut itself down cleanly, and you'll get your command-line prompt back.

Do *not* simply type Control-C to shut down the TiVoWeb process from the command line. There's a rather good chance that the TiVo will reboot itself. TiVoWeb is built on top of something called *TiVoSH* (the TiVo Shell), which doesn't like to be interrupted during database access.

 ## Scheduling a Recording with TiVoWeb

#66   Remotely scheduling a recording is just a few web pages away, thanks to the wonders of the TiVoWeb web interface.

Scheduling a recording with TiVoWeb is rather like doing so through TiVo's television interface. From the main TiVoWeb page or toolbar at the top of each page, click Search. You'll be presented with a page reminiscent of TiVo's *Search by Title* screen, as shown in Figure 5-10.

```
TiVo Web Project - TCL - v1.9.4
/Main Menu/ /Info/ /Logos/ /Logs/ /Mail/ /MFS/ /Phone/ /Resource Editor/ /Screen/
        /Search/ /Theme/ /User Interface/ /Web Remote/ /Restart/

                          Search
      Search By:     Title                              ▲▼
      Category       All                                ▲▼
      SubCategory    Don't specify a sub-category        ▲▼
      Search For:

        ☐  Include Channels You Don't Watch
        ☐  Display Empty (No Upcoming Episodes) Hits

                       ( Search )

                 Please enter the start of the title
   The search will match all titles starting with the text entered in "Search For:"
```

Figure 5-10. The TiVoWeb search interface

Because TiVoWeb has its fingers into the same hooks as the TiVo's WishLists, its search functionality is far more flexible than its TiVo counterpart. You can search not only by Title, but also by Keyword, Title Keyword, Actor, and by Director by simply changing the "Search By" field. You can further filter results by category (Movies, Educational, Western, etc.) and subcategory (under News and Business, for instance, you can select International, Magazine, Weather, etc.).

When you click the Search button, TiVo will chug on for a bit, finally returning anything it found matching your search criteria. Figure 5-11 shows some of the results of a search for the Title Keyword of "phoenix" when run on my TiVo.

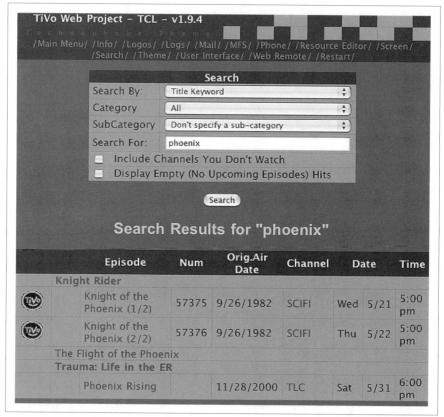

Figure 5-11. TiVoWeb search results

Select the program you're interested in from the list by clicking on its name—in my case, *Knight Rider*. As shown in Figure 5-12, you'll be presented with a list of all episodes already recorded on your TiVo, along with upcoming episodes.

Select the episode that you are interested in. You will be whisked away to the detailed information page for the episode and provided the option to Record or Get Season Pass (see Figure 5-13).

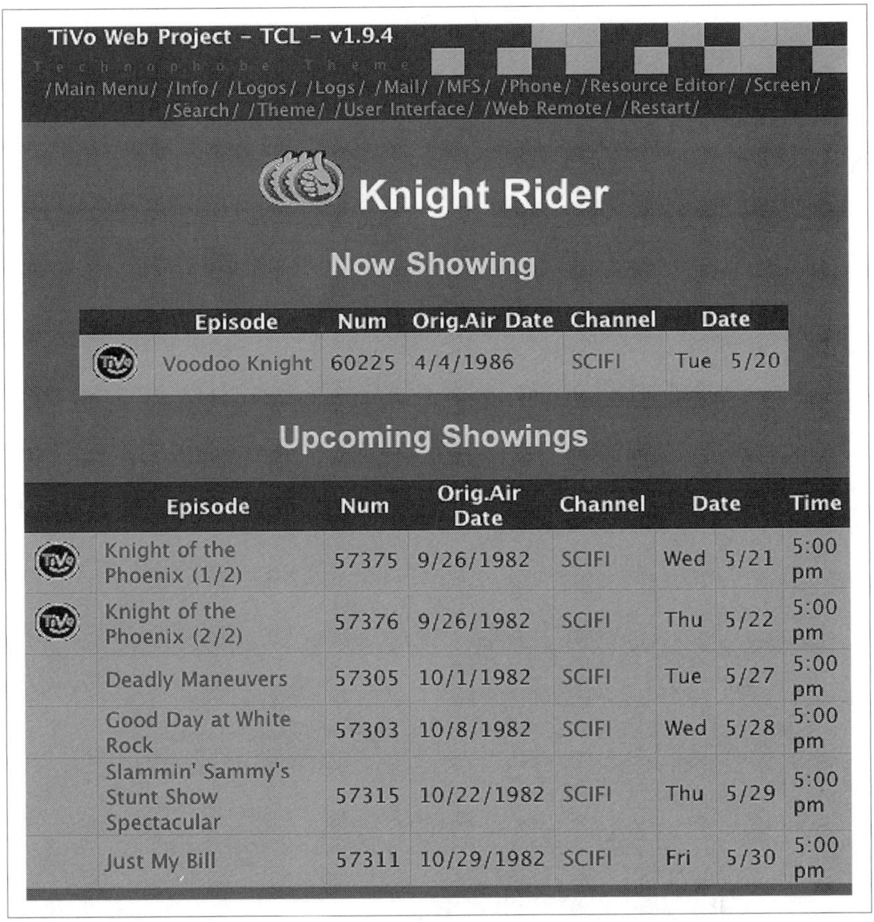

Figure 5-12. Recorded and upcoming episodes

Unlike the Home Media Option [Hack #64], the TiVoWeb is running right on your TiVo box itself. TiVoWeb will notice a conflict right away and tell you about it—no waiting for emails to find out if the scheduling happened or not. Talk about instant gratification. Set your Recording Options (see Figure 5-14), and click the Conflicts link to ask the TiVo to check whether it can actually record the show.

If you get to the magical *No Conflicts* screen, hit Record and you should be set. If you simply do not believe it, grab your TiVo remote, navigate to the *To Do List* (*Pick Programs to Record → To Do List*) on your television or on your computer [Hack #67], and you should see whatever you asked to record on the list.

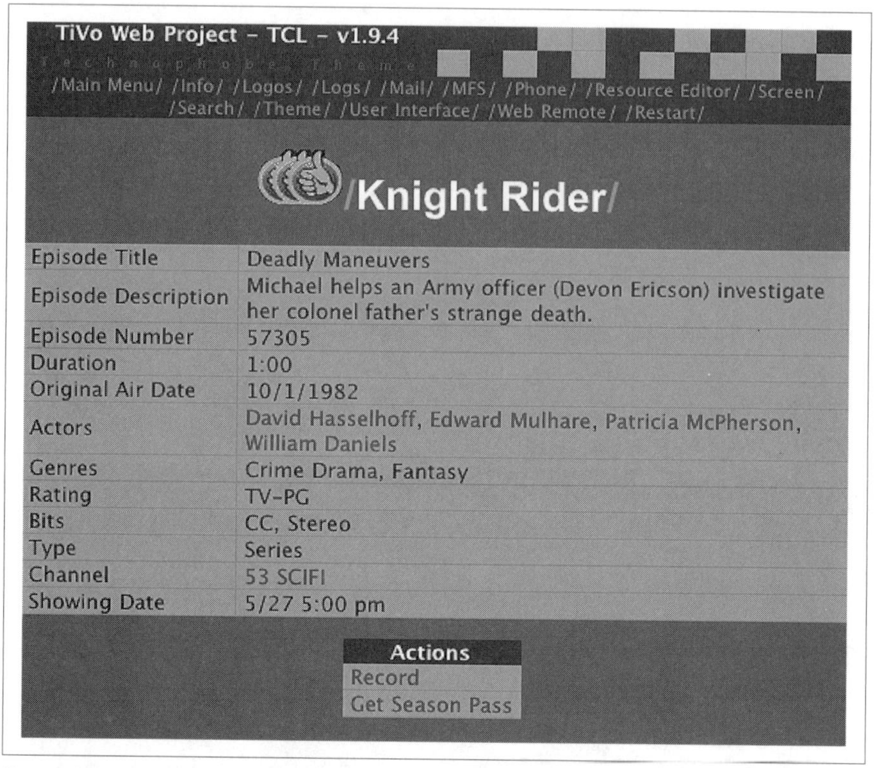

Figure 5-13. Recording a particular episode

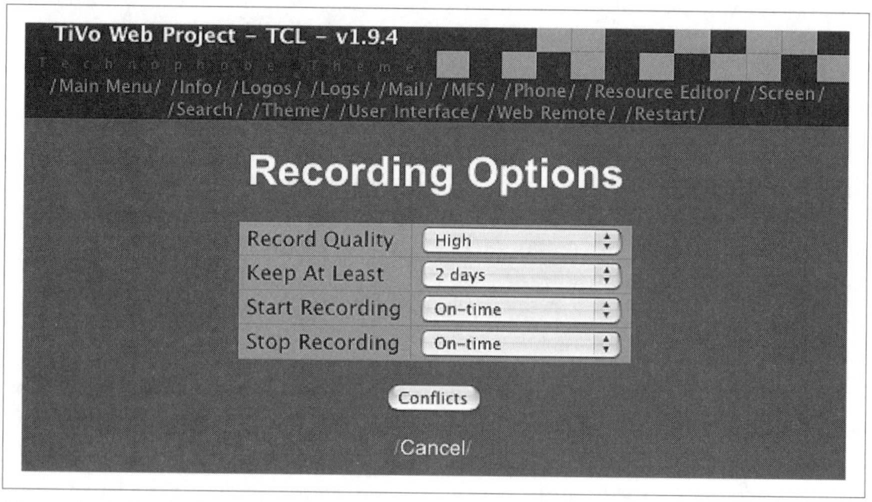

Figure 5-14. Setting Recording Options

What's on and beyond the To Do List?

Take a peek at what TiVo has in mind to record, both explicitly requested *To Do List* items and TiVo Suggestions.

Curious to know what your TiVo is going to record? Your TiVo maintains two lists of upcoming recordings. There's the *To Do List*: shows that you have asked it to record, including individually scheduled shows, Season Passes, and WishLists. Then there's the *Scheduled Suggestions List*: shows TiVo believes you'll find enjoyable, based on your recording history and Thumbs Up/Thumbs Down ratings.

The To Do List

The *To Do List* (*User Interface → To Do*), as displayed by TiVoWeb in Figure 5-15, should look familiar, as it is meant to look just like the *To Do List* on your TiVo itself. Along with program name, the list shows the episode title, date, time, and channel.

TiVo Web Project – TCL – v1.9.4

/Main Menu/ /Info/ /Logos/ /Logs/ /Mail/ /MFS/ /Phone/ /Resource Editor/ /Screen/ /Search/ /Theme/ /User Interface/ /Web Remote/ /Restart/

Date	Time	Channel	Program	Episode	
Sun 5/4	10:30 am	WCVB	This Week With George Stephanopoulos	No Episode Title	
Sun 5/4	5:00 pm	WLVI	Smallville	Witness	
Sun 5/4	6:30 pm	WCVB	ABC World News Tonight Sunday	No Episode Title	
Sun 5/4	7:00 pm	WLVI	Gilmore Girls	Run Away, Little Boy	
Sun 5/4	8:00 pm	WFXT	The Simpsons	Old Yeller Belly	
Sun 5/4	9:00 pm	WCVB	Alias	Second Double; The Telling	
Mon 5/5	6:30 pm	WCVB	ABC World News Tonight	No Episode Title	
Mon 5/5	9:00 pm	WLVI	Everwood	Episode 20	
Mon 5/5	10:00 pm	WBZ	CSI: Miami	Tinder Box	
Tue 5/6	3:35 am	WHDH	Late Night With Conan O'Brien	No Episode Title	
Tue 5/6	6:30 pm	WCVB	ABC World News Tonight	No Episode Title	
Tue 5/6	8:00 pm	WLVI	Gilmore Girls	Say Goodnight, Gracie	
Tue 5/6	9:00 pm	WFXT	24	Day 2: 5:00 – 6:00AM	
Wed 5/7	12:37 am	WHDH	Late Night With Conan O'Brien	No Episode Title	
Wed 5/7	6:30 pm	WCVB	ABC World News Tonight	No Episode Title	
Wed 5/7	8:00 pm	WLVI	Dawson's Creek	Joey Potter and Capeside Redemption	

Delete Shows

Figure 5-15. The To Do List, as displayed by TiVoWeb

The Scheduled Suggestions List

The *Scheduled Suggestions List* (*User Interface → Scheduled Suggestions*) looks exactly like the *To Do List*. However, the programs displayed are shows your TiVo has noticed—believing them to be shows you'd like—and is going to record for you. Figure 5-16 shows what my TiVo has in mind.

Date		Time	Channel	Program	Episode	Score	☐
Wed	5/21	10:00 am	TBS	Dawson's Creek	Detention	Explicit 3 255	☐
Wed	5/21	11:00 am	LIFE	Mad About You	Thanksgiving Show	Explicit 3 255	☐
Wed	5/21	11:30 am	LIFE	Mad About You	The Buried Fight	Explicit 3 255	☐
Wed	5/21	2:00 pm	TNN	Star Trek: The Next Generation	Where Silence Has Lease	Explicit 3 255	☐
Wed	5/21	5:00 pm	SCIFI	Knight Rider	Knight of the Phoenix	Explicit 3 255	☐
Wed	5/21	7:00 pm	WLVI	Friends	The One Where Rachel Has a Baby	Explicit 3 255	☐
Wed	5/21	7:30 pm	TBS	Friends	The One With Monica's Thunder	Explicit 3 255	☐
Thu	5/22	12:00 am	FOOD	Good Eats	Choux Shine	Explicit 3 255	☐
Thu	5/22	10:00 am	TBS	Dawson's Creek	Road Trip	Explicit 3 255	☐
Thu	5/22	11:00 am	LIFE	Mad About You	Farmer Buchman	Explicit 3 255	☐
Thu	5/22	2:00 pm	TNN	Star Trek: The Next Generation	Elementary, Dear Data	Explicit 3 255	☐
Thu	5/22	5:00 pm	SCIFI	Knight Rider	Knight of the Phoenix	Explicit 3 255	☐

TiVo Web Project – TCL – v1.9.4

/Main Menu/ /Info/ /Logos/ /Logs/ /Mail/ /MFS/ /Phone/ /Resource Editor/ /Screen/ /Search/ /Theme/ /User Interface/ /Web Remote/ /Restart/

Delete Shows

Figure 5-16. Scheduled Suggestions List, as displayed by TiVoWeb

Note that this list is slightly different than if you click on "Suggestions" from the *User Interface* menu. That web page displays everything your TiVo is considering, whereas this page shows what your TiVo has actually committed to recording.

Deleting Scheduled Recordings

HACK #68

TiVoWeb enables you to remove scheduled recordings from both the To Do List and TiVo's internal Scheduled Suggestions.

Notice the checkboxes next to the episode names (see Figure 5-15 and Figure 5-16) in both the *To Do List* and the *Scheduled Suggestions List*? In both cases, these checkboxes are used to delete shows from the list. Simply click the checkboxes associated with programs that you want to cancel, scroll down to the bottom of the screen, and click the Delete Shows button. TiVoWeb will pop up a confirmation screen, as shown in Figure 5-17. Click Yes to cancel the recording.

Date		Time	Program	Episode	Delete
Wed	5/21	10:00 pm	Sorority Life		☑
Wed	5/21	10:30 pm	Fraternity Life	How to Lose a Pledge in 10 Days: Welcome to Hell, Part 2	☑

TiVo Web Project – TCL – v1.9.4

/Main Menu/ /Info/ /Logos/ /Logs/ /Mail/ /MFS/ /Phone/ /Resource Editor/ /Screen/ /Search/ /Theme/ /User Interface/ /Web Remote/ /Restart/

Delete the following:?

Yes No

Figure 5-17. Deleting a scheduled recording

Undeleting Recordings

#69

So you've become a little trigger-happy and accidentally deleted something your spouse or roommate has asked you to keep. Reclaim recently deleted recordings before TiVo does away with them permanently.

Deleting a television program puts the show into the TiVo equivalent of limbo; while not actually deleted immediately, the show is effectively deleted, since it is no longer visible on your *Now Playing List*. In actuality, the location on the hard drive where the show lives is simply marked as available for reclamation; at any moment, TiVo can overwrite it with a new recording. This leaves you a small window of opportunity to reclaim that soon-to-be-lost show you deleted just a few minutes ago. But the window closes quickly, so don't expect to find that episode of *World News Tonight* you recorded three months ago still somewhere on your hard drive.

Just because TiVo doesn't expose the deleted program through its menus doesn't mean that TiVo doesn't have a handle on it; it very much does, as does TiVoWeb.

From the TiVoWeb main page or the top-of-the-page navigation bar, navigate to *User Interface → Deleted Shows*. Most of the time, TiVoWeb will report that you have "No shows available for undelete," but every so often you'll get lucky and see a screen like the one in Figure 5-18.

To actually undelete the show, just click on the recycling icon next to it. TiVoWeb will ask you if you are sure you want to undelete it. Click Yes, and that show will be added to your *To Do List* and removed from your *Deleted Shows* list.

TiVo Web Project – TCL – v1.9.4

/Main Menu/ /Info/ /Logos/ /Logs/ /Mail/ /MFS/ /Phone/ /Resource Editor/ /Screen/
/Search/ /Theme/ /User Interface/ /Web Remote/ /Restart/

Program	Episode	Date	
Family Guy	And the Wiener Is ...	Sun	5/18
Dawson's Creek	Kiss	Mon	5/19
Knight Rider	Knight of the Rising Sun	Mon	5/19
Friends	The One Where Chandler Crosses the Line	Mon	5/19
ABC World News Tonight	No Episode Title	Mon	5/19
Friends	The One Where Rachel Is Late	Mon	5/19
Late Night With Conan O'Brien	No Episode Title	Tue	5/20
Gilmore Girls	Those Are Strings, Pinocchio	Tue	5/20

To undelete a show click the icon next to its name

Figure 5-18. The shows available for undeletion

Renaming Recordings

#70 Amuse yourself and entertain your friends by editing show titles, episode names, and program descriptions.

You've probably dreamed of starring in a movie with Audrey Hepburn. Thanks to TiVoWeb's Edit Program functionality (*User Interface → Now Showing → Episode Title → Edit Program*), you can edit the title of a show, name of a particular episode, even the program description, to include your name. Make yourself the guest on *Late Night with Conan O'Brien* (see Figure 5-19), and watch your friends' eyes open with amazement.

Once you've made all the changes you'd like, just hit the Save button, pick up your TiVo remote, and surf to the *Now Playing List* and recording details screen to see your changes reflected.

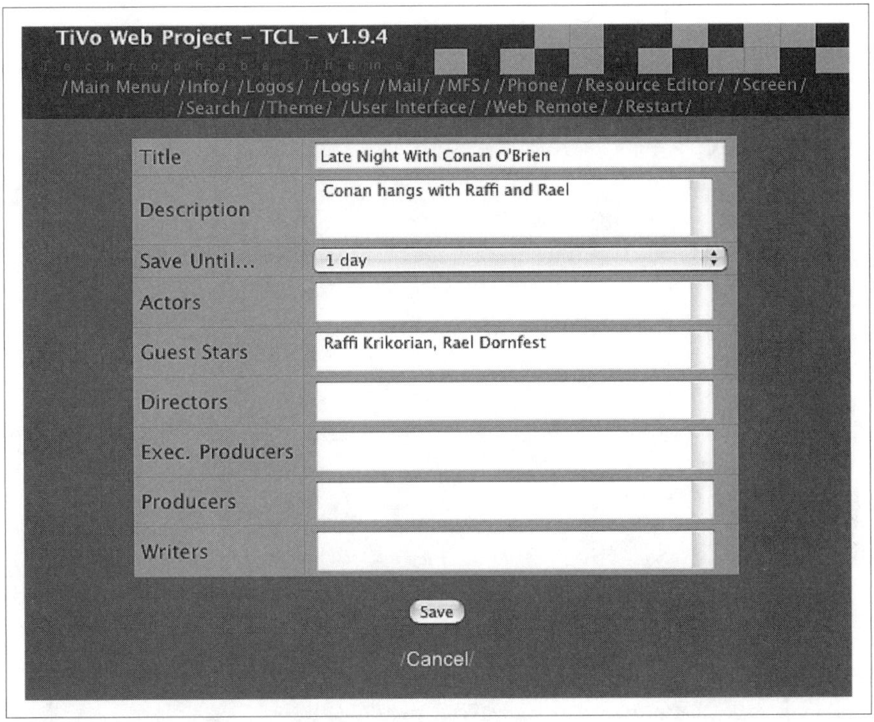

Figure 5-19. Editing the description of a recording

Editing Season Passes

#71

What TiVoWeb interface would be complete without the ability to manipulate your Season Passes?

TiVoWeb provides a full interface for manipulating existing Season Passes, whether they were originally set up via the TiVo television interface or TiVoWeb. From the TiVoWeb main screen or toolbar, navigate to *User Interface → Season Pass* for a list of your Season Passes. Figure 5-20 shows mine.

For each individual show in the list, you can edit the Season Pass parameters by clicking the icon next to a program name. You have full control over the recording quality, how long to keep episodes on your TiVo, whether to record repeats, and other Season Pass options found in the standard TiVo interface. Unfortunately, as of this writing, the only thing that the TiVoWeb interface cannot do is reorder the Season Passes; that much you are going to have to do from the remote control.

TiVo Web Project - TCL - v1.9.4

/Main Menu/ /Info/ /Logos/ /Logs/ /Mail/ /MFS/ /Phone/ /Resource Editor/ /Screen/ /Search/
/Theme/ /User Interface/ /Web Remote/ /Restart/

Pri	Title	Channel	KAM	Show Type
1	Dawson's Creek	WLVI	5	First Run
2	Alias	WCVB	5	First Run
3	Gilmore Girls	WLVI	5	Repeats & FR
4	24	WFXT	5	First Run
5	The West Wing	WHDH	5	First Run
6	Enterprise	WSBK	5	First Run
7	Friends	WHDH	5	First Run
8	ER	WHDH	5	First Run

To edit a season pass click the icon next to its name

Figure 5-20. TiVoWeb's Season Pass page

Emulating the TiVo Remote

HACK #72

TiVoWeb sports a working image map of a TiVo remote control that you can actually use to control your TiVo.

Cat got your remote? If so, for all but the latest models (the Series 2 DirecTiVo features a rudimentary control panel on the box itself) you're TiVo-less for the foreseeable future. Sure, you can purchase another at the TiVo Store (*http://store.tivo.com/Search.bok?category=Accessories*), but what will you do in the meantime?

While at first blush it may seem rather asinine, TiVoWeb's Web Remote (choose *Web Remote* from the main screen or toolbar) might just save primetime. Web Remote is fully functional, clickable, image-mapped picture of your TiVo remote control (see Figure 5-21). And that's your own remote control, mind you, not just a generic model; TiVoWeb actually goes to the trouble of choosing the right image for the right TiVo model.

If you click one of the buttons on this page, your TiVo will react precisely as it would have if you'd hit the respective remote control button. If you click the picture of the TiVo button while you're watching a television show, your

TiVo will whisk you away to TiVo Central. Press the **Power** button (for those TiVos that have it) to turn off your PVR.

Those with an aversion to mousing around with this faux remote can control their TiVo from the comfort of their very own computer keyboard. Through the magic of JavaScript, the *Web Remote* page captures keystrokes and translates them into remote control button presses. Table 5-1 summarizes the supported keystrokes and their associated remote control buttons.

Table 5-1. The TiVoWeb keystrokes and their associated remote control buttons

Keystroke	TiVo remote control button
Up arrow or Enter	▶
Right arrow or]	⏩
Left arrow or [	⏪
Spacebar or P	⏸
Down arrow or A	⏭
/ or ackspace	↻

At the time of this writing, this hack works only with certain browsers—Internet Explorer and Mozilla.

Emulating TiVo's Screens

#73 TiVoWeb's web browser emulation of the current TiVo screen allows you to control TiVo through the traditional interface without being anywhere near your TV.

The Web Remote [Hack #72] allows you to move about through TiVo's menus, but you have to be sitting in front of your television to see what's happening. Not so if you use the Screen emulator.

Select *Screen* from the TiVoWeb main page or toolbar, and you'll find yourself on a page showing all the menu options that are currently being displayed by the TiVo. For example, if your box is displaying the *TiVo Central* screen, then the *Screen* page in your browser will show a menu with the same choices available through the *TiVo Central* screen. Clicking an option will both cause your TiVo to display that menu on the television screen and also show a representation of that menu in your browser. Figure 5-22 shows the Screen emulator in action.

If you click on any link in the Screen emulator, not only will the web page change, but the television screen will also reflect the changes. Those links on the bottom of Figure 5-22 are persistent throughout the entire emulator.

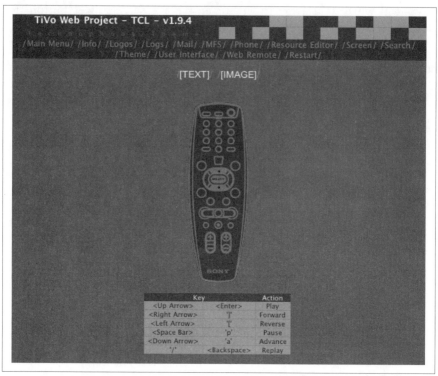

Figure 5-21. The TiVoWeb Web Remote on a Sony SVR-2000

You can always hit the 📺 button, hit the **Back** button, or refresh the screen in case the TiVo has changed out from under the web page.

There are a few limitations to keep in the back of your mind when using this hack:

- TiVo models that can actually be turned off will be unresponsive to the Screen emulation until the TiVo box itself is powered up.

- Search screens (e.g., *Search by Title*) and the Season Pass Manager have not yet been implemented, at least not at the time of this writing. So, while you can surf to these screens via this hack, you will not be able to interact with them. This really shouldn't be much of a problem, though, as you can use some of the other hacks to get at the same functionality.

H A C K   Using TiVo Mail
#74

TiVoWeb turns your web browser into a web mail client so you can read and delete your TiVo mail.

Falsify messages from TiVo, Inc., threatening friends and family that their TiVos will stop recording their favorite shows! Or leave yourself notes some-

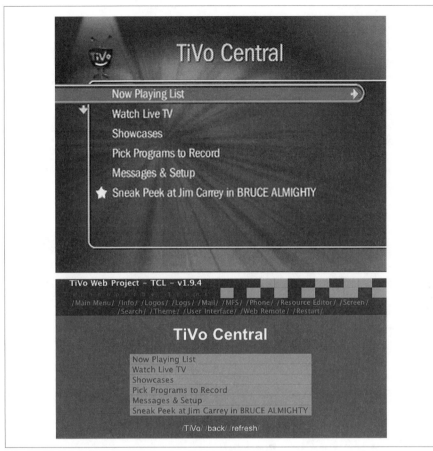

Figure 5-22. Actual TiVo screen and browser emulation

where you will be very likely to read them: right on your television screen. Welcome to TiVo mail.

Before we dive into writing new mail, first let's figure out how to read the mail that TiVo, Inc. might leave you first. Surf to *Mail → View/Delete Existing Mail* from the main web page or the menu bar. If your TiVo has mail or messages, you'll be able to read them from here. But, of course, it's hard to test this, right? How often do you get TiVo mail anyway? So, let's create some mail to read first.

Go back to that *Mail* menu and select *Create New Mail*. As shown in Figure 5-23, just enter in the message you want.

When mail pops up on the message board, you get that envelope icon on the *TiVo Central* menu next to "New TiVo Messages & Setup." You've proba-

TiVo Web Project – TCL – v1.9.4

/Main Menu/ /Info/ /Logos/ /Logs/ /Mail/ /MFS/ /Phone/ /Resource Editor/ /Screen/
/Search/ /Theme/ /User Interface/ /Web Remote/ /Restart/

Enter new email message

Priority:	Medium
Destination:	Pre–TiVo Central
Expire:	in 2 weeks
Subject:	Warning
From:	TiVo
Body:	Warning, Raffi – We at TiVo have been noticing that your television watching habits are horrendous. Starting effectively, we are dropping your TiVo subscription as we are just too embarassed to have you as a customer.

Send Mail

Figure 5-23. Leaving a TiVo message destined for Pre-TiVo Central and forging it from TiVo

bly already seen the envelope icon used for channel lineup changes and the like. The more exciting way to send a message—also a way to force the message to come up—is to post the message to "Pre-TiVo Central," as this is bound to get the TiVo user's attention. When somebody hits the 🏆 button, this message is going to come up on the screen first (see Figure 5-24). Just be sure to delete the message; otherwise, it will just keep coming up.

HACK #75 Changing Channel Logos

Fiddle with the channel logos shown in the *Now Playing List* and program info bars.

While flipping through channels or browsing the *Now Playing List*, you'll notice that certain programs sport the logo of the channel from which they were recorded. On my TiVo, these are usually network channels like NBC and specialty channels like the Discovery Channel. These channel logos are stored on the TiVo itself, and TiVoWeb exposes access to all those logos and the facilities to assign them.

Navigate to the *Logos* menu (either from the main TiVoWeb screen or the toolbar). You should see your entire channel lineup, with logos associated with some of the channels. Figure 5-25 shows a typical channel lineup with some channel logos. The first column of logos are those seen in the black information bar that overlays either the recorded or the live program, and

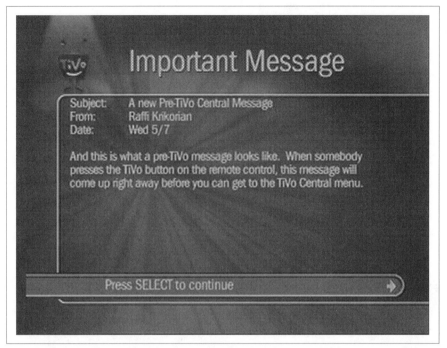

Figure 5-24. The display of the message sent in Figure 5-23.

the second column are the images that you see in the *Now Playing List* next to the episode titles.

Browsing the Available Logos

Before we do anything else, let's take a quick look at all the logos that the TiVo already has on it. Don't worry, we won't change anything yet. We are just going to poke around to see what's there.

Click the Change link associated with the first channel in the list. The logo chooser page will list all the logos available to you (see Figure 5-26). The first group contains the channel logos, and the second contains the logos for the *Now Playing List*. Quite a few of them, no? It's curious they are not assigned in the first place.

Assigning a Logo

Let's try assigning a logo to a channel. Find a logo on the list for a channel that you know you receive but which doesn't currently appear to have an assigned logo. In my case, ABC doesn't have an assigned logo, even though I see it among the available channel logos. Back up to the *Logos* page—that

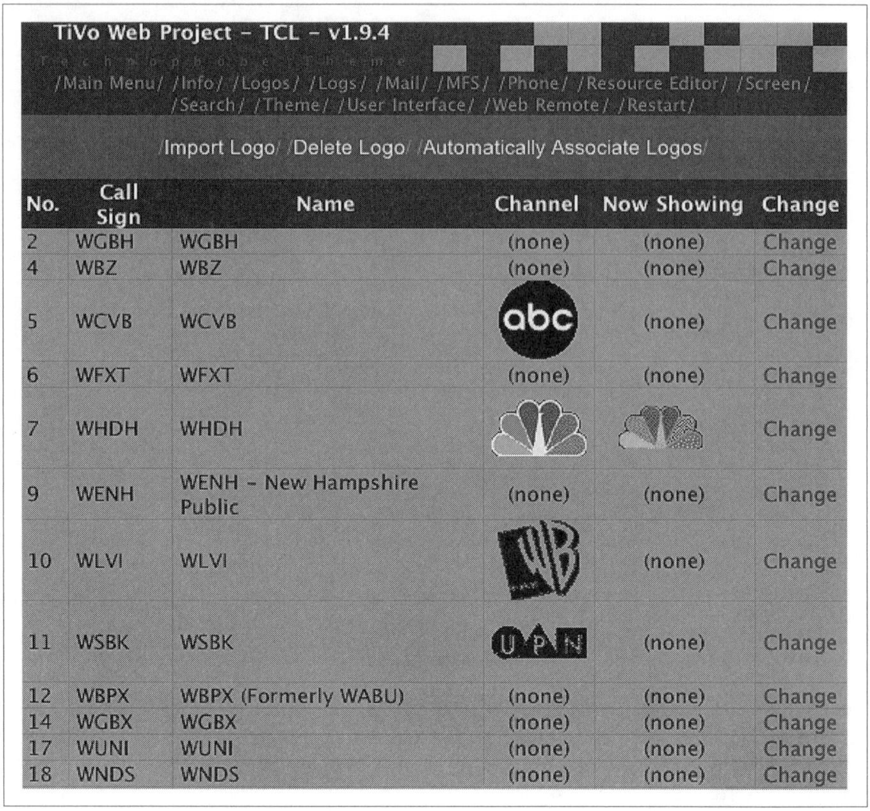

TiVo Web Project - TCL - v1.9.4

/Main Menu/ /Info/ /Logos/ /Logs/ /Mail/ /MFS/ /Phone/ /Resource Editor/ /Screen/ /Search/ /Theme/ /User Interface/ /Web Remote/ /Restart/

/Import Logo/ /Delete Logo/ /Automatically Associate Logos/

No.	Call Sign	Name	Channel	Now Showing	Change
2	WGBH	WGBH	(none)	(none)	Change
4	WBZ	WBZ	(none)	(none)	Change
5	WCVB	WCVB	abc	(none)	Change
6	WFXT	WFXT	(none)	(none)	Change
7	WHDH	WHDH			Change
9	WENH	WENH - New Hampshire Public	(none)	(none)	Change
10	WLVI	WLVI	WB	(none)	Change
11	WSBK	WSBK	UPN	(none)	Change
12	WBPX	WBPX (Formerly WABU)	(none)	(none)	Change
14	WGBX	WGBX	(none)	(none)	Change
17	WUNI	WUNI	(none)	(none)	Change
18	WNDS	WNDS	(none)	(none)	Change

Figure 5-25. Channel logos associated with your channel lineup

listing of all the channels you receive—and click the Change link next to your ABC affiliate (for the Bostonians out there, I have channel 5, WCVB). Now, find the ABC logo, point, and click. TiVoWeb should redirect you back to the main *Logos* page, and you should now see the logo next to your ABC channel. I have only an ABC channel logo; my *Now Showing List* logo is listed as "(empty)." Of course, if your TiVo does not have the ABC logo available to it, you can always substitute another in its place.

Unfortunately, before you see the logo appear on the TiVo itself, you are going to have to reboot your machine. Be sure that your TiVo is not recording anything before you reboot (some of you might have to reach around back and pull the plug). Wait a second or two for the spinning of the hard drives to die down, and then plug the cord back in. When your TiVo comes back up, go to live TV and surf your way to the ABC channel. On the top-right of your screen, you should see the logo you chose. Figure 5-27 shows my new ABC logo, now appearing on the information bar.

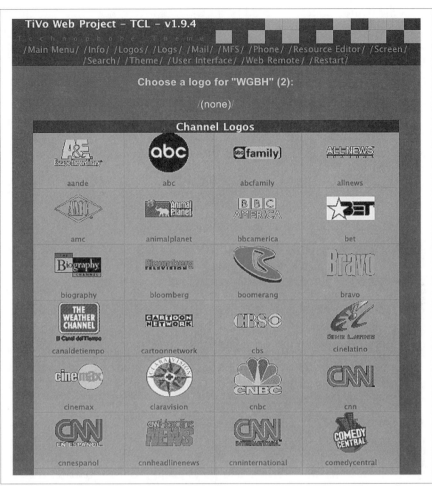

Figure 5-26. Some of the available channel logos

Figure 5-27. Information bar sporting a newly assigned ABC channel logo

HACK #76 Automatically Assigning All Logos

If TiVo already has all these logos on board, why doesn't it just use them?

I personally have over 150 program and Now Playing logos already installed on my TiVo, and you probably have somewhere in the same ballpark if you are in the United States. It would be a major inconvenience to have to install each and every logo one at a time using the steps outlined in "Changing Channel Logos" [Hack #75]. Thankfully, TiVoWeb has that functionality already built in.

Toward the top of the *Logos* page, you should notice an Automatically Associate Logos link. Click it. TiVoWeb asks to confirm that you want it to automatically associate the images it has with the appropriate channels. Eyeball the list, just to make sure all seems as it should, and click the Associate button at the bottom. TiVoWeb will do all the association for you fairly quickly.

Of course, you still need to reboot your box to have the new logos appear on the TiVo itself.

Creating Your Own Custom Logos

#77 If you have a creative flair and want your TiVo to have a little more of its own personality, you might try creating your own custom channel logos.

If the default channel logos don't please your artistic eye, or if the one logo you were looking for isn't onboard (Now Playing logos are typically missing), you can simply import our own custom logos to use on your TiVo.

All you need is your favorite graphics application. Find one that can intelligently manipulate palettes and spit out PNG files; Photoshop or the Gimp (*http://www.gimp.org/*) will do just fine.

There are two keys to creating channel logos properly. The first is size/resolution; channel logos must be 65 pixels wide by 55 pixels high, while Now Playing logos are 100 pixels wide by 35 pixels high. The second is the restrictive color palette. Rather than build an appropriate palette, the best route is to open an existing logo in your graphics application and use it as a template for building new ones.

For this example, I have chosen to replace the bland black-and-white MTV logo with a slightly more colorful one I came across on the Web. Load a page on TiVoWeb with a colorful logo on it; NBC is probably the best bet, as most TiVos will already have it installed somewhere on the *Logos* page. Right-click or Control-click on the icon to save it to disk, and then pop open the logo in Photoshop. Then, open the logo you found on the Web and resize it so that it fits within the NBC logo's bounding box, as shown in Figure 5-28 with my new MTV logo. Erase the NBC logo with the eraser tool (a Select All and Delete should also do just fine). Next, copy and paste the new logo in its place. The act of pasting the new logo into the old NBC image causes the palette to be remapped, which is exactly what we want it to do.

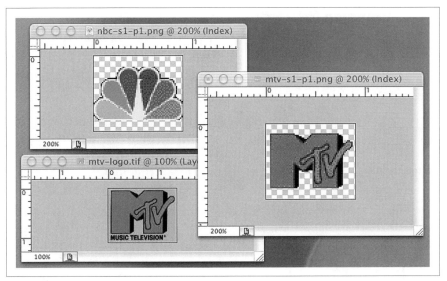

Figure 5-28. Using the existing NBC logo to create the new, custom, color-mapped MTV logo in Photoshop

Creating the Now Playing logo is done in the same way.

 Pay attention to properly centering the image inside the bounding box.

That done, you should save the file, naming it according to the following conventions: use the channel initials and *–s1-p1* for channel logos, and use *-s2-p2* for Now Playing logos. Be sure to assign the right extension: *.png*. For example, I named my files *mtv-s1-p1.png* and *mtv-s2-p2.png*. Save the file as a noninterlaced PNG.

Finally, we are ready to make the switch. Navigate TiVoWeb once again to the *Logos* page, click the Import Logo link at the top, and click the Choose File button. You'll be prompted for custom files to upload; select one of the files you just created and click the Import button to send it to your TiVo. You'll have to do this for both the channel and Now Playing logo files.

TiVoWeb now knows about these custom logos, and you can associate them [Hack #75] with any channel you choose.

Dropping New Extensions into TiVoWeb

#78   TiVoWeb is more than just a web server; it's an application server. Extending
its functionality is as simple as dropping a module into the right directory.

One really great feature of TiVoWeb is the simplicity of adding more functionality. Think of this as "hacking the hack."

Every item you see on the main screen is actually linked to something called
a *module*. If you meander over to */var/hack/tivoweb-tcl/modules* on your
TiVo, you should see *itcl* files, reminiscent of each of TiVoWeb's menu
items: *ui.itcl* controls the *User Interface*, *search.itcl* administers requests to
the *Search* page, and so on.

If you find a module that you want to load into TiVoWeb and run (unfortunately, there is no master list, so you'll just have to keep an eye on bulletin
boards like *http://www.tivocommunity.com*), just drop the file into the */var/
hack/tivoweb-tcl/modules* directory and select *Restart → Quick Reload* from
TiVoWeb's main screen. This asks TiVoWeb to restart and load any new
modules. Once that's done, you'll see any new menu item associated with
the module among TiVoWeb's menus.

Personally, I really like the *Now Playing with Sort and Folders* and
DisplayText modules, which we'll take a look at now.

Now Playing with Sort and Folders

One of the biggest problems associated with adding hard drive space to your
TiVo (see Chapter 2) is that the *Now Playing List* quickly becomes unman-
ageable. The ability to sort the list on the television **[Hack #10]** or in the
TiVoWeb helps, but sometimes it's just not general enough. This is where
LJ's *Now Playing with Sort and Folders* TiVoWeb module (*http://www.ljs.
nildram.co.uk/tivo.html*) comes in.

LJ's module allows you to create folders to sort your recorded shows into.
By default, all episodes fall into an *All Programs* folder, in which you can not
only sort as your TiVo does (all shows are sorted by recording date, with the
recommended shows at the end), by expiration date, or alphabetically, but
you can also sort by duration and genre.

Creating new folders is like adding your own custom genres to the television shows you record. What if you could bring up your TiVoWeb and ask
it to display only shows that you classify as "Sunday morning favorites"? In
the language of LJ's module, you just create a *Sunday morning favorites*
folder and assign a couple of television shows to it. Later, when you come
back to TiVoWeb, you can access the module to search and browse through
that folder.

Installation of LJ's module shows just how easy it is to install TiVoWeb modules. Download *folders.itcl* from his site and upload it to your TiVo. I suggest you just use your web browser to get a copy of the *itcl* file, and then use the TiVo FTP server [Hack #55] to move the file to your */var/hack/tivoweb-tcl/modules* directory on the TiVo. *Restart → Quick Reload* will coerce the server to reload all its modules, and that's it!

Go to TiVoWeb's main screen, and you should see the new link in the menu and menu bar, as shown in Figure 5-29. Cool, huh?

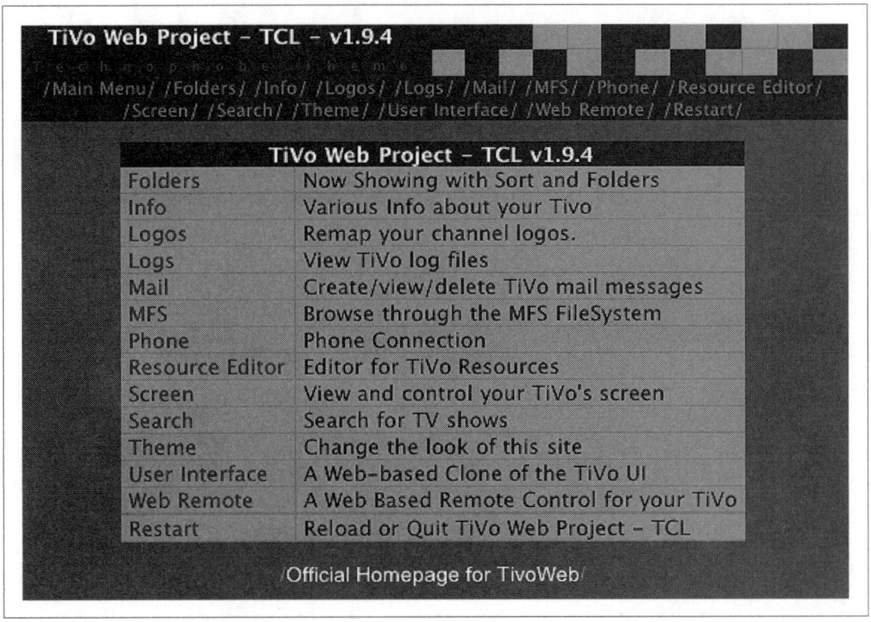

Figure 5-29. TiVoWeb home page, with LJ's Now Playing with Sorts and Folders module installed

DisplayText

What if you could have a really simple web interface for putting text on the screen? One *DisplayText* TiVoWeb module coming right up!

First, though, you'll need to be sure that you have installed *newtext2osd* [Hack #41]. Then, grab Gary Davis's *DisplayText* module from *http://www. webguild.com/tivo/default.aspx*, and extract the *displaytext.itcl* file into the */var/hack/tivoweb-tcl/modules* directory, just as described for the *Now Playing with Sorts and Folders* module. Reload TiVoWeb to have the *DisplayText* item show up in the menus.

Select *DisplayText* from TiVoWeb's home page or menu bar, and you'll be presented the simple form shown in Figure 5-30. Fill out the form, click the Display Text button, and poof!—the text you typed pops up on your television set. Won't that be a surprise to your supposedly geek-worthy friends watching TV? The *DisplayText* module allows you to type in the text, positioning, and colors into a web page and then display it on the television, all with a press of a button.

TiVo Web Project – TCL – v1.9.4

/Main Menu/ /DisplayText/ /Info/ /Logos/ /Logs/ /Mail/ /MFS/ /Phone/ /Resource Editor/
/Screen/ /Search/ /Theme/ /User Interface/ /Web Remote/ /Restart/

Enter Text Message and Parameters

Text Message:			
Delay:	30		
X Position:	0	Y Position:	0
FG Color:	153	BG Color:	1

Display Text

Figure 5-30. The DisplayText module

Starting TiVoWeb with TiVo

HACK #79

You certainly don't want to have to start TiVoWeb from the command line every time you reboot your TiVo. Instead, have it start up when TiVo boots.

Getting the TiVoWeb server to start automatically when you boot your TiVo itself is just a matter of adding the right invocation to the initialization system.

You'll need command-line access to your TiVo [Hacks #30, #52]. Once you're logged in, be sure that the root partition is mounted read/write:

```
mount -o remount,rw /
```

Next, you'll simply append the same command used to start TiVoWeb [Hack #65] manually to the startup script, */etc/rc.d/rc.sysinit*, like so:

```
echo "/var/hack/tivoweb-tcl/tivoweb" | cat /etc/rc.d/rc.sysinit
```

To commit your changes, remount the filesystem as read-only:

```
mount -o remount,ro /
```

Reboot your TiVo. After you get past the *Almost there* startup screen, TiVoWeb should be up and running and accessible through your web browser.

Putting Your TiVo on the Web

All your TiVoWeb usage thus far has probably been done from the comfort of your own home network. But the true magic lies in reaching your TiVo from anywhere in the world.

You're probably itching to put your TiVo on the Web so that it can be accessed from anywhere in the world. Otherwise, why would you go through the trouble of web-enabling your TiVo box, rather than simply standing in front of your television set, remote control in hand?

While you have about all you need to put your TiVo on the Web, beware of the dragons there. Simply giving your TiVo one of your broadband account's static IP addresses and opening it to the world is fraught with dangers. While I have been crowing the TiVo as a Linux PC's little brother, I've been glazing over the fact that the TiVo's networking is not quite up to the level of its big brother. The simplest denial-of-service attack against your TiVo can take it out of commission. There's no built-in firewall, and it has not been battle-hardened against network intrusions. Authentication—allowing only discriminating access to your programming—is primitive at best.

And this assumes you even have the ability to run servers on your broadband connection, know something about IP addresses and port-forwarding, and so forth.

For these reasons, it's best to leave your TiVo behind your home network's firewall. Just access it from the inside, where things are safe and friendly.

Where's the fun in that?

There are three real options for getting your small box to a place that the Web can see it, and each option has its pros and cons. Think of these options as a continuum, trying to balance the simplest to setup with the most secure infrastructure.

Port Forwarding and Security by Obscurity

If you have a broadband router (DSL or cable modem) in your home that can connect multiple computers to the Internet, chances are that your router can do something called *port-forwarding*. This means telling your router to route requests received on a particular port (think of channels) to a particular computer on your home network.

You can use this functionality to route requests on a particular port to your networked TiVo. Choose a port number that you will remember but that most people won't guess; my personal favorites are numbers like 8080, 8008, or the more obscure 8013, to pick one at random. Tell your router to forward all such requests to port 80—the standard web server port on which TiVoWeb runs—on your TiVo box, and access TiVoWeb by pointing your web browser at your router's IP address and port you chose to forward.

Bear in mind that security by obscurity is in no way real security. If someone guesses your IP address and port at which your TiVo is reachable, they're in like Flynn.

TiVoWeb's Rudimentary Password Protection

For a little more protection from somebody who stumbles upon your Internet-accessible TiVo and decides to queue up lots of television shows for you to watch, TiVoWeb does have some rudimentary password-control mechanisms built into it. Set up your TiVo and router for port-forwarding, but then coerce your TiVoWeb to ask for a password every time.

To assign a username/password pair to your TiVoWeb server, you need to change the first two lines of your *tivoweb.cfg* file in the */var/hack/tivoweb-tcl* directory:

```
Username =
Password =
```

You actually need to assign a username and a password on these two lines. If you have an editor on your TiVo [Hack #38], [Hack #39] then you can just edit that file directly. No editor? No problem! Just execute the following commands on your TiVo:

```
bash-2.02# cd /var/hack/tivoweb-tcl
bash-2.02# echo Username = raffik >> tivoweb.cfg.hold
bash-2.02# echo Password = pass >> tivoweb.cfg.hold
bash-2.02# cat tivoweb.cfg | tail -5 >> tivoweb.cfg.hold
bash-2.02# mv tivoweb.cfg.hold tivoweb.cfg
```

But you probably want to change the username/password pair from raffik/ pass to something else. The preceding commands create a temporary file named *tivoweb.cfg.hold*, whose first two lines are the username and password lines. Now, if you look at the *tivoweb.cfg* file, you'll notice that it is seven lines long. The second-to-last line will append to the *tivoweb.cfg.hold* file the last five lines of *tivoweb.cfg*. Good to go. Now, just copy your new file over the old one.

Once you have made these changes, reset your TiVoWeb (*Restart* → *Quick Reload*). If all goes well, the next time you try to access TiVoWeb, you'll be prompted for a username and password before being able to go any further.

Proxy Pass-Through with Apache

Now, while port-forwarding with passwords works and is probably safe, it still exposes the TiVoWeb and the TiVo itself directly to the vagaries of the Internet—something that should not necessarily be done lightly. In almost every case, it is probably OK to do so. But if you want to be extra secure, or if you are running PPP over the serial port, then setting up the Apache web server (downloadable from *http://www.apache.org*) to proxy pass-through is the way for you. In reality, any modern web server should be able to be configured for proxy pass-throughs.

Doing this will certainly take more hardware than the other two options. You are going to need another computer somewhere on your network that is prepared to be exposed to the Internet. That machine will accept all messages on the TiVo's behalf and then make the TiVo's request on the behalf of the requestor on the Internet. Because the computer's TCP/IP stack is more robust, it can handle erroneous or malicious connections. The computer processes connections that it deems as OK, and then it establishes its own connections to the TiVo (which are almost guaranteed not to be malicious) and passes the data back and forth.

Think of this process like having a body guard: your body guard makes sure that malicious people do not get to you. Your bodyguard provides all the protection, but every once in a while he is going to get a question about you that he cannot answer. He will then turn to you, ask the question, and relay the answer to who ever asked the question. Yeah, Apache is like the TiVo's bodyguard.

The following instructions assume you have Apache up and running on a computer on your home network and have port-forwarded requests on some port to this computer. I also assume that you already have Apache serving web pages from inside your network to the rest of the Internet.

We are going to use *mod_proxy*, a fairly standard Apache extension module designed to handle connection forwarding.

Edit your Apache server's *httpd.conf* file, commonly found at */etc/httpd/conf* under Unix, */etc/httpd* on Mac OS X, and in the *conf* subdirectory of your Apache installation on Windows. Make sure the following two lines are uncommented (i.e., they are not preceded by a # character at the beginning of the line):

```
LoadModule proxy_module    modules/libproxy.so
...
AddModule mod_proxy.c
```

These two directives will have Apache load the proxy module at startup.

Now, we need to map TiVoWeb into a portion of your Apache server's namespace. For example, if you can reach your web server on the Net as *http://your.web.server*, then you want to connect to your TiVoWeb installation by pointing your web browser to *http://your.web.server/tivoweb*. Obviously, your computer has a different name than *your.web.server*, and you might want it to have a different directory at the end of the URL.

Add the following lines to the end of your *httpd.conf* file, but replace *tivo* in *http://tivo* with the IP address of your TiVo, and replace */tivoweb* with the directory where you want it to be:

```
ProxyPass /tivoweb http://tivo/
ProxyPassReverse /tivoweb http://tivo/
```

Lastly, we need to tell TiVoWeb that it is operating behind Apache in a specific directory. Again, the magic is in the *tivoweb.cfg* file. Either edit it using an editor on your TiVo to set the Prefix line to the name of the directory, or run the following commands on your TiVo:

```
bash-2.02# cd /var/hack/tivoweb-tcl
bash-2.02# head -3 tivoweb.cfg tivoweb.cfg.hold
bash-2.02# echo Prefix = tivoweb tivoweb.cfg.hold
bash-2.02# cat tivoweb.cfg | tail -3 tivoweb.cfg.hold
bash-2.02# mv tivoweb.cfg.hold tivoweb.cfg
```

Restart TiVoWeb and your Apache server. Now, all requests going to *http://your.web.server/tivoweb* should bring up TiVoWeb in your browser.

One last thing to consider is the use of Apache's password. In either case, be sure to turn off password protection on TiVoWeb if you turned it on, as it'll be prompting Apache, the middle man, for the username/password.

Password-protect the */tivoweb* path by adding the following lines to the end of your Apache installation's *httpd.conf* file:

```
<Location /tivoweb>
 AuthType Basic
 AuthName tivo
 AuthUserFile /etc/httpd/passwd
 Require user tivo
</Location>
```

Restart Apache again for this change to take effect.

All that's left is to assign our TiVo user, specified in the aforementioned password-protection directives. Under Unix and Mac OS X, type:

```
% htpasswd -c /etc/httpd/passwd tivo
```

You'll be prompted for a password and then prompted again to confirm it.

Apache will now be password-protecting the */tivoweb* URL and looking for a valid username and password pair from the */etc/httpd/passwd* file before allowing access to TiVoWeb.

See Also

For more information on how to restrict access under Apache, see the *mod_auth* documentation (*http://httpd.apache.org/docs/mod/mod_auth.html*).For more on the Apache Web server, you might want to consult *Apache: The Definitive Guide* (*http://www.oreilly.com/catalog/apache3/*).

## CHAPTER SIX

Working with Videos
Hacks 81–87

Your TiVo is great at making all the television you watch "yours." But it's yours only insofar as it's the programming you most wanted on your television—and nowhere else. Perhaps you'd like to archive all those shows taking up valuable hard drive space, and saving them to VCR tape just isn't something you can bring yourself to do. What about that six-hour plane ride next week; what could possibly be better than a mix of your favorite sitcoms and soaps to keep you company? All of this requires somehow sucking that programming right out of your TiVo and working with the videos directly.

Thankfully, TiVo records everything to MPEG-2 format on its hard drive or drives. All that remains is to extract those videos, convert them to something more appropriate, and pass them to your basement PC's DVD burner for archiving or laptop for taking on the road with you.

Limitations

There are a couple of constraints on video extraction, the first of which may stop you in your tracks, while the latter two are just a matter of a little hackery, sufficient bandwidth, and storage space.

Series 1 only

Unfortunately, while video is kept "in the clear" on Series 1 TiVo units and is eminently extractable, the newer Series 2s scramble the video, keeping only encrypted versions on the hard drive. This means that Series 2 users are out of luck when it comes to video extraction.

Bandwidth

Don't bother trying the hacks in this chapter if you don't have a high-speed network connection running to your TiVo [Hack #49]. The files that we're talking about here are monstrous, and getting them out—even via a 115-kilobaud connection to your serial port [Hack #47]—is just not an option. If you were even contemplating sending one hour of television over the serial port to your PC, that's about one day's transfer time. Note that we're not talking about your network connection to the outside world; it's the connection between your TiVo and PC (and, indeed, other TiVos in your home) that matters.

Storage space

Video takes an inordinate amount of storage space on your hard drive or removable media like a writeable DVD. The rule of thumb is that one hour on your TiVo takes about one gigabyte of storage on your hard drive.

Pulling Video from Your TiVo over FTP

#81 Extract recorded television shows from TiVo's Media File System using *mfs_ftp* and your garden-variety FTP application.

By this time you should be pretty comfortable FTPing [Hack #55] stuff back and forth to your TiVo. Most of your file transfers have, up to now, been one way and rather simple—moving small files and software to your network-enabled TiVo [Hack #49]. Let's raise the bar a little and siphon some of that recorded television programming out of the TiVo.

No matter how hard you look, you're not going to find those recorded television shows anywhere on your TiVo's filesystem [Hack #29]. The reason is simple: you're not seeing the entire filesystem.

TiVo's hard drives are organized in two ways: there's the standard Linux filesystem you are seeing when you telnet in [Hack #52], and then there is the Media Filesystem (MFS) that actually holds all the recordings. The regular old FTP server (*tivoftpd*) doesn't have access to the MFS, but Riley Cassel's *mfs_ftp* (*http://alt.org/forum/index.php?t=getfile&id=81*) does.

Installing mfs_ftp

Before getting *mfs_ftp* going, you'll need to get a hold of a few support programs: *mfs_stdinsert*, *mfs_tarstream*, *mfs_stream*, and *mfs_export*. Thankfully, all of these programs are available in one convenient package at *http://alt.org/forum/index.php?t=getfile&id=86&rid=24*.

Move the entire *mfs_ftp_support_files.tar.gz* archive over to your TiVo, drop it into */var*, and unpack it:

```
bash-2.02# cd /var
bash-2.02# gzip -d mfs_ftp_support_files.tar.gz
bash-2.02# cpio -i -H tar -create-directories < mfs_ftp_support_files.tar
bash-2.02# cd mfs_ftp
bash-2.02# chmod 755 mfs_* ftpf
```

I know I've been making a habit of putting all our hacks into
/var/hack, but the authors wrote this hack to be different and
everything is based in the */var/mfs_ftp* directory.

Once they're all across and in place, kill off your standard FTP daemon.
There is no pretty, built-in way to shut down the FTP daemon, so you'll
have to do it the Unix way. Figure out the process ID of the FTP server
(*tivoftpd*) and kill it:

```
bash-2.02# ps auxw | grep tivoftpd
root    1220 0.0 0.0   0   0 ? SW  01:21  0:00 /var/hack/bin/tivoftpd
root    1233 0.0 0.0   0   0 p0 SW  01:21  0:00 grep tivoftpd
bash-2.02# kill -9 1220
```

You don't have to kill off *tivoftpd*; you can run it alongside
mfs_ftp. They serve different purposes and it may be useful
to have them both running simultaneously. I suggest shutting down *tivoftpd* only so you can use the standard FTP port
in the following examples.

Now start up the *mfs_ftp* daemon , invoking it on the command line, like so:

```
bash-2.02# /var/mfs_ftp/mfs_ftp.tcl 21 &
```

It'll start up, listening on port 21 (the standard FTP port) for incoming connections. If you have the tail Unix utility installed [Hack #34], you can watch
the *msf_ftp* server running, if you're so inclined:

```
bash-2.02# tail -f /var/mfs_ftp/ftp.log
00:00:00 - entering init_mfs_ftp
00:00:01 - entering background
00:00:01 - ping - mfs_ftp running on 127,0,0,1 : 21
00:00:01 - mfs_ftp version 1.2.5.9 - checking tivo system sw
00:00:01 - version 3.0-01-1-010
00:00:01 - setting mfspath to /Recording/NowShowingByClassic
00:00:01 - insert throttle is  0, == 0 ms
00:00:01 - extract throttle is 0, == 0 ms
00:00:01 - entering reset_mfs_ftp
00:00:01 - port 21 control socket initialized - ready for connections
00:00:01 - entering build_dir_LIST
00:00:01 - entering update_rec_fsids
00:00:01 - getting current rec_fsids list
00:00:01 - rec_fsids doesn't match cached_rec_fsids, deleting cached info
00:00:01 - entering build_rec_list
00:00:01 - from mfs "/Recording/NowShowingByClassic"
.................................................................
00:00:07 - build_rec_LIST complete
```

The tail utility will continue watching the *ftp.log* file, sending updates to the screen as it deals with FTP traffic. Stop tail at any time by pressing Control-C.

A Tour of mfs_ftp's Filesystem

Now that we have the *mfs_ftp* server up and running, use your favorite FTP program to FTP into your TiVo and take a look around. The directory structure of the server is as follows:

txt

Plain text files containing the same information as TiVo's *Now Showing* menu.

xml

Almost the same information as that found in the *txt* directory, this time in XML format. A typical file in this directory—this one representing a *Friends* episode (*1686510 Friends—The One With The Embryos.xml*)— looks something like this:

```
<?xml version="1.0" tivoversion="3.0-01-1-010"?>
<Object type="Recording" id="_top">
 <SubObject type="RecordingPart" id="Part">
  <Begin>0</Begin>
  <CommercialSkipOffset>0</CommercialSkipOffset>
  <End>1313822</End>
 </SubObject>
 <SubObject type="RecordingPart" id="Part">
  <Begin>1314323</Begin>
  <CommercialSkipOffset>0</CommercialSkipOffset>
  <End>1798965</End>
 </SubObject>
 <RecordQuality>75</RecordQuality>
 <SubObject type="Showing" id="Showing">
  <Bits>35</Bits>
  <Date>12198</Date>
  <Duration>1800</Duration>
 <Object type="Program" id="Program">
  <Actor>Aniston|Jennifer</Actor>
  <Actor>Cox|Courteney</Actor>
  <Actor>Kudrow|Lisa</Actor>
  <Actor>LeBlanc|Matt</Actor>
  <Actor>Perry|Matthew</Actor>
  <Actor>Schwimmer|David</Actor>
  <AltEpisodeNum>466611</AltEpisodeNum>
  <ColorCode>4</ColorCode>
  <DescLanguage>English</DescLanguage>
  <Description>Phoebe undergoes a procedure so she can serve as a ↵
   surrogate mother.</Description>
  <EpisodeNum>85</EpisodeNum>
  <EpisodeTitle>The One With the Embryos</EpisodeTitle>
  <ExecProducer>Bright|Kevin S.</ExecProducer>
```

```
    <ExecProducer>Kauffman|Marta</ExecProducer>
    <ExecProducer>Crane|David</ExecProducer>
    <Genre>91</Genre>
    <Genre>1002</Genre>
    <GuestStar>Ribisi|Giovanni</GuestStar>
    <GuestStar>Rupp|Debra Jo</GuestStar>
    <IsEpisode>1</IsEpisode>
    <NetworkSource>synd</NetworkSource>
    <OriginalAirDate>10241</OriginalAirDate>
    <Object type="Series" id="Series">
     <Episodic>1</Episodic>
     <Genre>91</Genre>
     <Genre>1002</Genre>
     <ServerId>16645</ServerId>
     <ServerVersion>310</ServerVersion>
     <ThumbData>268633087</ThumbData>
     <Title>Friends</Title>
     <TmsId>SH115127</TmsId>
    </Object>
    <ServerId>16805</ServerId>
    <ServerVersion>42</ServerVersion>
    <ShowType>5</ShowType>
    <SourceType>2</SourceType>
    <Title>Friends</Title>
    <TmsId>EP1151270091</TmsId>
   </Object>
   <Object type="Station" id="Station">
    <Affiliation>WB Affiliate</Affiliation>
    <AffiliationIndex>53</AffiliationIndex>
    <CallSign>WLVI</CallSign>
    <City>Boston</City>
    <Country>United States</Country>
    <DmaName>Boston, MA-Manchester, NH</DmaName>
    <DmaNum>6</DmaNum>
    <FccChannelNum>56</FccChannelNum>
    <LogoIndex>131303</LogoIndex>
    <Name>WLVI</Name>
    <ServerId>1387</ServerId>
    <ServerVersion>16</ServerVersion>
    <TmsId>11659</TmsId>
    <ZipCode>02125</ZipCode>
   </Object>
    <Time>79200</Time>
    <TvRating>4</TvRating>
   </SubObject>
   <StartDate>12198</StartDate>
   <StartTime>79198</StartTime>
   <StopDate>12198</StopDate>
   <StopTime>80999</StopTime>
   <StreamFileSize>720896</StreamFileSize>
   <SubPriority>268633087</SubPriority>
   <UsedBy>1</UsedBy>
  </Object>
```

As you can see, all the metadata about the television program—including the episode description, actors, station on which it was broadcast, and oodles more—is encoded in this file.

ty

Recorded shows are stored as *ty* files, the most appropriate file type from which to extract the videos.

tmf

TiVo Media Format (*tmf*) files are similar to the *ty* variety and are particularly useful for extracting files with an eye to later reinserting them into TiVo.

tyx

Next generation *tmf* files, not yet ready for primetime because the software to use them is not as stable as one would like.

shutdown

More of a trigger than a directory, the very act of navigating into this folder will shut down the *mfs_ftp* server.

phoenix

Like the *shutdown* directory, moving into the *phoenix* directory will restart the server (read: kill off *mfs_ftp* and start a new version in its place). Think "phoenix rising from the ashes"—geek humor again, I'm afraid.

> In actuality, these directories are created on-the-fly by the *mfs_ftp* daemon for your convenience, making browsing the contents of the filesystem that much easier. The real MFS is not packaged nearly as nicely.

Transferring Video Files

Since our goal here is to grab video files over FTP, switch to the *ty* directory and download a television program you're interested in.

> The *mfs_ftp* server supports only one connection at a time. Feel free to create a queue of television shows and configure your FTP client to grab them serially, but don't expect to be able to download more than one program at a time.

Extraction speed can vary quite a bit; some users have reported speeds as slow as 20 KB per second (quite slow and probably a sign of defective hardware), while others have been lucky enough to reach speeds of 1 MB per second and faster. About the only factor you can influence is the speed of the

Ethernet connection; I recommend that Series 1 users get their hands on a TurboNET adapter [Hack #49], with its onboard 100 megabit Ethernet port, and extract either directly to a 100 megabit–enabled PC or Mac or over a 100 megabit network.

Go To

Those extracted *ty* files aren't going to do you much good without a media player [Hack #83] to read them or some way to convert them [Hack #85].

H A C K   Pulling Video from Your TiVo via Web Interface
#82

Clean and simple downloading of recorded shows through your web browser is just a *TiVoWeb* module away.

If you're rather attached to your browser—as I am—and would prefer a nice web interface for downloading recorded TV shows, John Sproull's *MfsStream* module (*http://www.dealdatabase.com/forum/attachment. php?s=&postid=77818*) for TiVoWeb [Hack #65] is for you.

> If you are passing *TiVoWeb* through an Apache proxy (see "Proxy Pass-Through with Apache" in "Putting Your TiVo on the Web" [Hack #80]), the *MfsStream* module won't work for you right out of the box. I'll show you why at the end of this hack.

Grab the *mfsstreamweb98b.zip* archive from the previously mentioned URL and expand it on your PC. The archive contains plenty of files, only a few of which we'll be needing. FTP [Hack #55] the *mfs_stream* file to your TiVo's */var/hack/tivoweb-tcl* directory; this is the program that talks to TiVo's Media Filesystem (MFS), where recorded programming is actually kept.

MfsStream was originally written to send video directly to the command line for capturing in a regular file. What's needed is some way to proxy it, rerouting it to the network. The *tyhttpd* program included in the *MfsStream* archive does just that. Copy it to TiVoWeb's */var/hack/tivoweb-tcl* directory. Lastly, transfer the contents of the *modules* directory (extracted from the archive) to */var/hack/tivoweb-tcl/modules*. These scripts add a new *MfsStream* menu item to *TiVoWeb*.

Let's give it a whirl, shall we? From the command line, launch *tyhttpd*:

```
bash-2.02# /var/hack/tivoweb-tcl/tyhttpd 2000 1 >> /dev/null &
```

This command will run the *ty* file server in the background on port 2000. The 1 specifies the number of streams you can concurrently download off your TiVo. Chances are that you'll never really need any more than the one stream, given the size of the files and how quickly downloading more than one will exhaust available bandwidth.

Restart *TiVoWeb* from its menu and take a gander at the updated home page. As shown in Figure 6-1, you should find a new *MfsStream* menu, listed both on the main list of menus and in the menu bar.

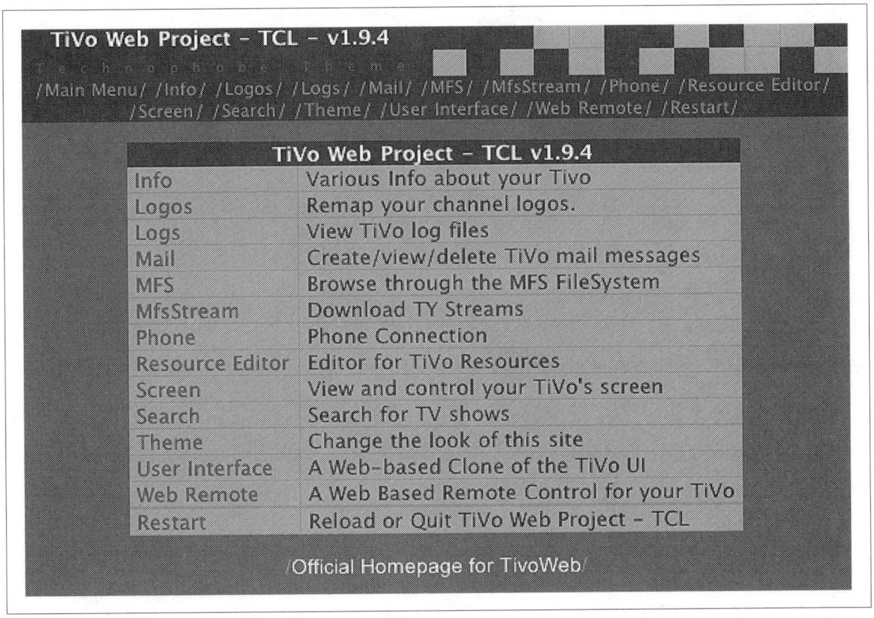

Figure 6-1. The TiVoWeb home page with the new MfsStream module installed

Click the *MfsStream* menu item, and you'll come to a screen that looks a lot like the *Now Showing* list (see Figure 6-2). The difference is your ability to download the show (as *ty* file) simply by clicking on its now-hyperlinked title.

Now that we're done testing and all seems to be working as expected, have *tyhttpd* run automatically at TiVo startup by appending [Hacks #38, #39] the appropriate invocation to */etc/rc.sysinit*. I'm being a little lazy and using the echo command to append the line to *rc.sysinit* without using a text editor:

```
bash-2.02# mount -o remount,rw /
bash-2.02# echo '/var/hack/tivoweb-tcl/tyhttpd 2000 1 >> /dev/null ⏎
&' >> /etc/rc.d/rc.sysinit
bash-2.02# mount -o remount,ro /
```

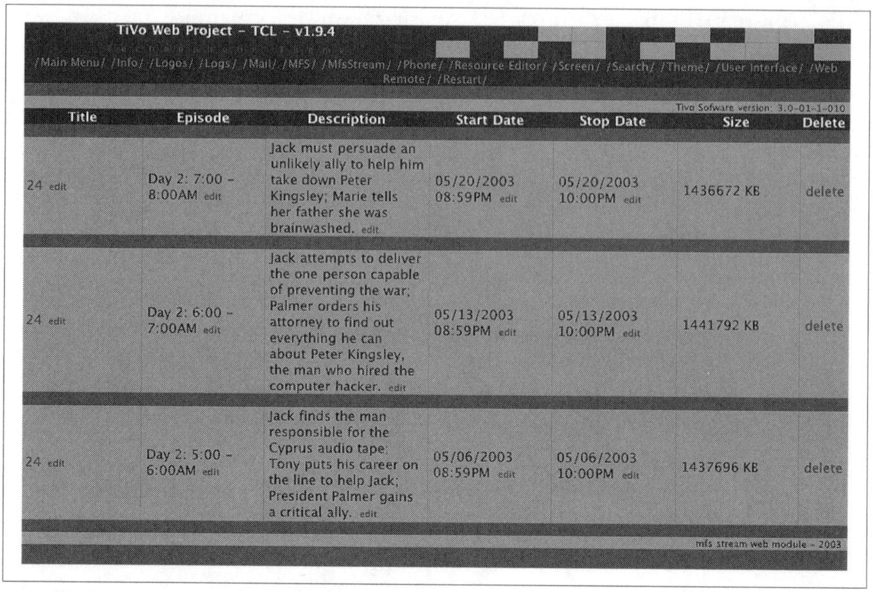

Figure 6-2. Hyperlinked titles for downloading recorded shows at the click of a mouse

MfsStream and Proxying TiVoWeb Through Apache

The heart of the reason why you can't use *MfsStream* when proxying TiVoWeb through Apache is because *tyhttpd* opens its own port instead of using the port that we are already proxying. Assuming your TiVoWeb is running through Apache at *http://tivo.apache.your.domain.com:8080/ tivoweb*, when you click on a program name in the *MfsStream* module, your TiVo starts downloading from something that starts with *http://tivo.apache. your.domain.com:2000/*. Note that *2000*; that's the port that we have set up *tyhttpd* to be running on. But also note that your Apache installation is not proxying that port out. Your web browser is stuck, attempting to make a connection to a port that is refusing connections.

This problem is actually quite easy to fix by asking Apache to forward *tyhttpd*'s port too. Just place the following lines in your Apache server's *httpd.conf* file:

```
NameVirtualHost *
Listen 2000
<VirtualHost *:2000>
ProxyPass / http://tivo:2000/
ProxyPassReverse / http://tivo:2000/
</VirtualHost>
```

This asks your Apache installation to open and listen on port 2000, but then to forward all requests to your TiVo's port 2000, exactly where *tyhttpd* is running.

For more on the Apache Web server, you might want to consult *Apache: The Definitive Guide* (*http://www.oreilly.com/catalog/apache3/*).

Go To

Those extracted *ty* files aren't going to do you much good without a media player [Hack #83] to read them or some way to convert them [Hack #86].

HACK #83 Playing Extracted Video
Now that you do have the video on your computer, what do you do with it?

So, you've extracted a handful of TV shows from TiVo, filling your PC's hard drive with these massive *ty* files. Now, how do you watch them?

As of this writing, there is only one program that can play the *ty* files directly: Chris Wingert's *TiVo MPlayer* (*http://tivo-mplayer.sourceforge.net/*). Based on the original MPlayer (*http://www.mplayerhq.hu/*) movie player for Linux, Wingert's version adds extra code for reading, decoding, and playing back streams in real time. The TiVo MPlayer site provides Windows binaries using Cygwin (*http://www.cygwin.com*), and instructions for compiling the player under Mac OS X and other varieties of Unix .

Working with the Windows version, extract the contents of the ZIP file in WinZip or some file-decompression utility. You're also going to need to work the MS-DOS prompt at this point, because there is no fancy GUI. You won't need Cygwin preinstalled, because Wingert carefully included all the files you need in the ZIP file. However, if you already have Cygwin installed, make sure that the version of *cygwin1.dll* in your installation is current.

To play back an episode of TechTV's *Fresh Gear* from *fresh_gear.ty*, invoke TiVo MPlayer from the command line, like so:

```
C:\Program Files\mplayer> mplayer fresh_gear.ty
```

The show should pop up in a new window and start playing immediately. Use the arrow keys on your keyboard to fast forward and rewind. For full-screen mode, use the –fs command-line argument :

```
C:\Program Files\mplayer> mplayer -fs fresh_gear.ty
```

Once compiled, TiVo MPlayer behaves in the same way under Mac OS X and other Unix platforms.

Streaming Video Directly from TiVo

#84

Why download massive videos and take up local hard drive space when you can stream them right from your TiVo over your home network?

Playing downloaded streams from your TiVo is just one way to use Wingert's TiVo MPlayer [Hack #83]. The whole reason he extended the original MPlayer was to enable you to stream videos right from your TiVo to your PC.

You'll need a program called *vserver* to pull off this hack. Download *http://tivo-mplayer.sourceforge.net/releases/vserver-1.2.tar.gz* and unpack the archive. Inside, you'll find a whole slew of files. Look for a binary called *vserver-ppc-s1-exec*. Move and rename the file to */var/hack/bin/vserver* on your TiVo. Start it up:

```
bash-2.02# ./vserver
waiting for connections on port 8074
```

Launch *MPlayer* as in the previous hack, only this time passing it the URL tivo://*tivo_ip_address*/list, replacing *tivo_ip_address* with the IP address of your TiVo [Hack #51]. That magical tivo URL handler up front (the tivo:// bit) makes sure that MPlayer talks to the *vserver* on the right port with the right protocol. The list bit, as you might imagine, requests a list of available programming. Here, I'm asking my TiVo (at IP address 192.168.0.3) for its *Now Showing* list:

```
C:\Program Files\mplayer> mplayer -quiet -cache 8192⏎
tivo:// 192.168.0.3/1662160
Playing tivo://tivo/list
Listing streams in /Recording/NowShowingByTitle
[1662160][3][24][Day 2: 7:00 - 8:00AM]
[1651148][3][24][Day 2: 6:00 - 7:00AM]
[1636997][3][24][Day 2: 5:00 - 6:00AM]
[1623225][3][24][Day 2: 4:00 - 5:00AM]
[1220239][13][9/11][(null)]
[1670974][2][ABC World News Tonig][(null)]
[700897][4][The Armenians: A Sto][(null)]
[1684169][2][Coming Attractions][(null)]
[1651146][5][Dawson's Creek][All Good Things ... Must Come to an End]
...
```

Those numbers in the first column are the filesystem IDs (FSIDs) for the recorded streams, TiVo's way of indexing recorded videos. They're also used by *vserver* to select a show to stream:

```
C:\Program Files\mplayer> mplayer tivo://192.168.0.3/1662160
```

And up comes the final episode of *24*. To stop playback and quit *MPlayer*, press Control-C on the command line. *mplayer* is unfortunately quite computationally intensive, so the other flags on the command line are about less-ing the load on your PC. -quiet supresses *mplayer*'s output on the command line, giving your PC more computational cycles for the video. The -cache line asks your PC to cache 8 MB of video data at all times while it is playing to protect your PC against the unpredictability of networks

With *vserver* running, you also can extract *ty* streams directly from TiVo using *mplayer* [Hack #85]. On the command line, invoke *mplayer*, specifying an output file and the FSID of the stream you want to extract:

```
$ mplayer -dumpfile out.ty -dumpstream tivo://192.168.0.3/1692481
```

When you're done, don't forget to also kill the *vserver* process on your TiVo with a Control-C.

HACK #85 Converting Extracted Video

Coerce those TiVo *ty* files into a more standard video format.

Video file formats proliferate, but there are a few standards supported by the lion's share of media players, MPEG, DiVX, and AVI being among the most common. TiVo's *ty* files are just not one of them. So, in order to play them just about anywhere, we need to coerce those files into a more standard video format.

You have a couple of options here, both of which have varying degrees success. Both solutions are still under development and have received their fair share of complaints.

MPlayer

If you compiled your own version of TiVo–MPlayer [Hack #83], you also have a copy of the bundled *mencoder* application, a perfectly fine option for simple encoding.

mencoder can take a *ty* file specified on the command line and encode the audio and video using a variety of different codecs. In my opinion, the best tradeoff of quality, space, and resolution is to encode the video using the DiVX 5.0 codec (*http://www.divx.com*) and audio into MP3 using *lame* (*http://lame.sourceforge.net/*). I like to resize the output to 352 by 240 pixels, because that is approximately the resolution of a video CD; anything larger may be a waste, and anything smaller loses information. You can also deinterlace the resulting AVI file at the same time. Instead of transmitting every line on your television at one time, all the odd lines are transmitted first, followed by all the even lines. While this looks fine on a television set, it looks horrendous on a computer screen; deinterlacing cleans that up.

As an example, here I encode an episode of TechTV's *Fresh Gear*:

```
$ mencoder fresh_gear.ty -ovc lavc -lavcopts vcodec=mpeg4↵
-vop scale=352:240,pp=lb -oac mp3lame -o fresh_gear.avi
```

I'm afraid that *mencoder's* command-line options are notoriously convoluted. Specify the appropriate *ty* file first. We're using the audio/video codec libraries to handle the output video. The ovc command-line option specifies which output video codec you want to use—in this case, MPEG4 (DiVX). The vop option says that we'll be toggling the video options; we are rescaling the video and deinterlacing it. Similar to ovc, the oac option controls the output audio codec. We are using lame to do the MP3 encoding of the sound.

After a while, depending on how fast your CPU is, *mencoder* will spit out a file called *fresh_gear.avi*, which you can then drag-and-drop into just about any popular media player to watch.

> If your media player doesn't support DiVX 5.0 right out of the box, you can download the DiVX 5.0 codec for most platforms to integrate into Windows Media Player, Quick-Time, MPlayer, and the like.

If you prefer a really high-quality encoding, you might want to do something called a *three-pass encode*, which requires three calls to *mencoder*:

1. Encode only the audio from the *ty* file into MP3 format. The audio has to go into a file called *frameno.avi*; it won't work any place else, so don't change that filename.

   ```
   $ mencoder -ovc frameno -o frameno.avi -oac mp3lame fresh_gear.ty
   ```

2. Extract and compute bitrate information from the *ty* file. With this added information, the next step can make a better guess at the quality at which to encode the video for a higher quality, yet smaller-sized file.

   ```
   $ mencoder -nosound -oac copy -ovc lavc -lavcopts vcodec=mpeg4:vpass=1↵
   -vop scale 352:240,pp=lb -o /dev/null fresh_gear.ty
   ```

3. Encode the *ty* file as a DiVX AVI using the hints generated from step 2. And, while you're at it, include the MP3 generated from step 1.

   ```
   $ mencoder -oac copy -ovc lavc -lavcopts vcodec=mpeg4:vpass=2↵
   -vop scale=352:240,pp=lb -o fresh_gear.avi fresh_gear.ty
   ```

The *mencoder* also encodes to most other popular formats, such as MPEG-1 and OGM. For further information, see the *mplayer* home page (*http:// www.mplayerhq.hu/*).

TyStudio

One problem with *mencoder* is its inability to edit your streams before encoding them. What if you want to create an AVI or MPEG of your favorite show, excluding the commercials? Or perhaps you'd like to capture one particular segment of a favorite talk show featuring your favorite singer, actress, or crocodile hunter?

TyStudio (*http://dvd-create.sourceforge.net/tystudio/*) allows you to do just that. You'll find both Linux and Windows versions, with one for Mac OS X in the works.

While I'm using the Windows version (shown in Figure 6-3) for the rest of this hack, these instructions also apply rather well to the other releases.

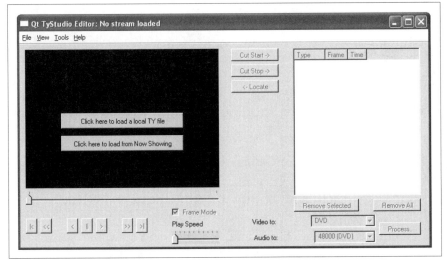

Figure 6-3. The TyStudio interface

 Don't be fooled by TyStudio's bare interface. Great power is hidden within its menus.

As with *mplayer* and *mencoder*, we can load *ty* files either from the filesystem or directly from the TiVo itself. You can either click the "Click here to load a local TY file" button and select a *ty* file, or you can grab their *tyServer* (*http://dvd-create.sourceforge.net/tystudio/tyserver.ppc.sh*) and run it on your TiVo to give TyStudio direct access. Either way, you'll end up with a *ty* file that is ready for editing.

Use the slider under the viewer pane to move forward and backward through the stream; the video will update as you do so. When you come to the beginning of a section you want to remove from the final video, click the Cut Start button, slide forward to the end of what you want to remove, and click the Cut Stop button. You'll see the time codes for the block destined for the cutting-room floor appear in the pane to the right. If you make a mistake and want to add a cut back into your video, select it in the right pane and click the Remove Selected button. ("Remove" means "remove from the to-be-cut list," not "remove from the video.")

Now to generate the edited video. Notice the "Video to" and "Audio to" pull-down menus on the lower-right side of the interface. You have a couple of options, depending on exactly what you plan to do with the resulting video file:

Generic MPEG2
An MPEG stream, playable by any software and most hardware MPEG players. Be sure to set "Audio to" to "No Transcoding."

DVD
A DVD-compliant MPEG stream. If you have a South African or United Kingdom TiVo, set the "Audio to" to either "DVD" or "AC3 DVD." However, the AC3 option is recommended only if you have a DVD player capable of playing AC3 audio. DirecTiVo owners should set "Audio to" to "No Transcoding."

SVCD
An SVCD-compliant MPEG stream. Set "Audio to" to "44100."

Elementary Stream
Produces a raw video file and a raw audio file. You will most likely use this if you want to edit the files separately in another program—a DVD-authoring program, for instance. You may wish to "Transcode" the audio; just follow the same audio steps you would follow if you were making a DVD or an SVCD.

Click the Process button and wait a while—though not nearly as long as with *mencoder*.

You should have an MPEG-2 file of your television show—sans whatever you edited out—that you can open in almost any DVD-player application on your computer. In a pinch, you can easily convert the MPEG-2 to MPEG-1 using programs like *TMPGEnc (http://www.tmpgenc.net)*.

Putting Videos Back into TiVo

You have all these great videos you've been archiving from your TiVo, but you miss watching them on your TV; let's put them back into your TiVo.

No coverage of extracting video from your TiVo would be complete without talking about how to put them back in. While you can't really put *ty* files back into your TiVo box, you can extract and reinject those *tmf* files [Hack #81] we mentioned earlier. Those are magic files you can take off and put back onto your TiVo at any time.

Let's say you already have the *mfs_ftp* server running on your TiVo. Let's also say that you have some *tmf* files you extracted on your PC and since deleted from your TiVo. It sure would be nice to see them on the 36" screen again. No problem. Open an FTP connection to your TiVo, navigate to the *tmf* directory where you found the files in the first place, and upload them again. Wait about ten minutes per hour you want to upload. Visit your TiVo's *Now Playing* menu, and your shows should once again be there, ready for playing.

Does this mean that every time you want to do anything interesting with extracted video, yet still be able to put shows back, you need to extract both a *ty* and the corresponding *tmf* file? Not at all! The *tmf* file is actually composed of the *ty* file or files containing the television program itself and the XML show information. The combination of the two is what allows your TiVo to accept a new file into its *Now Showing* pile. So, the question remains: how do you separate them out? Simply treat them as a TAR archive, a common, ZIP-like form of archive used on Unix systems. Append a *.tar* extension to the end of the file, run it through WinZip, UnStuffit, or tar on the command line, and out pops out an *xml* file and *ty* files. You can take a quick peek using tar's tvf option, which lists, but does not extract, the contents of the archive:

```
$ tar tvf 1694436\ Good\ Eats\ -\ Tomatoes.tmf
-rw-r--r-- tivo/tivo      2077 2003-06-06 11:01:33 showing.xml
-rw-r--r-- tivo/tivo 536870912 2003-06-06 11:01:33 part00.ty
-rw-r--r-- tivo/tivo 201326592 2003-06-06 11:12:28 part01.ty
```

Don't be surprised if there are more than one *ty* file in the archive. The TiVo breaks up all recorded programs into a bunch of streams that it stores on its drive; MPlayer [Hack #84] and the rest just clump it together into one big file. *mfs_ftp* does its best to keep everything just the way TiVos like it, so putting it back onto TiVo goes smoothly.

Moving Shows Between TiVo Units

Of course you could just extract a television show from one TiVo and insert it into another, but there's an easier way to transfer from one unit to another.

With a growing archive of *tmf* files on your PC, you can easily shuffle shows from one TiVo to another in your home: *The Love Boat* in the bedroom, *Serpico* in the media room, and *Blue's Clues* in the playroom. Think of the collaborative scheduling possibilities: if two television shows are on at the same time, have one TiVo record one, have another TiVo record the other show, extract the *tmf* files, and move them about at will. Stock the family TiVo with only family-friendly programming, keeping those *X-Files* episodes away from your 5-year-old.

There's really no need to FTP extract [Hack #81] files from one TiVo to your PC, only to insert them [Hack #86] into another TiVo—unless, of course, you want to archive the files in the process. Thanks to an extension of FTP called FXP, you can cross-transfer between two FTP servers, using your FTP client only as the middleman for making the introductions, controlling the connection, and deciding what goes where. No data is ever actually sent to or stored on your PC. Your FTP client simply asks one TiVo to send files to the other, and vice versa. The most popular Windows FTP application, WS_FTP (*http://www.ipswitch.com/Products/WS_FTP/index.html*) supports FXP transfers quite nicely. Open up two TiVos in two windows, select the *tmf* file to transfer, drag, and drop. LundFXP (*http://www.lundman.net/unix/lundfxp.html*) is an FXP client (still in alpha testing at the time of this writing) for Mac OS X, Windows, and Unix variants.

## CHAPTER SEVEN

Writing Code
Hacks 88–100

We've run the gamut of the kinds of tips, tricks, and hacks it takes to become a TiVo power user, but we haven't taught you to build anything yourself yet. Up to this point, the extent to which you've hacked your TiVo's software has only meant borrowing and running other people's code.

Let's change that.

While this chapter will not magically turn you into a TiVo code jockey, it will whet your appetite, providing a reasonable primer on the concepts you'll need to understand if you're going to start stringing together pieces of code to suit your purposes. To sit at the feet of the masters, hang out at some of the user forums, such as *http://alt.org/forum*, devoted to open source TiVo development. Be forewarned, though, that most contributors there are pretty advanced. But that shouldn't stop you from listening in and learning.

As is usually the case with hacking, there's more than one way to do just about everything. There are two programming languages on TiVo you usually stumble over:

Tcl

Tcl (pronounced "tickle") is the glue language of the TiVo world, passing commands between interactive applications, and providing a lower learning and development curve to building lightweight TiVo applications.

C

C performs much of the heavy lifting in TiVo. TiVo's main brains (read: binaries) are written in C. C is harder to write correctly, but it's compiled for speed and let's you do so much more in terms of interfacing with the TiVo hardware.

Which language you choose is for you to decide, depending on the task at hand, balancing rapid versus more stringent development, and taking into account your level of programming skill.

To write Tcl, all you really need is a text editor [Hacks #38, #39] on your TiVo, or you can edit on your PC and FTP [Hack #55] the files across, or use a shared NFS directory [Hack #56]. Once set up to write the code, run your creations from the command line using the onboard Tcl interpreter.

C code needs to be compiled before it'll run. It's generally not a good idea to run the compiler on your TiVo itself, because the horsepower drained will seriously affect the operation of the box: video stutters, menus become unresponsive, and so forth. Think of it like running the MP3 player [Hack #46], but worse. Instead, get your hands on a cross-compiler [Hack #100] that, while it runs on another computer, generates executables that run on the TiVo platform. At *http://tivoutils.sourceforge.net/*, you'll find cross-compilers for x86, Mac OS X, and some that run natively on the TiVo.

A Crash Course in Tcl

This section provides a quick overview of the Tcl language, just enough for you to understand the hacks in this chapter. It assumes you have a rudimentary understanding of some form of programming language—whether C, Perl, Java, or Basic—or at least have a willingness to learn. For a more complete reference, take a look at a Tcl reference manual (*http://tmml. sourceforge.net/doc/tcl/*), the object-oriented *[incr Tcl]* reference (*http://www. tcl.tk/man/itcl3.1/*), and The Tcler's Wiki (*http://mini.net/tcl/*).

You can play along with the code either interactively or by writing Tcl scripts and running them from the command line. To interact with Tcl directly, run *tclsh* (the Tcl shell) on a Unix machine or *tivosh* (the TiVo shell, a derivative of the Tcl shell) on your TiVo command line. To turn any text file full of Tcl code into a script, make sure the first line has the magic incantation. Use the following line for *tclsh* on a Unix machine:

```
#!/usr/bin/tclsh
```

Use this line for the TiVo shell:

```
#!/tvbin/tivosh
```

And don't forget to make that script executable, like so:

```
bash-2.02# chmod 755 my_script.tcl
```

Variables

In many programming languages, variables are prefixed with a special character. For example, in Perl, a $ indicates simple text or a number. Other languages, usually compiled languages like C, have no prefix at all. In Tcl, it's mixed, with variables referred to as *$myvar* and sometimes simply *myvar*, depending on the context. The distinction is whether you are talking about the value of the variable or the variable itself. Here, the first line sets the *myvar* variable to 1, while the second prints its value (notice the $ prefix when referring to the value of the variable):

```
% set myvar 1
% puts $myvar
```

It seems simple enough now, but it's easy to slip up and add a $ where you shouldn't.

Expressions

Everything in a programming language can reduce to an expression at one point or another. Anything that Tcl can work with is an expression, including mathematical statements, strings, and so forth.

The expr expression computes the value of whatever it's fed—in this case, 2 + 2:

```
% expr 2 + 2
4
```

This result, as one might hope, is 4, the value of the sum of 2 + 2.

The puts expression, rather than attempting to compute anything, simply prints whatever it's given—once again, 2 + 2 in this case, this time in quotes:

```
% puts "2 + 2"
2 + 2
```

To include an expr within a quoted string passed to puts, you can't simply embed the expr and hope for the best:

```
% puts "2 plus 2 is expr 2 + 2"
2 plus 2 is expr 2 + 2
```

As you can see, this prints 2 plus 2 is expr 2 + 2—not quite what we we're after. To nest an expression, enclose it in square brackets, [and]. The nested expression is evaluated first, its results incorporated into the string sent to puts, like so:

```
% puts "2 plus 2 is [expr 2 + 2]"
2 plus 2 is 4
```

Lastly, { and } are used for grouping expressions. Double quotes are one way of grouping; they tell Tcl to treat everything within them as one object, a string. { and } are very similar; but, unlike grouping through double quotes, Tcl won't try to automatically evaluate anything within curly braces, even if it thinks it knows how to evaluate the expression. Because of this, the following prints exactly what's inside the curly braces, with no further processing:

```
% puts {2 + 2 = [expr 2 + 2]}
2 + 2 = [expr 2 + 2]
```

Flow Control

It's amazing how much time hackers spend on conditionals. If this, then that; otherwise, if that, then such-and-such. Typical Tcl (or Perl, C, or Java, for that matter) flow control looks like this:

```
if {$myvar > 0} {
        puts "$myvar is greater than zero"
} elseif {$myvar == 0} {
        puts "$myvar is equal to zero"
} else {
        puts "$myvar is less than zero"
}
```

This code says: if the value of variable $myvar is greater than 0, then evaluate the first block—all the code between curly braces—and be done with it. If, instead, $myvar is equal to 0, then run the second block. Finally, for all other values of $myvar (read: all negative values), run the last block.

Procedures

You don't have to be satisfied with using only the expressions Tcl provides you. The proc expression allows you to create your own procedures (read: expressions), pass them arguments, retrieve the values they return, and generally use them whenever and wherever you would usually use a built-in Tcl expression. Here's a simple procedure called test:

```
% proc test {arg1} {
    puts "hi, world"
    if {$arg1 > 0} {
        puts "The argument was: $arg1"
    } elseif {$arg1 == 0} {
        puts "Lets see what happens here: [test2 $arg1]"
    } else {
        puts "The absolute value of the argument is: [expr abs$arg1)]"
    }
    return 1
}
```

The proc expression takes three arguments: a name for your new expression, the list of arguments you want it to accept, and a block of curly-brace-delimited code to be evaluated whenever the expression is called. Our new test procedure takes one argument named arg1, here enclosed in curly braces. The third argument—everything between the second set of curly braces, from puts "hi, world" to return 1– is the procedure's code.

Now that our new test procedure is defined, let's try it out:

```
% test 1
hi, world
The argument was: 1
1
```

Notice the 1 printed as the last line of output. The result of the last expression in the procedure—in this case, 1, because of that return 1—is always printed.

Notice that call to another, *nonexistent* procedure, test2, in one branch of the if tree:

```
} elseif {$arg1 == 0} {
    puts "Lets see what happens here: [test2 $arg1]"
```

Surely that should raise some sort of alarm? Not so; it really doesn't matter to the Tcl interpreter at all until that block of code is executed. As long as you always call test with a value greater than 0, the block of code is never executed and the call to a nonexistent procedure never noticed. Let's try feeding our test procedure a 0, to call the bogus test2:

```
% test 0
hi, world
invalid command name "test2"
```

Finally, if you call test without any parameters at all, it won't have an arg1 argument to evaluate and will produce an error:

```
% test
no value given for parameter "arg1" to "test"
```

That should provide you with enough rudimentary knowledge of Tcl programming to at least skim through the Tcl code in this chapter and understand something of what it's trying to do.

HACK #88 Navigating the Media Filesystem

The Media Filesystem (MFS) is the database and filesystem that the TiVo uses to hold all of its useful information.

Alongside its Linux filesystem, TiVo runs a custom hybrid filesystem and database called the Media Filesystem (MFS). The MFS is where the TiVo stuffs all its recorded programming and knowledge. Here you'll find the programs appearing in your *Now Playing List*, databases of famous actors, your Thumbs Up/Thumbs Down show ratings, WishLists, Season Passes, messages—everything that makes your TiVo a TiVo.

The reason for using a custom filesystem is not fully known, but most people speculate it's twofold. First, it allows for very large video files to be stored safely. If you've ever turned off your computer without shutting it down, you've no doubt noticed just how long it takes to come up the next time. It's checking to make sure its filesystem is intact and nothing's out of step or just plain corrupt. With its specialized filesystem, TiVo gets around this problem and manages to boot in a reasonable amount of time, which is vital for something considered more of an entertainment system component than a computer.

Second, the MFS allows for rich metadata to be associated with media files, including Thumbs Up ratings, lists of actors, directors, genres, and so forth—everything TiVo makes available to us about the shows we're watching and TiVo, Inc. about our preferences. On the whole, TiVo's MFS is both a simple filesystem and a rich media database at the same time. You'll find it packed with directories (*tyDir*), objects (*tyObj*), files, and streams—each and every item with its own unique key, the filesystem ID (FSID) **[Hack #84]**.

The mls Command

The standard TiVo shell provides us with an analog of the Unix ls ("list directory contents") command: mls ("MFS ls"). mls provides a listing of the contents of a particular directory. There's one caveat, however: the *tivosh* environment is rather primitive and has no concept of a current directory (the directory you're in). This means you have to provide a full path every time you call mls. So, whether you're actually in */Recording/NowShowingByTitle* (where all the recorded television shows under TiVo OS 3.x are kept) or elsewhere, you still need to type mls /Recording/NowShowingByTitle to see its contents.

Let's take a look around at the bounty TiVo has brought us, shall we? From the Bash prompt, launch the TiVo shell and use mls to list the contents of */Recording/NowShowingByTitle*:

```
bash-2.02# tivosh
% mls /Recording/NowShowingByTitle
Directory of /Recording/NowShowingByTitle starting at ''

    Name Type
    FsId Date Time Size
    ---- ---- -
    --- ---- ---- ----
```

```
        1:2003 MTV MOVIE AWARDS:87788:91001:1717520         tyDb    1717520  06/
08/03 15:33    1172
        1:24:87806:96401:1662160                            tyDb↵
        1662160   06/05/03 21:14    1028
        1:AMAZING RACE 4:87791:13601:1692463                tyDb↵
        1692463   06/06/03 17:02    1032
        1:ARMENIANS A STORY OF SURVIVAL:88341:24401:700897  tyDb↵
        700897   08/11/02 14:44    1076
        1:COMING ATTRACTIONS:87794:74801:1699840                  tyDb↵
        1699840   06/06/03 05:36    900
        1:DAWSONS CREEK:87813:13601:1651146                       tyDb↵
        1651146   05/15/03 01:59    1236
    ...
```

Essentially, TiVo looks in */Recording/NowShowingByClassic* for shows in reverse chronological order to compile its *Now Playing List*. MPlayer [Hack #84] does the same thing to get a list of all programming available for streaming.

Note that mls will list only the first 50 entries in a directory. You can get beyond the first 50 as they happen to appear in alphabetical order by specifying a prefix and/or wildcard for mls to use when selecting which files to show. For example, to see all the shows that start at *Kojak* (alphabetically speaking), you'd type:

```
% mls "/Recording/NowShowingByTitle/1:KOJAK*"
```

Note the use of double quotes and the wildcard (*).

We've previously explored only a small section of the MFS via FTP [Hack #81]. There's a lot more to meander and explore. Table 7-1 lists some of the more interesting nooks and crannies.

Table 7-1. A listing of the more interesting MFS directories and their contents

MFS directory	Contents
/Component	Infrared codes for the IR blaster and programmable remote
/Famous	A list of famous actors and directors
/GuideIndexV2	The indexes used to sort shows by title, keyword, actor, and so forth—useful for finding particular airings of a program
/MenuItem	The "extra" menu item you sometimes see appear on the *TiVo Central* menu, telling you about new previews and products
/MessageItem	The mail you receive from TiVo, Inc.
/Person	Definitions of actors, directors, and writers, used by the preferences engine
/Preference	Your Thumbs Up/Thumbs Down ratings

Table 7-1. *A listing of the more interesting MFS directories and their contents (continued)*

MFS directory	Contents
/Recording	Listings of all recordings scheduled by the viewer and automatically by the TiVo, organized by show title, date, and so forth
/Resource	The fonts, images, sounds, and backgrounds used in constructing the TiVo user interface
/Schedule	Guide data, organized by station and day
/SeasonPass	All the information about your Season Passes
/SwSystem	Information about the specific version of the TiVo OS you are running
/Theme	The viewer's WishLists

If you have TiVoWeb [Hack #65] installed, you can alternatively use your browser to navigate this terrain. From the TiVoWeb main menu, select *MFS* for the built-in MFS web-based browser, shown in Figure 7-1.

Everything is nicely laid out with the same information you'd see on the command line. Instead of letting your typing fingers do the walking, you can just click your way through the MFS.

Starting out from the root directory (/) you can keep using mls or TiVoWeb to explore subdirectories until you run into MFS objects [Hack #89], inspected in quite a different manner.

Inspecting MFS Objects
#89

Embedded in the *tyDirs* are the *tyDbs*. This is where the real data is actually hiding out.

While poking through the MFS [Hack #88] you are inevitably going to run into objects. The objects, or *tyDbs* as they are called, are the database objects holding the real information that the filesystem directories (*tyDirs*) are just organizing into a simple hierarchy.

You can peek at an object using the TiVo shell's dumpobj command. dumpobj does exactly as its name suggests: reach into the MFS database for a specified filesystem ID (FSID), extract appropriate metadata, and dump it to the screen in human-readable form.

Let's take a look at a rundown of the first television show in my */Recording/ NowShowingByTitle* directory. From the TiVo shell (type tivosh at the Bash prompt if you're not already in *tivosh*), run it on one of your FSIDs, like so:

```
% dumpobj 1717520
Recording 1717520/10 {
  ActualShowing  = 1717520/16
```

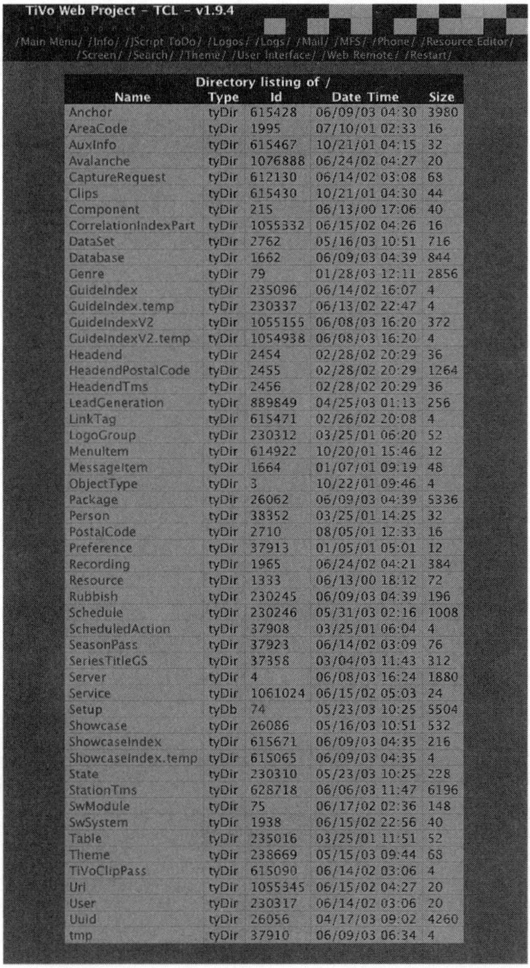

Name	Type	Id	Date Time	Size
Anchor	tyDir	615428	06/09/03 04:30	3980
AreaCode	tyDir	1995	07/10/01 02:33	16
AuxInfo	tyDir	615467	10/21/01 04:15	32
Avalanche	tyDir	1076888	06/24/02 04:27	20
CaptureRequest	tyDir	612130	06/14/02 03:08	68
Clips	tyDir	615430	10/21/01 04:30	44
Component	tyDir	215	06/13/00 17:06	40
CorrelationIndexPart	tyDir	1055332	06/15/02 04:26	16
DataSet	tyDir	2762	05/16/03 10:51	716
Database	tyDir	1662	06/09/03 04:39	844
Genre	tyDir	79	01/28/03 12:11	2856
GuideIndex	tyDir	235096	06/14/02 16:07	4
GuideIndex.temp	tyDir	230337	06/13/02 22:47	4
GuideIndexV2	tyDir	1055155	06/08/03 16:20	372
GuideIndexV2.temp	tyDir	1054938	06/08/03 16:20	4
Headend	tyDir	2454	02/28/02 20:29	36
HeadendPostalCode	tyDir	2455	02/28/02 20:29	1264
HeadendTms	tyDir	2456	02/28/02 20:29	36
LeadGeneration	tyDir	889849	04/25/03 01:13	256
LinkTag	tyDir	615471	02/26/02 20:08	4
LogoGroup	tyDir	230312	03/25/01 06:20	52
MenuItem	tyDir	614922	10/20/01 15:46	12
MessageItem	tyDir	1664	01/07/01 09:19	48
ObjectType	tyDir	3	10/22/01 09:46	4
Package	tyDir	26062	06/09/03 04:39	5336
Person	tyDir	38352	03/25/01 14:25	32
PostalCode	tyDir	2710	08/05/01 12:33	16
Preference	tyDir	37913	01/05/01 05:01	12
Recording	tyDir	1965	06/24/02 04:21	384
Resource	tyDir	1333	06/13/00 18:12	72
Rubbish	tyDir	230245	06/09/03 04:39	196
Schedule	tyDir	230246	05/31/03 02:16	1008
ScheduledAction	tyDir	37908	03/25/01 06:04	4
SeasonPass	tyDir	37923	06/14/02 03:09	76
SeriesTitleGS	tyDir	37358	03/04/03 11:43	312
Server	tyDir	4	06/08/03 16:24	1880
Service	tyDir	1061024	06/15/02 05:03	24
Setup	tyDb	74	05/23/03 10:25	5504
Showcase	tyDir	26086	05/16/03 10:51	532
ShowcaseIndex	tyDir	615671	06/09/03 04:35	216
ShowcaseIndex.temp	tyDir	615065	06/09/03 04:35	4
State	tyDir	230310	05/23/03 10:25	228
StationTms	tyDir	628718	06/06/03 11:47	6196
SwModule	tyDir	75	06/17/02 02:36	148
SwSystem	tyDir	1938	06/15/02 22:56	40
Table	tyDir	235016	03/25/01 11:51	52
Theme	tyDir	238669	05/15/03 09:44	68
TiVoClipPass	tyDir	615090	06/14/02 03:06	4
Uri	tyDir	1055345	06/15/02 04:27	20
User	tyDir	230317	06/14/02 03:06	20
Uuid	tyDir	26056	04/17/03 09:02	4260
tmp	tyDir	37910	06/09/03 06:34	4

Figure 7-1. Browsing the MFS through TiVoWeb

```
  BitRate        = 0
  Bookmark       = 1717520/19
  DeletionDate   = 24855
  ExpirationDate = 12213
  ExpirationTime = 9000
  IndexPath      = /Recording/Active/1:12211:08998:1717520 /Recording/
NoReRecord/12919640:2:99999:01717520 /Recording/TmsId/SH5785730000:87788:
91001:1717520 /Recording/NowShowingByClassic/2:87788:91001:1717520 /
Recording/NowShowingByExpiration/2:12213:09000:1717520 {/Recording/
NowShowingByTitle/1:2003 MTV MOVIE AWARDS:87788:91001:1717520} /Recording/
DiskUsed/10/1717520:2842624
  IndexUsed      = 1717520/11 1717520/12
  NSecondsWatched = 3539
```

```
       NVisit          = 1
       Part            = 1717520/13 1717520/15 1717520/17 1717520/18 1717520/20
    1717520/21
       RecordQuality   = 75
       RecordingBehavior = 1717520/12
       Score           = 0
       SelectionType   = 3
       Showing         = 1717520/11
       StartDate       = 12211
       StartTime       = 8998
       State           = 4
       StopDate        = 12211
       StopTime        = 16200
       StreamFileSize  = 2842624
       UsedBy          = 1
       Version         = 56
    }
```

Out comes all the attributes associated with this television show. Notice the title fragment "MTV MOVIE AWARDS" (/Recording/NowShowingByTitle/1:2003 MTV MOVIE AWARDS), the number of seconds I've already watched (NSecondsWatched = 3539), and other assorted details.

It's also worth mentioning that our friend TiVoWeb will do the same thing. Use the web-based MFS browser to click your way to one of the *tyDb* objects, and you should see something like Figure 7-2.

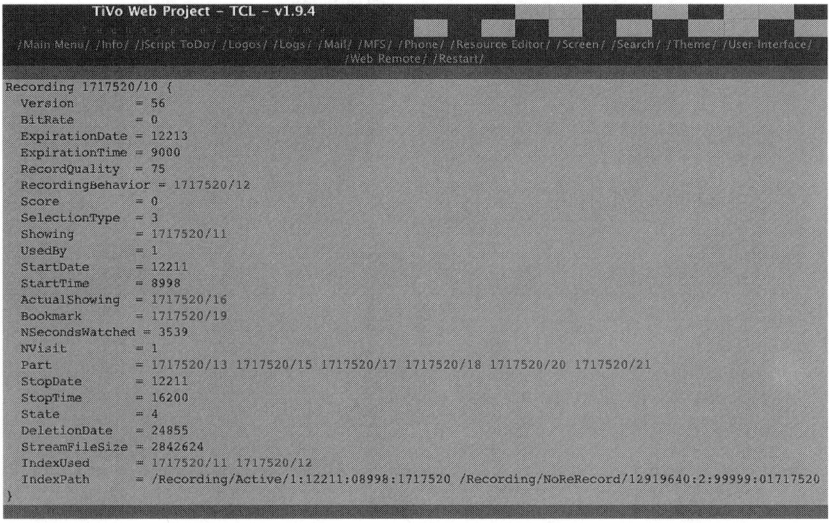

Figure 7-2. Looking at the same tyDB object through TiVoWeb

That said, if all data about the show is in the MFS database, where's the full title of the show? The guest stars? Television channel from which it was recorded? If you look closely at the object dump, you may well see what appear to be FSIDs; in fact, that's what they are.

This is where the TiVo shell and command line has one leg up on TiVoWeb. You could go through and dumpobj each of the associated FSIDs, but you'll no doubt find even more to comb through. You could also click through on TiVoWeb, but that is just going to get frustrating. There is a short cut: dumpobj takes a closure flag, telling it to dump all the FSIDs it finds along the way, starting with the FSID you provide. It's a long list but a pirate's booty of information:

```
% dumpobj -closure  1717520
Recording 1717520/10 {
   ActualShowing  = 1717520/16
   BitRate        = 0
   Bookmark       = 1717520/19
   DeletionDate   = 24855
   ExpirationDate = 12213
   ExpirationTime = 9000
   IndexPath      = /Recording/Active/1:12211:08998:1717520 /Recording/
NoReRecord/129196
40:2:99999:01717520 /Recording/TmsId/SH5785730000:87788:91001:1717520 /
Recording/NowSho
wingByClassic/2:87788:91001:1717520 /Recording/NowShowingByExpiration/2:
12213:09000:171
7520 {/Recording/NowShowingByTitle/1:2003 MTV MOVIE AWARDS:87788:91001:
1717520} /Record
ing/DiskUsed/10/1717520:2842624
   IndexUsed      = 1717520/11 1717520/12
   NSecondsWatched = 3539
   NVisit         = 1
   Part           = 1717520/13 1717520/15 1717520/17 1717520/18 1717520/20
1717520/21
   RecordQuality  = 75
   RecordingBehavior = 1717520/12
   Score          = 0
   SelectionType  = 3
   Showing        = 1717520/11
   StartDate      = 12211
   StartTime      = 8998
   State          = 4
   StopDate       = 12211
   StopTime       = 16200
   StreamFileSize = 2842624
   UsedBy         = 1
   Version        = 56
}

Showing 1717520/16 {
```

```
    Bits          = 2
    Date          = 12211
    Duration      = 7200
    Program       = 1691635/-1
    Station       = 2086/-1
    Time          = 9000
}

Bookmark 1717520/19 {
    TimeMs        = 4171221
}

Showing 1717520/11 {
    Bits          = 2
    Date          = 12211
    Duration      = 7200
    IndexUsedBy   = 1717520/10
    Program       = 1691635/-1
    Station       = 2086/-1
    Time          = 9000
}

RecordingBehavior 1717520/12 {
    DiskBehavior  = 5
    IndexUsedBy   = 1717520/10
    PresentationBehavior = 1
    ProgramGuideBehavior = 1
    TunerBehavior = 1
}

RecordingPart 1717520/13 {
    Begin         = 0
    CommercialSkipOffset = 0
    End           = 1318759
    File          = 1717637
}

RecordingPart 1717520/15 {
    Begin         = 1319259
    CommercialSkipOffset = 0
    End           = 2652833
    File          = 1717645
}

RecordingPart 1717520/17 {
    Begin         = 2653334
    CommercialSkipOffset = 0
    End           = 3984672
    File          = 1717665
}

RecordingPart 1717520/18 {
    Begin         = 3985172
```

```
  CommercialSkipOffset = 0
  End           = 5316511
  File          = 1717666
}

RecordingPart 1717520/20 {
  Begin         = 5317011
  CommercialSkipOffset = 0
  End           = 6646248
  File          = 1717667
}

RecordingPart 1717520/21 {
Begin           = 6646848
  CommercialSkipOffset = 0
  End           = 7201392
  File          = 1717668
}

Program 1691635/11 {
  ColorCode     = 4
  DescLanguage  = English
  Description   = {The Shrine Auditorium in Los Angeles; hosts Justin
Timberlake and Seann William Scott.}
  Genre         = 9 100 1000
  IndexPath     = /Server/12919640
  IsEpisode     = 1
  OriginalAirDate = 12208
  Series        = 1691634/-1
  ServerId      = 12919640
  ServerVersion = 4
  ShowType      = 3
  SourceType    = 1
  Title         = {2003 MTV Movie Awards}
  TmsId         = SH5785730000
  Version       = 1
}

Station 2086/15 {
  Affiliation   = Satellite
  AffiliationIndex = 39
  CallSign      = MTV
  City          = {New York}
  Country       = {United States}
  DmaNum        = 0
  IndexPath     = /StationTms/10986:826 /Server/928
  LogoIndex     = LogoSpace=Tivo    LogoIndex=0
  Name          = {MTV - Music Television}
  ServerId      = 928
  ServerVersion = 80
  State         = NY
  TmsId         = 10986
  Version       = 10
```

```
    ZipCode        = 10036
}

Series 1691634/11 {
    Episodic       = 0
    Genre          = 9 100 1000
    IndexPath      = /Server/12919853
    ServerId       = 12919853
    ServerVersion  = 2
}
```

The Program node (FSID 1691635) holds the title and full description of the show. The Station node (FSID 2086) tells us that the show was recorded off MTV. And that's absolutely everything TiVo knows about the object we asked for. The question is, what do you do with it? See the following hacks for some answers.

Extracting Your Now Showing List

#90

Ask TiVo's MFS database for your Now Showing List, including title, description, and date and time the show aired.

Curious about what's showing? Want to keep track of your television viewing habits (or at least what's been recorded for you) over time? You can ask the TiVo MFS with some pretty trivial data mining. We'll start with the *Now Showing List* and everything TiVo knows about the shows we currently have queued up for watching. We'll write the title, description, and date and time the show aired to a file and save it. You can even automate this using *cron* [Hack #44] and write the files to your PC's NFS-mounted [Hack #56] drive if you are truly serious about archiving that data.

Let's go over what we already know. We know that recorded programs are all held in */Recording/NowShowingByTitle*, and we know that each of these programs has all the information we want somewhere in its closure of objects. Therefore, we can easily find the date the show aired, the name of the program, and the name of the episode.

Before we write the code, let's actually find all this information in the closure listed in "Inspecting MFS Objects" [Hack #89]. The date and time the show aired are listed in the top Recording object under StartDate and StartTime; conveniently, this is listed under the FSID of the object in */Recording/ NowShowingByTitle*. The rest of the information seems to be in the Program object. The path between the Recording object and the Program object seems to pass through Showing. We want to grab the Recording object, follow through the Showing attribute to a Showing object, and follow that out to a Program attribute.

Seems simple enough. All we need to do is express this in Tcl. The heart of the program just makes use of mfs commands to maneuver through the directories and then uses dbobj commands to dig into the database. To get a rundown of some of the commands that people know about (remember that these things are discovered, not documented), take a gander at Table 7-2 and Table 7-3.

Table 7-2. Some of the mfs commands used to manipulate files on the Media Filesystem

Filesystem command	Purpose
mfs find <path>	Look for an item in the MFS and return its FSID and type
mfs mkdir <path>	Make a named directory
mfs rmdir <path>	Remove a named directory
mfs streamsize <fsid>	Get the size of a recording stream
mfs moddate <fsid>	Return the last time an object was modified, in seconds since the Unix epoch time
mfs size <fsid>	Return the size of a given MFS object
mfs scan <path> [-start string] [-count number] [-backward]	List up to a certain number of items in a specific MFS directory that optionally starts with a specified string

Table 7-3. Some of the dbobj commands used to manipulate database objects

Database object command	Purpose
dbobj equal <dbobj> <dbobj>	Test the equality of two database objects
dbobj <dbobj> fsid	Return the FSID of a database object
dbobj <dbobj> subobjid	Return the subobjid of a database object
dbobj <dbobj> type	Return the type of a database object
dbobj <dbobj> attrs	Return the attributes of a database object
Dbobj <dbobj> attrtype <attr>	Get the type of an attribute of a database
dbobj <dbobj> get [-noerror] <attr> [<index>]	Get the value of a specific attribute of this type
dbobj <dbobj> add <attr> <tclobj>	Append an attribute of a given name to a database object
Dbobj <dbobj> remove <attr> [<tclobj>]	Remove the last attribute of a given name from a database object
dbobj <dbobj> delete	Delete a particular database object (be careful with this one)
dbobj <dbobj> clear	Clear out a particular database object
dbobj <dbobj> removeat <attr> <index>	Remove a specific attribute from a database object. The index is used when there are multiple attributes with the same name
dbobj <dbobj> copyfrom <dbobj>	Copy a database object

The Code

You'll need my *tivotime* library (*http://www.bitwaste.com/ tivo/tivotime.tar.gz*) to handle time in a manner TiVo understands. Download it, extract *tivotime.tcl* from the archive, and drop it **[Hack #36]** into */var/hack/lib/tcl* on your TiVo.

```
#!/tvbin/tivosh

# include code to do a timezone conversion back into our time format
source /var/hack/lib/tcl/tivotime.tcl

# open the database
set db [dbopen]

# pull out the first 50 recorded shows from the database
set recdir "/Recording/NowShowingByTitle"
transaction {
    set files [mfs scan $recdir -count 50]
}

while { [llength $files] > 0 } {
    # iterate through the shows we extracted
    foreach rec $files {
        # grab the FSID of the program from the list
        set fsid [lindex $rec 0]

        transaction {
            # get the object that represents this recording and the
            # object that represents this episode.
            set recordingobj [db $db openid $fsid]
            set episodeobj [dbobj [dbobj $recordingobj get Showing]↵
            get Program]

            # pull out the date the show aired
            # convert it to something a bit more
            # human-readable using the tivotime library
            set showtime [::tivotime::converttime \
                           [dbobj $recordingobj get StartDate] \
                           [dbobj $recordingobj get StartTime] ]
            set showtime [clock format $showtime -format "%m/%d/%Y %H:%M"]

            # pull out the show's name and episode title
            regsub -all "\[\{\}\]" [dbobj $episodeobj get Title] ""↵
            programname
            regsub -all "\[\{\}\]" [dbobj $episodeobj get↵
            EpisodeTitle] episodename
        }

        # output a pipe (|) delimited list containing the date,
        # show name, and episode title
```

```
        puts "$showtime | $programname | $episodename"
}

# and grab the next 50 television shows
set lastName [lindex [lindex $files end] 1]
transaction {
        set files [mfs scan $recdir -start $lastName -count 50]
}

if { $lastName == [lindex [lindex $files 0] 1] } {
        set files [lrange $files 1 end]
}
}
```

Save the code as *nowshowing.tcl* in TiVo's */var/hack/bin* directory and make
it executable:

```
bash-2.02# chmod 755 /var/hack/bin/nowshowing.tcl
```

Running the Hack

From TiVo's command line [Hacks #30, #52], invoke the script, like so:

```
bash-2.02# /var/hack/bin/nowshowing.tcl
06/07/2003 21:29 | 2003 MTV Movie Awards |
05/20/2003 19:59 | 24 | Day 2: 7:00 - 8:00AM
06/05/2003 18:59 | The Amazing Race 4 | It Doesn't Say Anything About First
Come, First Served. And We're Bigger
12/02/2001 15:59 | The Armenians: A Story of Survival |
06/02/2003 01:59 | Coming Attractions |
05/14/2003 18:59 | Dawson's Creek | All Good Things ... Must Come to an End
05/07/2003 18:59 | Dawson's Creek | Joey Potter and Capeside Redemption
04/30/2003 18:59 | Dawson's Creek | Goodbye, Yellow Brick Road
04/16/2003 18:59 | Dawson's Creek | Lovelines
04/09/2003 18:59 | Dawson's Creek | Love Bites
02/12/2003 19:59 | Dawson's Creek | Castaways
02/05/2003 19:59 | Dawson's Creek | Clean and Sober
01/15/2003 19:59 | Dawson's Creek | Day Out of Days
12/11/2002 19:59 | Dawson's Creek | Merry Mayhem
11/20/2002 19:59 | Dawson's Creek | Everything Put Together Falls Apart
11/13/2002 19:59 | Dawson's Creek | Spiderwebs
11/06/2002 19:59 | Dawson's Creek | Ego Tripping at the Gates of Hell
10/30/2002 19:59 | Dawson's Creek | Living Dead Girl
10/23/2002 18:59 | Dawson's Creek | The Impostors
10/16/2002 18:59 | Dawson's Creek | Instant Karma!
06/07/2003 02:59 | East Meets West | Sushi 303
06/04/2003 14:29 | Epicurious | Dim Sum
06/05/2003 01:29 | Food 911 | Two Guys, a Girl and a Brisket!
06/04/2003 01:29 | Food 911 | Empanadas to Go
06/02/2003 19:59 | For Love or Money |
06/05/2003 03:29 | The Galloping Gourmet | Mantay
05/13/2003 18:59 | Gilmore Girls | Here Comes the Son
05/06/2003 18:59 | Gilmore Girls | Say Goodnight, Gracie
```

```
06/04/2003 15:29 | Great Chefs of the World | Stuffed Mushrooms; Hazelnut
Napoleon
06/04/2003 14:59 | Great Chefs of the World | Shrimp Ceviche; Lamb; Banana
Pudding
04/18/2003 19:59 | John Doe | Remote Control
06/04/2003 19:59 | Junkyard Wars | Manic Mud Racers
06/06/2003 23:37 | Late Night With Conan O'Brien |
05/25/2003 20:59 | Single in the Hamptons |
03/02/2003 16:59 | Smallville | Rosetta
02/23/2003 16:59 | Smallville | Fever
02/16/2003 16:59 | Smallville | Prodigal
02/09/2003 16:59 | Smallville | Rush
06/08/2003 14:59 | Star Trek: The Next Generation | A Fistful of Datas
05/07/2003 19:59 | The West Wing | Commencement
04/23/2003 19:59 | The West Wing | Evidence of Things Not Seen
02/26/2003 20:59 | The West Wing | Red Haven's on Fire
02/19/2003 20:59 | The West Wing | California 47th
```

To capture the *Now Playing List* as a pipe-delimited text file, use the > redirect symbol and supply the name of a file to which to write. For example, sending output to a file called *nowshowing.out* in the */var/out* directory would look like this:

```
bash-2.02# /var/hack/bin/nowshowing.tcl > /var/out/nowshowing.out
```

HACK #91 Discovering Your Favorite Actors

Ever think about who your favorite stars of the small screen are? I don't mean those you can think of off the top of your head. I mean based on actual television viewing habits.

We already have a framework to key off and siphon data from the television shows in the Now Playing List **[Hack #90]**. Now, let's gather some slightly different data. We'll make an account of all the actors and actresses in the television shows we watch, perhaps spotting trends in those we tend to gravitate toward.

Programmatically, this isn't any more than grabbing the `Actor` rather than the `Title` and `EpisodeTitle` attributes from the `Program` object. The `Actor` object lists all the stars of a particular show, which we'll parse to draw out the individual names and tally up the number of times they show up in your *Now Playing List*.

The Code

```
#!/tvbin/tivosh

# open the database, and for each television show,
# extract the date it aired, the title of the show,
# and the episode title
```

```
set db [dbopen]

# pull out the first 50 recorded shows from the database
set recdir "/Recording/NowShowingByTitle"
RetryTransaction {
    set files [mfs scan $recdir -count 50]

}

set actors { }
while { [llength $files] > 0 } {
    # iterate through the shows we extracted
    foreach rec $files {
        # grab the FSID of the program from the list
        set fsid [lindex $rec 0]

        RetryTransaction {
            # get the object that represents this recording and the
            # object that represents this episode.  wrap it in a
            # catch just in case it doesn't work
            set recordingobj [db $db openid $fsid]
            set episodeobj [dbobj [dbobj $recordingobj get Showing] get
Program]

            # pull out the list of actors in this show
            set epactors [dbobj $episodeobj get Actor]

        }

        # transform the actors names into strings and append them to
        # our list of all the actors on our TiVo
        foreach epactor $epactors {
            set slashpos [string first "|" $epactor]
            set repactor \
                "[string range $epactor 0 [expr $slashpos - 1]],"
            set repactor \
                "$repactor [string range $epactor [expr $slashpos + 1] end]"
            lappend actors $repactor

        }

    }

    # and grab the next 49 television shows
    set lastName [lindex [lindex $files end] 1]
    RetryTransaction {
        set files [mfs scan $recdir -start $lastName -count 50]

    }
    if { $lastName == [lindex [lindex $files 0] 1] } {
        set files [lrange $files 1 end]
    }
```

```
    }

    # create a new list called factors that is the frequency count of the
    # actors on the shows we have watched
    set factors { }
    foreach l $actors {
        if ![ info exists a($l) ] {
            set a($l) 0

        }
        incr a($l)

    }
    foreach i [ array names a ] {
        lappend factors [list $i $a($i)]
    }

    # and let's quickly alphabetically sort then print the list.⏎
      set factors [lsort -index 0 $factors]
    foreach factor $factors {
        puts "[lindex $factor 0] | [lindex $factor 1]"

    }
```

Save the code to a file called *actors.tcl* in TiVo's */var/hack/bin* directory and make it executable:

```
bash-2.02# chmod 755 /var/hack/bin/actors.tcl
```

Running the Hack

Run the script from TiVo's command line [Hacks #30, #52]:

```
bash-2.02# /var/hack/bin/actors.tcl
Ackles, Jensen | 4
Agena, Keiko | 2
Berkeley, Xander | 1
Bernard, Carlos | 1
Bishop, Kelly | 2
Bledel, Alexis | 2
Brook, Jayne | 1
Burton, LeVar | 1
Carradine, Ever | 1
Channing, Stockard | 4
Corbett, John | 1
Cuthbert, Elisha | 1
Dorn, Michael | 1
Esposito, Giancarlo | 1
Forsythe, William | 1
Frakes, Jonathan | 1
Gardell, Billy | 1
Glover, John | 4
Graham, Lauren | 2
```

```
Gunn, Sean | 2
Haysbert, Dennis | 1
Herrmann, Edward | 2
Hill, Dule | 4
Holmes, Katie | 15
Hudson, Oliver | 5
Humes, Mary-Margaret | 1
Jackson, Joshua | 15
Janney, Allison | 4
Jerald, Penny Johnson | 1
Jones III, Sam | 4
Jones, John Marshall | 1
Kajlich, Bianca | 5
Kreuk, Kristin | 4
Lowe, Rob | 4
Mack, Allison | 4
Malina, Josh | 1
McCarthy, Melissa | 2
McFadden, Gates | 1
Moloney, Janel | 4
...
```

To capture your list of favorite actors as a pipe-delimited text file, use the >
redirect symbol and supply the name of a file to which to write. For example, sending output to a file called *actors.out* in the */var/out* directory would
look like this:

```
bash-2.02# /var/hack/bin/actors.tcl > /var/out/actors.out
```

HACK #92   Discovering Your Favorite Writers, Producers, and Directors

Do you tend to favor the work of a particular director? Do the words of a
particular writer keep you riveted to the screen? Chances are that you
haven't given your favorite creatives much thought. Thankfully, TiVo keeps
track of them for you.

A variation on "Discovering Your Favorite Actors" [Hack #91], let's give a little
credit to the creatives—the writers, producers, and directors—while at the
same time learning a little more Tcl.

The Code

```
#!/tvbin/tivosh

global creatives
proc addcreative { c type } {
    global creatives
    foreach epcreative $c {
        set slashpos [string first "|" $epcreative]
        set repcreative \
```

```
                    "[string range $epcreative 0 [expr $slashpos - 1]],"⏎
            set repcreative \
                    "$repcreative [string range $epcreative [expr $slashpos + 1]⏎
                    end]"
            set repcreative \
                    "$repcreative | $type"
            lappend creatives $repcreative
    }


}

# open the database
set db [dbopen]

# pull out the first 50 recorded shows from the database
set recdir "/Recording/NowShowingByTitle"
RetryTransaction {
    set files [mfs scan $recdir -count 50]
    }

set creatives { }
while { [llength $files] > 0 } {
    # iterate through the shows we extracted
    foreach rec $files {
        # grab the FSID of the program from the list
        set fsid [lindex $rec 0]

        RetryTransaction {
            # get the object that represents this recording and the
            # object that represents this episode.  wrap it in
            # a catch just in case
            # it doesn't work
            set recordingobj [db $db openid $fsid]
            set episodeobj [dbobj [dbobj $recordingobj get Showing] get
Program]

            # pull out the list of writers, directors, and producers of the
            # shows.  none of these are guaranteed to be here
            set epwriters [dbobj $episodeobj get Writer]
            set epdirectors [dbobj $episodeobj get Director]
            set epproducers [dbobj $episodeobj get ExecProducer]
        }

        # add all those creatives to a list to work with
        addcreative $epwriters "Writer"
        addcreative $epdirectors "Director"
        addcreative $epproducers "ExecProducer"
    }

    # and grab the next 49 television shows⏎
    set lastName [lindex [lindex $files end] 1]
    RetryTransaction {
        set files [mfs scan $recdir -start $lastName -count 50]
```

```
        }
        if { $lastName == [lindex [lindex $files 0] 1] } {
            set files [lrange $files 1 end]
        }
    }

    # create a new list called fcreatives that is the frequency count
    # of the creatives on the shows we have watched
    set fcreatives { }
    foreach l $creatives {
        if ![ info exists a($l) ] {
            set a($l) 0
        }
        incr a($l)
    }
    foreach i [ array names a ] {
        lappend fcreatives [list $i $a($i)]
    }

    # and let's quickly alphabetically sort then print the list
    set fcreatives [lsort -index 0 $fcreatives]
    foreach fcreative $fcreatives {
        puts "[lindex $fcreative 0] | [lindex $fcreative 1]"
    }
```

Save the code as *creatives.tcl* in TiVo's */var/hack/bin* directory and make it executable:

```
bash-2.02# chmod 755 /var/hack/bin/creatives.tcl
```

Running the Hack

Run the script from TiVo's command line [Hacks #30, #52]:

```
bash-2.02# /var/hack/bin/creatives.tcl
Babbit, Jamie | Director | 1
Beeman, Greg | Director | 1
Berlanti, Greg | ExecProducer | 15
Berman, Rick | ExecProducer | 1
Braga, Brannon | Writer | 1
Bruckheimer, Jerry | ExecProducer | 1
Camp, Brandon | ExecProducer | 1
Cochran, Bob | ExecProducer | 1
Fattore, Gina | Writer | 5
Foy, John | ExecProducer | 1
Fricke, Anna | Writer | 3
Friedman, Maggie | Writer | 3
Garcia, Liz | Writer | 1
Gereghty, Bill | Director | 1
Gough, Al | Writer | 1
Gough, Alfred | ExecProducer | 4
Jackson, Joshua | Director | 1
```

```
Kapinos, Tom | Writer | 3
Kowalski, Peter | Director | 1
Kroll, Jon | ExecProducer | 1
Lange, Michael | Director | 3
Leahy, Janet | Writer | 1
Leder, Mimi | ExecProducer | 1
Marshall, James | Director | 1
McNeill, Robbie | Director | 2
Millar, Miles | ExecProducer | 4
Millar, Miles | Writer | 1
Moore, Jason | Director | 1
Nash, Bruce | ExecProducer | 1
Nelson, Todd | ExecProducer | 1
...
```

To capture your list of favorite writers, producers, and directors as a pipe-delimited text file, use the > redirect symbol and supply the name of a file to which to write. For example, sending output to a file called *creatives.out* in the */var/out* directory would look like this:

```
bash-2.02# /var/hack/bin/creatives.tcl > /var/out/creatives.out
```

Take note that people can be listed under more than one role, and they can also be listed more than once for a given role. Take a look at Miles Millar; he was credited four times as an Executive Producer and once as a writer. If we gather enough of this information over time, we can create our own Internet Movie Database (*http://www.imdb.com*) from our television listings alone.

HACK #93   Turning Favorites Lists into JavaScript

With a little Tcl, you can query TiVo for your favorite actors, preferred creatives, Now Showing List, and so forth. Syndicate those lists to your web site or weblog with a little JavaScript and the magic of TiVoWeb.

The problem with pipe-delimited lists [Hacks **[Hack #90]**, **[Hack #91]** is that you have to get them off your TiVo to another machine and run yet another script to either process the list for display or generate something that you can manipulate. Seems a little complicated to me.

What if what you want is really simple? You just want to have a live version of your *To Do List* on your web site or weblog. You want anybody who goes to your site to see what's of interest to you on the tube—or at least what TiVo will be recording for you—over the next couple of days. What if I told you it was dirt simple and required none of that pipe-delimited nonsense?

Remember TiVoWeb **[Hack #65]** from Chapter 5? It has access to your To Do List **[Hack #67]**. Why not just write a module **[Hack #78]** that generates some JavaScript to be included in the web page of your choosing? That's exactly what we are going to do.

In fact, writing a TivoWeb module is decidedly simple, as you can see in the following code. TiVoWeb already has a database handle available for use by a module, and all we have to do is write whatever we are planning to write with a call to puts. Whatever you write will get shoved out the socket, right to the browser visiting your site.

The Code

```
proc action_jtodo { chan path env } {
    global db
    global tzoffset
    eval $env

    # pull out the first 50 todo list shows from the database
    set tododir "/Recording/Active"
    set prefix "4"
    transaction {
        set files [mfs scan $tododir -start $prefix -count 50]
    }

    while { [llength $files] > 0 } {
        # iterate through the shows we extracted
        foreach rec $files {
            # grab the FSID of the program from the list
            set fsid [lindex $rec 0]

            RetryTransaction {
                # get the object that represents this recording and
                # the object that represents this episode. wrap it
                # in a catch just in case
                # it doesn't work
                set recordingobj [db $db openid $fsid]
                set showingobj [dbobj $recordingobj get Showing]
                set episodeobj [dbobj $showingobj get Program]
                set behaviorobj [dbobj $recordingobj get RecordingBehavior]

                # pull out the date the show aired -- also convert
                # it to something a bit more human readable
                set showtime [expr ( [dbobj $showingobj get Date] * 86400 )↵
                + \ [dbobj $showingobj get Time] + $tzoffset ]
                set showtime [clock format $showtime -format "%m/%d"]

                # pull out the show's name and episode title
                regsub -all "\[\{\}\]" [dbobj $episodeobj get Title] ""↵
                programname
                regsub -all "\[\{\}\]" [dbobj $episodeobj get EpisodeTitle]
"" \
                episodename

                # get the data to figure out whether this a
                # scheduled recording or a suggested recording
```

```
                    set presbehavior [dbobj $behaviorobj get↲
                    PresentationBehavior]
                }

                # output some javascript -- if presbehavior is 6, that
                # means we are looking at a suggested recording
                if { $presbehavior != 6 } {
                    puts $chan "document.write( \"<span class=\\\"episodedate\\\↲
                    ">$showtime</span> - <span↲
                    class=\\\"showtitle\\\">$programname</span> <span class=\\\↲
                    "episodetitle\\\">$episodename</span><br/>
\" );"
                }

            # and grab the next 50 television shows
            set lastName [lindex [lindex $files end] 1]
            transaction {
                set files [mfs scan $tododir -start $lastName -count 50]
            }
            if { $lastName == [lindex [lindex $files 0] 1] } {
                set files [lrange $files 1 end]
            }
        }
    }

    # register the module as JScript ToDo with a friendly
    # description for inclusion in TiVoWeb's main menu
    register_module "jtodo" "JScript ToDo" "Generate Javascript with the ToDo
    list"
```

Save this file as *jtodo.itcl* in the */var/hack/tivoweb-tcl/modules* directory on your TiVo. Restart TiVoWeb by choosing *Restart → Full Reload* from its menu bar. The module should be noticed and activated when TiVoWeb starts back up.

Running the Hack

Simply insert the following line into your HTML document where you'd like the *To Do List* to appear:

```
<script
language="JavaScript"
src="http://my_tivo/jtodo">
</script>
```

Replace *my_tivo* with the hostname or IP address of your TiVo.

Upon encountering this tag, JavaScript-enabled web browsers (most modern browsers) will grab a fresh copy of the *To Do List* from your TiVo, inserting it right into the page.

The JavaScript source version of my current *To Do List* looks like this:

```
document.write( "<span class=\"episodedate\">06/08</span> - <span class=\
"showtitle\">Lucky</span> <span class=\"episodetitle\">The Method</span><br/
>" );
document.write( "<span class=\"episodedate\">06/09</span> - <span class=\
"showtitle\">Advanced Paid Program</span> <span class=\"episodetitle\"></
span><br/>" );
document.write( "<span class=\"episodedate\">06/09</span> - <span class=\
"showtitle\">Teleworld Paid Program</span> <span class=\"episodetitle\"></
span><br/>" );
document.write( "<span class=\"episodedate\">06/09</span> - <span class=\
"showtitle\">Surf Girls</span> <span class=\"episodetitle\"></span><br/>" );
document.write( "<span class=\"episodedate\">06/09</span> - <span class=\
"showtitle\">Surf Girls</span> <span class=\"episodetitle\"></span><br/>" );
document.write( "<span class=\"episodedate\">06/09</span> - <span class=\
"showtitle\">ABC World News Tonight</span> <span class=\"episodetitle\"></
span><br/>" );
document.write( "<span class=\"episodedate\">06/09</span> - <span class=\
"showtitle\">For Love or Money</span> <span class=\"episodetitle\"></span>
<br/>" );
document.write( "<span class=\"episodedate\">06/09</span> - <span class=\
"showtitle\">Road Rules</span> <span class=\"episodetitle\">South Pacific</
span><br/>" );
```

The module even provides you with stylesheet elements—episodedate, showtitle, and episodetitle—that you can color, size, and style any which way using standard CSS.

Figure 7-3 shows the result, my TiVo's *To Do List* incorporated into a page on my web site.

In actuality, you don't want to pull a fresh copy of your *To Do List* from your TiVo unit every time someone hits your web page. You'd be exposing your TiVo's hostname or address to the world—not a good thing to do, even if you're behind an Apache HTTP proxy (see "Proxy Pass-Through with Apache" in "Putting Your TiVo on the Web" [Hack #80]). You'll be placing undue strain on your TiVo and the TiVoWeb module as it serves up a response to all those visits to your ultrapopular home page. And then there's the fact that your *To Do List* doesn't change all that often, so brewing up a fresh copy each time is simply a waste of resources.

Instead, schedule the server on which your web site lives to fetch the JavaScript include once an hour or, better yet, once a day and serve up the local cached (read: saved) copy. You can do so using *cron* on Unix and Mac OS X servers, or Scheduled Events under Windows. In fact, if you go this direction, you might as well skip the JavaScript include altogether and alter the TiVoWeb module so that it produces plain old HTML:

```
puts $chan "<em>$programname</em>: $episodename ($showtime)<br />";
```

TiVo ToDo

06/09 - Surf Girls
06/09 - Surf Girls
06/09 - ABC World News
Tonight
06/09 - For Love or Money
06/09 - Road Rules South
Pacific
06/09 - Surf Girls
06/09 - Family Guy
European Road Show
06/10 - Late Night With
Conan O'Brien
06/10 - ABC World News
Tonight
06/10 - The Real World
Paris
06/10 - The Osbournes
06/11 - Late Night With
Conan O'Brien
06/11 - ABC World News
Tonight
06/12 - Late Night With
Conan O'Brien
06/12 - Teleworld Paid
Program
06/12 - Teleworld Paid
Program
06/12 - ABC World News
Tonight
06/12 - The Amazing Race
4 I Wasn't Even Going to
Touch You Until You
Slammed My Head
Backwards
06/13 - Late Night With
Conan O'Brien

Figure 7-3. TiVo's To Do List, JavaScript-included in a web page

This line replaces the line beginning with puts $chan "document.write in the previous module code.

This HTML fragment can easily be incorporated into a web page using Server-Side Includes (*http://hoohoo.ncsa.uiuc.edu/docs/tutorials/includes.html*) or the like. Here, I include a copy cached as *tivo_todo.html* into my home page, *index.shtml*:

```
<!--#include virtual="./tivo_todo.html" -->
```

HACK   How Do You Watch TV?
#94
Compute your hunt-and-peck percentage to truly find out what kind of a viewer you are.

Are you a watch-the-show-all-the-way-through kind of TiVo user, or do you hunt and peck, watching 5 minutes of a show and moving on? Do you never finish watching what is on your *Now Showing List*? Continuing our personal data mining, let's find out what kind of person you are—at least according to your TiVo. We'll compute your hunt-and-peck percentage—what percentage, on average, of a show you typically watch—down to the second. And with a little JavaScript magic, we'll share the outcome with the world on your web page.

The Code

```
proc action_huntandpeck { chan path env } {
   global db

   # pull out the first 50 todo list shows from the database
   set tododir "/Recording/NowShowingByTitle"
   RetryTransaction {
      set files [mfs scan $tododir -count 50]
   }

   set nshows 0
   set pshows 0
   while { [llength $files] > 0 } {
      # iterate through the shows we extracted
      foreach rec $files {
        set fsid [lindex $rec 0]

        RetryTransaction {
         # get the object that represents this recording.
         # also figure out of the person has played this
         # program then stopped -- if they did, the
         # bookmark will be set
         set recordingobj [db $db openid $fsid]
         set bookmark [dbobj $recordingobj get Bookmark]
         if { $bookmark != "" } {
           incr pshows
         }
         incr nshows
       }
      }

      # and grab the next 50 television shows
      set lastName [lindex [lindex $files end] 1]
      RetryTransaction {
         set files [mfs scan $tododir -start $lastName -count 50]
      }
      if { $lastName == [lindex [lindex $files 0] 1] } {
         set files [lrange $files 1 end]
      }
   }
   puts $chan "document.write( \"<span class=\"hptext\">My TiVo↵
   Hunt-and-Peck Ratio is</span> <span class=\"hpnum\">↵
   [expr ( $pshows * 1.0 ) / ( $nshows * 1.0 )]</span>\" );\

}

register_module "huntandpeck" "HuntAndPeck" "Are you a hunter or a pecker?"
```

This hack is in the form of another TiVoWeb module [Hack #93]. Save this code as *huntandpeck.itcl* in the */var/hack/tivoweb-tcl/modules* directory on your TiVo. Restart TiVoWeb by choosing *Restart → Full Reload* from its menu bar. The module should be noticed and activated when TiVoWeb starts back up.

Running the Hack

Simply insert the following line into your HTML document where you'd like your hunt-and-peck percentage to appear:

```
<script
language="JavaScript"
src="http://my_tivo/huntandpeck">
</script>
```

Replace *my_tivo* with the hostname or IP address of your TiVo.

Upon encountering this tag, JavaScript-enabled web browsers (most modern browsers) will grab a fresh copy of your hunt-and-peck ratio from your TiVo, inserting it right into the page, like so:

```
document.write( "<span class=\"hptext\">My TiVo Hunt-and-Peck Ratio⏎
is</span><span class=\"hpnum\"> 0.204081632653</span> " );
```

Apparently, I hunt and peck 20% of the time. Who'd have thunk it?

> In actuality, you don't want to pull a fresh copy of your hun-
> and-peck ratio from your TiVo unit every time someone hits
> your web page. See the end of "Turning Favorites Lists into
> JavaScript" [Hack #93] for further discussion and solutions.

HACK #95 Browsing Through TiVo's Resources

Groups of resources are loaded by TiVo's main programs at runtime. Hacking these resources allows customization of the TiVo software without recompiling or any such complex shenanigans.

Resource groups are external definitions of strings that the main program can load at runtime, allowing programmers to customize applications in various ways without touching the executable applications themselves. Normally these resources are meant for TiVo, Inc. programmers, but now they in the hands of hackers.

You can browse the current crop of resource groups on your TiVo in */SwSystem/ ACTIVE*. Use mls [Hack #88] to inspect the file. Then use dumpobj [Hack #89] to view their contents:

```
% mls /SwSystem/ACTIVE
Directory of /SwSystem starting at 'ACTIVE'
```

```
Name Type FsId Date Time Size
---- ---- ---- ---- ---- ----
ACTIVE tyDb 1054901 06/14/02 07:04 652
```

```
% dumpobj /SwSystem/ACTIVE
SwSystem 1054901/11 {
  Active          = 1
  IndexPath       = /SwSystem/3.0-01-1-010 /SwSystem/ACTIVE /Server/6406408
  Module          = 1054552/-1 1054554/-1 1054556/-1 1054558/-1 1054560/-1
1054562/-1 1054564/-1 1054566/-1 1054902/-1
  Name            = 3.0-01-1-010
  ResourceChecksum = 2561393d51da083831d2f0714914888a
  ResourceGroup   = 1054757/-1 1054758/-1 1054889/-1 1054761/-1 1054766/-1
1054767/-1 1054890/-1 1054772/-1 1054775/-1 1054776/-1 1054779/-1 1054891/-1
1054784/-1 1054787/-1 1054892/-1 1054792/-1 1054795/-1 1054796/-1 1054800/-1
1054893/-1 1054803/-1 1054806/-1 1054807/-1 1054808/-1 1054809/-1 1054894/-1
1054810/-1 1054895/-1 1054896/-1 1054897/-1 1054811/-1 1054812/-1 1054813/-1
1054814/-1 1054815/-1 1054816/-1 1054817/-1 1054818/-1 1054821/-1 1054898/-1
1054826/-1 1054899/-1 1054831/-1 1054900/-1 1054840/-1 1054841/-1 1054850/-1
1054851/-1 1054854/-1
  ServerId        = 6406408
  ServerVersion   = 51
  Version         = 2
}
```

FSIDs of all the available resource groups are listed under ResourceGroup. Here, you'll find all the text in the TiVo user interface, constants that control your MPEG encoder bitrate, the backdoor password [Hack #8], a veritable cornucopia of default values, and a host of things nobody has yet figured out.

The Code

The following script is based on a conversation at *http://alt.org/forum/index.php?t=msg&th=34*. It walks through all the resources in the TiVo and prints them out with their identification numbers

```
#!/tvbin/tivosh

set outformat "%3s %3s %s"
puts [format $outformat "GID" "IID" "Resource"]
puts [format $outformat "---" "---" "--------"]

set db [dbopen]
RetryTransaction {
    set active [db $db open "/SwSystem/ACTIVE"]
    set rgroup [dbobj $active get ResourceGroup]
    set groupn 0
    foreach group $rgroup {
        set items [dbobj $group get Item]
        set itemn 0
        foreach item $items {
```

```
    regsub -all "\[\{\}\]" [dbobj $item get String] "" resource↵
    puts [format $outformat $groupn $itemn "\"$resource\""]↵
    incr itemn
    }
    incr groupn
  }
}
```

Save the code as *dump.tcl* in your TiVo's */var/hack/bin* directory and make it executable, like so:

```
bash-2.02# chmod 755 /var/hack/bin/dump.tcl
```

Running the Hack

Run the script from TiVo's command line [Hacks #30, #52]. You're sure to see lots of familiar strings flow by.

```
bash-2.02# /var/hack/bin/dump.tcl
...
  1   5 "Now Playing List"
  1   6 "TiVo Central"
  1   7 "TiVo's Suggestions"
  1   8 "TiVolution Magazine"
  1   9 "Showcases"
  1  10 "Pick Programs to Record"
  1  11 "To Do List"
  1  12 "Messages & Setup"
  1  13 "DIRECTV Menu"
  1  14 "No programs"
  1  15 "TiVolution Magazine is currently unavailable. It will be updated
the next time your Recorder makes a daily call to the TiVo Service. "
  1  16 "Custom"
  1  17 " Channel %s"
  1  18 " Search By Title"
  1  19 " Browse By Channel"
  1  20 " Browse By Time"
  1  21 " Search Using WishLists"
  1  22 " Manually Record Time/Channel"
...
```

Just makes you want to reach out and fiddle [Hack #96], doesn't it?

Making Recordings Start Late and End Early

#96

Only interested in your local news for tomorrow's weather report, but you find yourself having to fast forward through the whole thing every night? By altering TiVo's resources, you can allow scheduled recordings of only the portion of a show you're interested in.

While scanning your TiVo's mind (a.k.a. *resources*) can make for some interesting reading, there are actually all sorts of things you can do by writing to it. This hack does more than make a cosmetic change to a menu or tweak a display setting; it actually changes the way TiVo works.

The script adds negative values to the Start Recording and Stop Recording options, allowing you to start recordings late and end them early, not just start early and end late. This is useful for recording tomorrow's weather forecast—the last 10 minutes of your local 10 o'clock news—without having to record the whole broadcast and fast forward your way through.

 As is, this hack will work only under TiVo OS 3.x.

The Code

Mike Baker wrote this *padhack.tcl* script, which modifies resource group 32, items 19 and 21, which supply values to the Start Recording and Stop Recording options.

```
#!/tvbin/tivosh

EnableTransactionHoldoff true

set db [dbopen]
RetryTransaction {
    # get handles to the right database entries
    set swsysa [db $db open "/SwSystem/ACTIVE"]
    set tmpgrp [dbobj $swsysa get ResourceGroup 32]

    # add new values for the start recording times
    set tmpres [dbobj $tmpgrp get "Item" 19]
    dbobj $tmpres set String "On-time|0|1 minute early|60|2 minutes↵
    early|120|3 minutes early|180|4 minutes early|240|5 minutes early|300|10↵
    minutes early|600|1 minute late|-60|2 minutes late|-120|3 minutes late|↵
    -180|4 minutes late|-240|5 minutes late|-300|10 minutes late|-600|"↵
    # add new values for the stop recording times↵
    set tmpres [dbobj $tmpgrp get "Item" 21]

    dbobj $tmpres set String "On-time|0|1 minute longer|60|2 minutes↵
    longer|120|5 minutes longer|300|15 minutes longer|900|30 minutes↵
    longer|1800|1 hour longer|3600|1 1/2 hours longer|5400|3 hours↵
    longer|10800|1 minute shorter|-60|2 minutes shorter|-120|3 minute↵
    shorter|-180|4 minutes shorter|-240|5 minutes shorter|-300|10 minutes↵
    shorter| 600|"

    dbobj $tmpgrp remove "CompressedFile"
}
```

To understand how this works, run *dump.tcl* [Hack #94] and find resource group 32. You'll see that item 19 dictates values for the Start Recording offset, and item 21 controls the Stop Recording offsets:

```
32 19 {On-time|0|1 minute early|60|2 minutes early|120|3 minutes early|180|4
minutes early|240|5 minutes early|300|10 minutes early|600|}
...
32 21 {On-time|0|1 minute longer|60|2 minutes longer|120|5 minutes
longer|300|15 minutes longer|900|30 minutes longer|1800|1 hour longer|3600|1
1/2 hours longer|5400|3 hours longer|10800|}
```

Save the code as *padhack.tcl* in TiVo's */var/hack/bin* directory and make it executable:

```
bash-2.02# chmod 755 /var/hack/bin/padhack.tcl
```

Running the Hack

Run the script from TiVo's command line [Hacks #30, #52]:

```
bash-2.02# /var/hack/bin/padhack.tcl
```

Reboot your TiVo, schedule a recording, and visit the *Recording Options* screen to see your changes in effect, as shown in Figure 7-4. Cool, huh? And it's useful if all you want to see is the Top 10 List at the beginning of a late night talk show, the weather report at the end of the news, headlines at the top of every hour on CNN, and so forth.

You have to run the script only once, because the altered settings persist through reboots.

Hacking the Hack

You're not confined to the changes you've just made. Take a closer look at the lines starting with dbobj $tmpres set in the *padhack.tcl* code. The groupings inside the { and } actually set the values for the TiVo. For example, On-time has an offset of 0, while a minute early has an offset of 60, and so forth.

We can insert any custom value that we want. Change it to look like this:

```
dbobj $tmpres set String "On-time|0|1 minute early|60|2 minutes early|120|3↵
minutes early|180|4 minutes early|240|5 minutes early|300|10 minutes↵
early|600|17 minutes early|1020|1 minute late|-60|2 minutes late|-120|3↵
minutes late|-180|4 minutes late|-240|5 minutes late|-300|10 minutes late|↵
-600|"
```

That new 17 minutes early|1020 segment adds the ability to the stop recording 17 minutes from the end of a program.

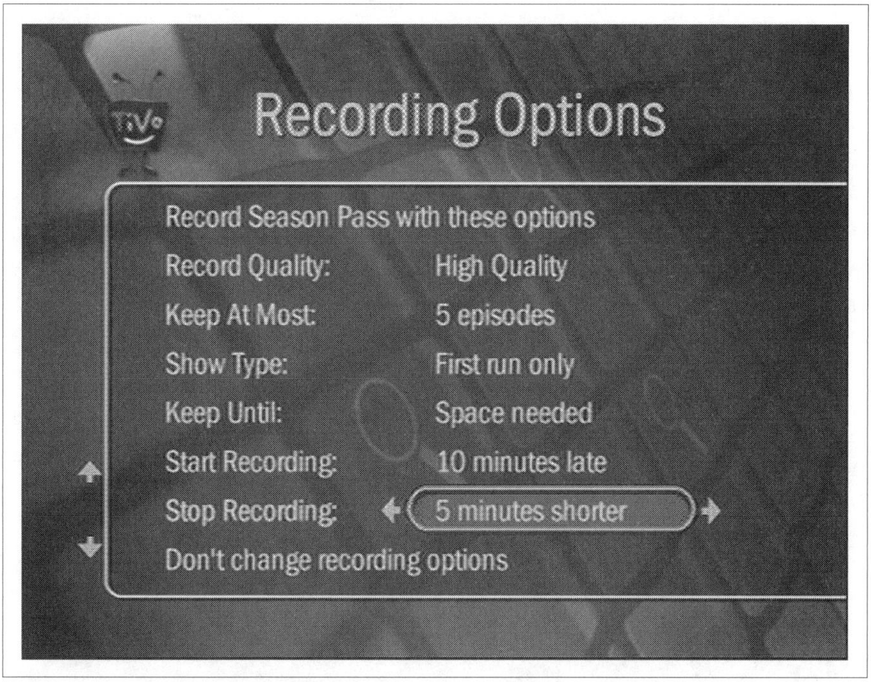

Recording Options

Record Season Pass with these options

Record Quality: High Quality

Keep At Most: 5 episodes

Show Type: First run only

Keep Until: Space needed

Start Recording: 10 minutes late

Stop Recording: ◀ ⬭5 minutes shorter⬭ ▶

Don't change recording options

Figure 7-4. Setting your Season Passes to start late and end early

HACK #97 Editing Resources with a Point and a Click

One of the easier ways to edit a resource [Hack #96] is just to make use of the TiVoWeb resource editor module.

Pick up your remote and surf to the *Search by Title* menu under *Pick Programs to Record*. Ever wanted to change the title on the screen? Trick it out to what you want it to say?

In the */var/hack/tivoweb-tcl/modules* directory of your TiVo, you should find a file called *tvres-3.0.res*.

> The *3.0* in the filename refers to the TiVo OS version you're running. If, for some reason, you are still running Version 2.0 or 2.5, take a look at the appropriately named file instead.

Add the following line to the file:

```
Words BrowseByTime 1 20
```

Check out the output of *dumpres.tcl* [Hack #95]. Scroll down until you find the line that starts: 1 20 {Browse By Time}. Those are the two numbers we are talking about here. We are telling TiVoWeb to expose that particular resource so that we can edit it.

For convenience, TiVoWeb is going to create a new grouping in its resource editor called Words, after the first token in the line we added. Then, the particular resource will be named after the second token, BrowseByTime.

To see TiVoWeb in action, go to TiVoWeb's [Hack #65] *Resource Editor*, click the Update Resources link, and restart the server (*Restart → Full Reload*). When you come back to the *Resource Editor*, you should find a new resource group (Figure 7-5).

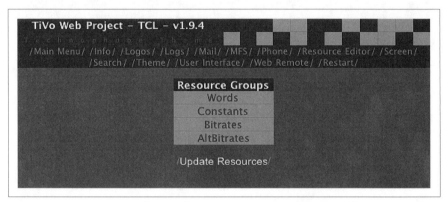

Figure 7-5. The Resource Editor, with a new resource group

Under that, the editor will provide a field for you to play with (Figure 7-6).

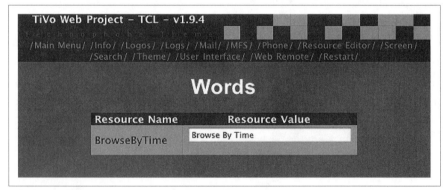

Figure 7-6. The TiVoWeb Resource Editor, providing an interface to change the new resource in the database

If you change this field, you will change the menu text that comes up in the *Browse By Time* screen. You can do this for anything that is hooked to a resource you can spot when using *dump.tcl*.

Catching TiVo Events

Instead of being one monolithic system, the TiVo is broken down into smaller programs that communicate with one another by passing messages around. If you intercept that message stream, you can get a clue into what the TiVo is doing.

One common software paradigm is to break up large pieces of code into smaller chunks of code that call one another when they need to interact. The TiVo software isn't much different. It has various subsystems, all talking to each other through a central event switcher. Think of the event switcher as a message board. An event is posted to the event switcher, which makes sure that everybody sees the event. Each software component can then choose if and how to react.

These events are structured in three parts: an event type, an event subtype, and the data carried. You can learn something about the event IDs through */tvlib/tcl/tv/Inc.tcl*. If you scroll far enough through that file, you'll see these lines:

```
namespace eval TmkEvent {
    # message enums taken directly from mom/event.h
    variable EVT_PAUSE                   0
    variable EVT_RESET                   1
    variable EVT_SHUTDOWN                2
    variable EVT_EOD                     3
    variable EVT_RESOURCE_UNAVAILABLE    4
    variable EVT_SHUTDOWN_COMPLETE       5
    variable EVT_READY                   6
    variable EVT_SET_POSITION            7
    variable EVT_SET_POSITION_RESULT     8
    variable EVT_OSD                     9
    variable EVT_RELEASE_RUN            10
    variable EVT_TRICKPLAY             11
    variable EVT_FLUSH                 12
...
```

These are all constant names assigned to the different event types. Unfortunately, none of this information is documented anywhere. To deduce anything, we'll have to see these events in action.

The Code

This script registers itself with the event switcher to receive a callback for events 0 through 74 listed in *Inc.tcl*. When it gets the call, it prints the event type it received, as well as all the data that came along with it.

```
#!/tvbin/tivosh

proc event_callback { type subtype } {
```

```
    global EventData
    binary scan $EventData I* idata
    puts "[format "%02d" $type] [format "%02d" $subtype] : $idata"
}

for {set x 0} {$x <= 74} {incr x} {
  event register $x event_callback
}

set StillWaiting 1
vwait StillWaiting
```

Save the code as *events.tcl* in your TiVo's */var/hack/bin* directory, and make
it executable:

```
bash-2.02# chmod 755 /var/hack/bin/events.tcl
```

Running the Hack

Run the script from TiVo's command line [Hacks #30, #52]. You might not see
anything at first. To give TiVo an event to react to, hit the 🍸 button. While
the details are sure to be different, you should see something like this:

```
bash-2.02# /var/hack/bin/events.tcl
28 01 : 5 1 1 1 245946781 1373220824
```

The second line represents the event sent out when the 🍸 button is pressed:
28 is the event type, 01 is the event subtype, and everything thereafter is
additional data. *Inc.tcl* says that event 28 maps to EVT_REMOTEEVENT, probably referring to a remote control event. If, instead, you press the **1** button on
your remote, you'll see something like this:

```
28 01 : 17 1 1 1 245946833 -889979864
```

Again, you capture an event of type 28, subtype 01. We can deduce that the
subtype doesn't detail which key is pressed. Perhaps that information is in
the data field? Let's see what happens when you press the **2** button instead:

```
28 01 : 18 1 1 1 245946847 395401288
```

Notice the change in the number after the colon; the **1** button generated a
17, while the **2** button generated an 18. As you work your way up the number scale on your remote, you'll see that data number increasing as you go.

And events spawn other events; you'll see other events as you go poking
about pressing buttons on the remote control. The 🍸 button, for instance,
is probably going to cause one of the subsystems to send out another event
telling whatever controls TiVo's menu and display systems to show the *TiVo
Central* menu on your television screen.

So, now that we've captured an event, let's see what can we do with it
[Hack #99].

HACK
99
Disabling the Live TV button

What good is limiting your children's viewing to the G-rated bounty TiVo's brought them if they can just meander into an R-rated neighborhood with a click of the Live TV button?

You've carefully crafted your children's television viewing to contain only television shows you believe are wholesome and good for them. But then they go mucking about with the **Live TV** button and catch some gruesome action flick or racy *Sex in the City* episode you'd rather they not see for a couple of years—or ever, for that matter. This hack is all about disabling that dastardly **Live TV** button on the kids' TiVo.

Now that you've learned all about events [Hack #98], it shouldn't surprise you to know that getting to Live TV is controlled by an event passing through the event switcher. Try it out by running *events.tcl* [Hack #98], and press the **Live TV** button on your remote. You should see something like this:

```
bash-2.02# /var/hack/bin/events.tcl
28 00 : 6 1 1 0 245947039 -971910840
27 00 : 6 2147480992 29693532 0 0 2147481008
28 01 : 6 1 1 1 245947039 -723092840
```

There are two event types here: type 28 is the remote control event, and type 27 is something called EVT_MW_STATUS. While you're running *events.tcl*, navigate to the *TiVo Central* menu, select *Watch Live TV*, and see what happens. You should see a few events float by, most notably this:

```
27 00 : 6 0 0 2138912008 0 2147480992
```

You might guess that an event type 27 with a first data value of 6 is telling TiVo to display live television. And you'd be right.

While it's tempting to simply squelch that event, we just can't do that—at least not without some serious programming know-how and developer-level knowledge of all the places the message is caught. But we can catch it and do something in retaliation. The plan of attack is to detect when the TiVo wants to display live television, asking it to put up the *TiVo Central* menu instead. This way, no matter how the TiVo attempts to get to live television—through the **Live TV** button, the *Watch Live TV* menu option on *TiVo Central*, or automatically after being on *TiVo Central* for too long—your TiVo will be asked to go back to the *TiVo Central* menu.

The Code

Because this code needs to be running at all times, it tends to be a little more on the complicated side. At its heart, it registers a callback to catch_livetv whenever an EVT_MW_STATUS event is noticed. If the event has a data value of

6, the script asks TiVo to simulate the pressing of the 📺 button, sending the viewer back to *TiVo Central*. (Do not pass Go. Do not collect $200). All the other code around the catch_livetv procedure is for support, to make this script as unintrusive as possible.

```
#!/tvbin/tivosh

# include some TiVo TCL libraries
source $tcl_library/tv/log.tcl
source $tcl_library/tv/sendkey.tcl

# disable the key sending from being put on the screen
set verboseSendKeyG 0

# the name of the file containing the PID
set pidfile "/tmp/livetv.pid"

# the callback function to call when we get a EVT_MW_STATUS event.
# whenever the TiVo attempts to switch into LiveTV, this event is sent
# out with a state number 6
proc catch_livetv { type subtype } {
    global EventData

    # pull out the state value -- if we get a state 6, then we send
    # the "TiVo" key
    binary scan $EventData I state
    if { $state == 6 } {
        SendKey "tivo"
    }
}

# see if we are supposed to be killing a version that is in the
# background.  if we are, read the PID file and kill the forked off
# process -- then delete the file
if { [lindex $argv 0] == "-stop" } {
    if { [file exists $pidfile] } {
        set pfchan [open $pidfile "r"]
        set lpid [gets $pfchan]
        close $pfchan
        file delete -force $pidfile
        try {
            kill $lpid
        } catch errCode { }
    }
    exit 0
}

# if livetv is already running, then put up a warning to that point
if { [file exists $pidfile] } {
    puts stderr "livetv is already running"
    puts stderr "if it is not, then delete /tmp/livetv.pid"
    exit 1
```

```
}

# if we get the -run flag, then we are going to create the pid file
# and start a process waiting for the right events
if { [lindex $argv 0] == "-run" } {
    set pfchan [open $pidfile "w"]
    puts $pfchan [pid]
    close $pfchan

    # register to watch EVT_MW_STATUS events
    event register 27 catch_livetv
    set StillWaiting 1
    vwait StillWaiting

} else {
    # fork off a copy of this script to be run in the background
    exec $argv0 "-run" "&"
}
```

Save the code as *disabletv.tcl* in TiVo's */var/hack/bin* directory, and make it executable:

```
bash-2.02# chmod 755 /var/hack/bin/disabletv.tcl
```

Running the Hack

Run the script from TiVo's command line [Hacks #30, #52], like so:

```
bash-2.02# /var/hack/bin/disabletv.tcl
```

This should return you to the prompt right away. If you take a look at the running processes, you should see that a version of this program is running in the background:

```
bash-2.02# ps auxw | grep disabletv
root       333  1.2  8.4  7936  1172 p1 S    02:47   0:01 tivosh /var/hack/
bin/disabletv.tcl -run
```

And it should be doing what it's programmed to do. Go ahead, push the **Live TV** button on your remote. Your television will show live television for an instant, followed immediately by the gentle "bling" sound of the 📺 button being pressed, and the *TiVo Central* menu will flicker right up on the screen. Any other way you attempt to get to live television will have the same effect.

To stop the hack, simply run the following command:

```
bash-2.02# /var/hack/bin/disabletv.tcl -stop
```

Your live television abilities will be returned to you.

HACK Cross-Compiling C Code for TiVo
100
Sometimes, you just need to use C. For those times, you'll need a compiler
that is capable of generating binaries to run on your Series 1 or Series 2 TiVo.

There are times that you realize why C is one of the most popular programming languages out there. If you use it right, it makes code that's small and
fast. Plus, there is already a lot of code out there written in C, including
most of the Unix utilities [Hack #34] we've been using in this book. Using a
cross-compiler is your best shot at turning your favorite little program into a
TiVo binary.

Cross-compiling is a black art that deserves a book unto itself, so we'll keep
to installing a cross-compiler and writing a small C program to satisfy ourselves that it works and provide yet another avenue for further TiVo hacking. If you look at *http://tivoutils.sourceforge.net*, you'll notice quite a few
cross-compilers listed—most notably, *http://prdownloads.sourceforge.net/
tivoutils/usr.local.powerpc-tivo.tar.bz2?download*. These are the cross-compilers that run under Linux and generate binaries to run on Series 1 and
Series 2 TiVos, respectively. Both are set up in basically the same way,
thanks to the hard work of M. Drew Streib.

Download the appropriate cross-compiler to a Linux PC, and unpack the
entire archive to */home/tivodev* (more than likely, you will have to do this as
root):

```
# bunzip2 usr.local.powerpc.tivo.tar.bz2
# tar xf usr.local.powerpc.tivo.tar
# mv tivodev /home
```

Once you have installed your cross-compiler, all the software you need for C
development for your TiVo (Series 1, in this case) will be available for your
coding pleasure. You have *gcc* (*/home/tivodev/root/bin/gcc*) as your compiler,
and a whole slew of libraries are already precompiled. However, in his
README, Streib makes it clear that "you may need to install additional
libraries, do some porting, etc., but that is par for the course. If you're not
prepared to get your hands in lots of Makefiles and a little bit of code, you're
in the wrong place."

Two libraries of note are also preinstalled: *libtivohack* and *ncurses*. Craig
Leres's *libtivohack* (*http://www.xse.com/leres/tivo/downloads/libtivohack/*)
fills in a bunch of the missing routines in the Series 1's system libraries with
dummy functions so that software can at least compile. As mentioned in
"Fetching Files from the Web" [Hack #53], the Series 1 is missing the ability to
perform domain name resolution, the appropriate routines dummied by
libtivohack.

ncurses is a simple, text-based windowing system. If you are planning any work in cross-compilation, this system is going to be a must for any of the more interesting programs out there.

The Code

As a quick hack, let's compile a really simple "hello world" C application. Save the following code as *compilertest.c*:

```
int main( int argc, char** argv ) {
  printf( "hello, tivo!\n" );
}
```

Compile it using the tools you just installed:

```
$ /home/tivodev/root/bin/gcc -o compilertest compilertest.c
```

Upload the resulting *compilertest* binary to TiVo's */var/hack/bin* directory, make it executable, and give it a whirl:

```
bash-2.02# chmod 755 /var/hack/bin/test
bash-2.02# test
hello, tivo!
```

Index

Symbols

* (asterisk), 203
\ (backslash), 70
>> bit, 60
^ (caret), 126
, (comma), 95, 108
{} (curly braces), 200, 201
$ (dollar sign), 199
= (equals sign), 134
| (pipe), 214, 217, 220
(pound), 95, 108
prompt, 44, 46, 50
/# prompt, 44, 46, 50
" (quotation marks), 12, 200, 203
> redirect symbol, 214, 217, 220
' (single quotes), 12
[] (square brackets), 199
~ (tilde), 96, 97

A

@accounts array, 137
active partition, 57, 60
active root image, 57
ActivePerl, 135, 137
ActiveState, 137
Actor object, 214
actors, discovering favorite, 214–217
Adaptec Easy CD Creator, 30
adapters
    null modem, 60, 64
    serial-to-USB, 64
    TurboNET, 186

USB-to-802.11b, 109
USB-to-Ethernet, 108
Y-power, 53
Adberg, Michael, 23–54
Advance button, 6
Advanced WishLists, 20
All Programs folder (TiVoWeb), 172
Apache Web server, 177–179, 186, 188, 189
archiving data, 210
aspect ratio, 80
asterisk (*), 203
ATA/66 IDE cable, 33
AT&T TCD130040, 25
audio
    listening to email, 138
    streaming, 130–134
authentication, 175
Automatically Associate Logos link, 170
AVI media players, 191

B

backdoor mode, 2, 9, 10–12
backdoor password, 227
backdoorpw utility, 10
backing out, 19
backslash (\), 70
backup partition (see inactive partition)
backup.bak file, 46, 48
backups
    adding drives and, 28
    backdoor hacks and, 1

We'd like to hear your suggestions for improving our indexes. Send email to *index@oreilly.com*.

Colophon

Our look is the result of reader comments, our own experimentation, and feedback from distribution channels. Distinctive covers complement our distinctive approach to technical topics, breathing personality and life into potentially dry subjects.

The tool on the cover of *TiVo Hacks* are jumper cables. Jumper cables are heavy duty electrical cables with alligator clips used to make a connection for jump starting a vehicle.

Sarah Sherman was the production editor and proofreader for *TiVo Hacks*. Brian Sawyer was the copyeditor. Genevieve d'Entremont and Colleen Gorman provided quality control. Lucie Haskins wrote the index.

Emma Colby designed the cover of this book, based on a series design by Edie Freedman. The cover image is a photograph taken from the Stockbyte Work Tools CD. Emma Colby produced the cover layout with Quark-XPress 4.1 using Adobe's Helvetica Neue and ITC Garamond fonts.

David Futato designed the interior layout. This book was converted by Andrew Savikas to FrameMaker 5.5.6 with a format conversion tool created by Erik Ray, Jason McIntosh, Neil Walls, and Mike Sierra that uses Perl and XML technologies. The text font is Linotype Birka; the heading font is Adobe Helvetica Neue Condensed; and the code font is LucasFont's TheSans Mono Condensed. The illustrations that appear in the book were produced by Robert Romano and Jessamyn Read using Macromedia Free-Hand 9 and Adobe Photoshop 6.

Other Hacks Titles Available from O'Reilly

By Tara Calishain
& Rael Dornfest
1st Edition
March 2003
352 pages
0-596-00447-8

By David A. Karp
1st Edition
August 2003
352 pages
0-596-00564-4

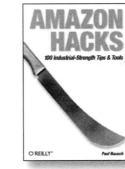

By Rael Dornfest
& Kevin Hemenway
1st Edition
March 2003
432 pages
0-596-00460-5

By Paul Bausch
1st Edition
August 2003
304 pages
0-596-00542-3

By Preston Gralla
1st Edition
August 2003
400 pages
0-596-00511-3

By Rob Flickenger
1st Edition
September 2003
304 pages
0-596-00559-8

O'REILLY®

To order: 800-998-9938 • *order@oreilly.com* • *www.oreilly.com*
Online editions of most O'Reilly titles are available by subscription at *safari.oreilly.com*
Also available at most retail and online bookstores.

How to stay in touch with O'Reilly

1. Visit our award-winning web site

http://www.oreilly.com/

★ "Top 100 Sites on the Web"—PC Magazine
★ CIO Magazine's Web Business 50 Awards

Our web site contains a library of comprehensive product information (including book excerpts and tables of contents), downloadable software, background articles, interviews with technology leaders, links to relevant sites, book cover art, and more. File us in your bookmarks or favorites!

2. Join our email mailing lists

Sign up to get email announcements of new books and conferences, special offers, and O'Reilly Network technology newsletters at:

http://elists.oreilly.com

It's easy to customize your free elists subscription so you'll get exactly the O'Reilly news you want.

3. Get examples from our books

To find example files for a book, go to:

http://www.oreilly.com/catalog

select the book, and follow the "Examples" link.

4. Work with us

Check out our web site for current employment opportunites:

http://jobs.oreilly.com/

5. Register your book

Register your book at:

http://register.oreilly.com

6. Contact us

O'Reilly & Associates, Inc.
1005 Gravenstein Hwy North
Sebastopol, CA 95472 USA
TEL: 707-827-7000 or 800-998-9938
　　　(6am to 5pm PST)
FAX: 707-829-0104

order@oreilly.com
For answers to problems regarding your order or our products. To place a book order online visit:

http://www.oreilly.com/order_new/

catalog@oreilly.com
To request a copy of our latest catalog.

booktech@oreilly.com
For book content technical questions or corrections.

corporate@oreilly.com
For educational, library, government, and corporate sales.

proposals@oreilly.com
To submit new book proposals to our editors and product managers.

international@oreilly.com
For information about our international distributors or translation queries. For a list of our distributors outside of North America check out:

http://international.oreilly.com/distributors.html

adoption@oreilly.com
For information about academic use of O'Reilly books, visit:

http://academic.oreilly.com

O'REILLY®

To order: 800-998-9938 • *order@oreilly.com* • *www.oreilly.com*
Online editions of most O'Reilly titles are available by subscription at *safari.oreilly.com*
Also available at most retail and online bookstores.